Nestor E. Terleckyj

Improvements

in the Quality

of Life

Estimates of Possibilities
in the United States, 1974-1983

National Planning Association
1975

IMPROVEMENTS IN THE QUALITY OF LIFE:
ESTIMATES OF POSSIBILITIES IN THE
UNITED STATES, 1974-1983
Report No. 142
Price: $10.00

Library of Congress
Catalogue Card Number: 74-82709

Contents

**Improvements in the Quality of Life:
Estimates of Possibilities
in the United States, 1974-1983**

by Nestor E. Terleckyj

Part II
ESTIMATES FOR SINGLE GOALS

Preface

The main objective of the present work is to develop an analytical system which could contribute to the understanding of changes in the quality of life. The secondary objective is to attempt some empirical estimates within the framework of this system.

Many complex relationships underlie changes which occur over a period of time in the various social conditions which are generally perceived as significant attributes of the quality of life. A formal analytical framework which can deal with these relationships simultaneously and in quantitative terms permits more meaningful comparisons between present conditions and possible improvements than verbal, impressionistic, incomplete, and even inconsistent information used in the absence of coherent conceptual formulations.

The dimensions of the quality of life are seen as goods in the sense that they are capable of satisfying human wants. The quantities of these distinct goods are measured by one or a few indicators each representing their principal characteristics. The analysis focuses on a series of projections of the productive possibilities which may exist for increasing the amount of these goods over a future period.

No attempt has been made to develop a complete or a theoretically consistent set of goods. However, a number of them are included, so that a simultaneous analysis of multiple changes could be developed. Included are goods such as "health" which are subject to direct productive efforts of the household and which directly affect the well-being of its members, public goods such as "science," and distributional characteristics of society such as "adequacy of income." Selection and identification of these goods for the present volume was quite pragmatic and followed a number of precedents which reflect, in the main, categorizations of consumer and governmental expenditures. Developing a priori a theoretically consistent set of goods would require, I think, major theoretical innovations especially in dealing with the collective and distributive goods. Also, any attempt to validate such a selection, e.g., for its conformance to preferences of individuals, would involve many empirical questions which can be approached only through future research.

These questions were left to the future and the effort was directed toward providing a conceptual system which would explicitly include the economic constraints and which, through a simultaneous approach to many dimensions of the quality of life, would permit exploration of the various interactions which may exist among them and among the means of their achievement.

In its focus on the quality of life, the analysis stresses results, or outcomes, rather than resources used. This emphasis on output is deliberate even though it is at variance with many of the prevailing conceptions used in examining consumer and governmental expenditures. The output orientation permits the analysis to focus not only beyond particular commodities but also beyond the institutional aggregates related to, but not identical with, broad concerns—thus stressing, for example, health rather than health services, education rather than schools. This formulation also brings the object of analysis closer to the objectives of families and individuals, and makes it possible to relate it to the body of recent research in the field of household behavior.

While the main emphasis has been on the formulation of concepts, attempts have been made throughout the development of these concepts to use the best available information to the extent to which data exist or the resources of the study permitted the development of data. Still, numerous interpolations and extrapolations had to be made from fragmentary data in order to place the information into a common framework. Experts who reviewed the individual chapters felt that the information used by and large represented the state of quantitative knowledge in these fields as of the time. The empirical content of this study can best be tested only through wide discussion and repeated efforts to develop estimates embodying additional or newly available information. However, not only the estimates but the analytical framework itself requires considerable testing and refinement.

The present volume embodies the results of two research projects which the author has conducted at the National Planning Association during the past seven years: the National Priorities Study, supported by a grant from the Ford Foundation and contributions from businesses and the AFL-CIO; and the Goals Accounting Study, supported by a research grant (No. SOC71-03642, formerly GS-29032) from the National Science Foundation. The empirical estimates produced in the National Priorities Study provided the starting points for the more extensive estimates included in the present work. The conceptual and theoretical materials pertaining to this analysis are being organized into a separate volume tentatively titled *An Economic Analysis of the Quality of Life*.

The National Priorities Study owed much of its conception to the late Gerhard Colm, NPA Chief Economist for many years. It has benefited from advice and counsel by members of the NPA Goals Research Advisory Committee: Curtis C. Aller, Neil W. Chamberlain, James S. Coleman, William W. Cooper, Richard M. Cyert (Chairman), Olaf Helmer, Clark Kerr, Edward S. Mason, the late Max Millikan, John R. Meyer, and William Riker. Much of the work of the staff of the National Priorities Study is embodied in the present report, which thus draws on the contributions of Joyce Powell and Daniel

Tunstall, permanent staff members of the National Priorities Study, and Geoffrey Davis, Lewis Ferguson, Eileen Mauskopf, and Philip Moss, who participated on a temporary basis.

The staff of the Goals Accounting Study participated extensively in research and in preparation of this report. Joyce Powell supervised data collection and processing and conducted the computer analyses in this project. Ms. Powell also conducted several independent substantive analyses, especially in the fields of education and earnings. Neil McMullen developed an analysis for calculating the interaction effects and the computer programs for this analysis. Mr. McMullen also made numerous substantive contributions at other points in the study. Philip Moss developed the analyses for adequacy and continuity of income and made several contributions in other parts of the study. Paul Farnham contributed the analysis of pollution control and several extensions of the analysis of resource availability and also conducted an extensive review of the estimates. Janice Zepik and Elizabeth Kosciw provided general research and editorial assistance and managed the administrative side of the project. Robert Costello assisted in research, data processing and editing of the manuscript. Jon Gabel, Albert Gillespie, Brandon Buteau, and Simin Royanian worked as research assistants. Albert Eckstein, consultant to the study, reviewed the report and made substantive contributions to the analysis of resource availability. B.J. Stone consulted in mathematical analysis and computer programming. Jo Tunstall was the editorial consultant for this report.

Throughout both studies, I have benefited greatly from numerous discussions with my colleagues at NPA: Phillip Golden, Leonard Lecht, Wilfred Lewis, John Miller, Everard Munsey, and others.

Over the years, I have discussed this work many times with Betty Bock, William W. Cooper, Harvey Garn, Michael Levy, Milton Moss, Andrew Rouse, and Daniel Tunstall, who generously gave of their time and thought and from whose advice and encouragement I have benefited immeasurably.

I would also like to thank Henry Aaron, Jack Besansky, Michael Boretsky, Vartkes Broussalian, Morris Cobern, Terrence Davies, Charles Friedman, Joseph Froomkin, Ivars Gutmanis, Martin Jones, Thomas Juster, Ronald Lee, Ruth Mack, Martin McGuire, Selma Mushkin, Sumner Myers, Richard Nelson, Chong Park, Steffen Plehn, Terry Pruden, Carl Rappaport, Edward Rhodes, Timothy Ruefli, Jack Schuman, Tibor Scitovsky, Julius Shiskin, Richard Speier, Robert Steadman, Peter Szanton, Nancy Teeters, Andrew Tershakovec, Milton Turen, Rowan Wakefield, Murray Weidenbaum, and Ian Wilson for numerous discussions and contributions that they have made in clarifying my thinking or helping me with various parts of the study.

This volume contains two distinct parts. Chapters 1-4 contain the conceptual core of the analysis, consisting of the multi-output productive relationships formulated in the activity-output and activity-cost matrices, the analysis of resource availability and estimation of the margin of discretionary resources, and the results of the least-cost calculations giving estimates of maximum achievement levels for different combinations of output which are consistent with the resource projection. The second part consists of Chapters 5-23 which contain detailed discussions of particular fields of social concerns, dealing with the choice of indicators and the estimation of the effects and costs of the activities relevant to each field of concern.

Nestor E. Terleckyj
Washington, D.C.
April 1975

PART I

SYSTEMATIC ANALYSIS
OF MULTIPLE GOALS

1

The analytical framework

Emergent interest in dimensions of the quality of life beyond the economic and the conventionally quantifiable, growing concern with the effectiveness of our institutions to cope with technological, social and physical challenges, and rising public expectations for the effective performance of institutions have placed heavy demands on our ability to analyze social change and to evaluate opportunities for achieving desirable change.

The present state of analysis in the social sciences cannot cope with these demands. A new type of analysis is required, capable, on the one hand, of dealing rigorously with many technical complexities and economic realities, and, on the other, of focusing on social conditions and human values.

For the past several years, a search has been under way in a number of fields for new approaches to provide better means by which social developments and institutional performance can be evaluated. This search has taken a number of directions.

One is the attempt by economists to extend measures of the gross national product (GNP) to reflect social and environmental costs and improvements, so that the measures of economic activity become better indicators of economic welfare than the presently measured volume of production of goods and services.[1] At the same time, social scientists have been developing systems of social indicators to measure directly conditions and changes in society.[2] Special official statistical reports have appeared in a number of countries, focusing exclusively on social statistics.[3]

1   F. Thomas Juster, "A Framework for the Measurement of Economic and Social Performance," *The Measurement of Economic and Social Performance,* Milton Moss, ed., Studies in Income and Wealth, Volume 38 (New York: National Bureau of Economic Research, Inc., 1973); James Tobin and William D. Nordhaus, *Economic Growth* (New York: National Bureau of Economic Research, June 1972).

2   Raymond A. Bauer, ed., *Social Indicators* (Cambridge: MIT Press, 1966); Eleanor B. Sheldon and Kenneth C. Land, "Social Reporting for the 1970's: A Review and Programmatic Statement," *Policy Sciences,* Vol. 3, No. 2 (New York: Russell Sage Foundation, July 1972), pp. 137-151.

3   In the United States: Executive Office of the President, Office of Management and Budget, *Social Indicators, 1973* (Washington, D.C.: U.S. Government Printing Office, 1974); in France: *Donnees*

(continued)

Another line of effort encompasses attempts to explicitly define national goals and national priorities and to measure the costs of achieving them.[4] Still another consists of attempts to define ways in which to assess the social impacts of business enterprises and, more generally, the effects of business activities on third parties, effects not reflected in financial accounts.[5]

Similarly, citizens, governmental officials and legislators have become increasingly mistrustful of expenditure as a criterion for governmental performance and have been looking for objective indicators of the effectiveness of public programs and institutions.[6]

Questions are also being raised in business administration about the relevance of currently prevailing concepts and accounting measurements to the actual objectives of business enterprises and of the traditional concepts of what constitutes products and markets to what the real product and market relationships may be as apparent from consumer use and producer competition in face of innovations.[7] Related questions resulting from the reevaluation of the nature of products and markets are being asked about the objectives of governmental regulation of business.[8]

(Footnote #3 continued)
Sociales, Premiere Edition, Institut National de la Statistique et des Etudes Economiques, 1973; in Germany: *Gesellschaftliche Daten, 1973* (Bonn: Presse und Informationsamt der Bundesregierung, 1973); in Japan: Government of Japan, Economic Planning Agency, *White Paper on National Life 1973–Quality of Life in Japan* (Tokyo: Overseas Data Service Co., Ltd., 1974); in the United Kingdom: *Social Trends,* No. 4, 1973, Muriel Nissel, ed. (London: Her Majesty's Stationery Office, 1973).

4 *Goals for Americans: The Report of the President's Commission on National Goals* (New York: Prentice-Hall, 1960); Gerhard Colm, "National Goals and the American Economy," *Financial Analysts Journal,* November-December 1964; Leonard A. Lecht, *Goals, Priorities and Dollars: The Next Decade* (New York: The Free Press, 1966), and "Dollars for National Goals," *Looking Ahead,* Vol. 21, No. 8, January 1974; Nestor E. Terleckyj, "Measuring Progress Towards Social Goals: Some Possibilities at National and Local Levels," *Management Science,* Vol. 16, No. 12, August 1970.

5 Eli Goldston, *The Quantification of Concern: Some Aspects of Social Accounting* (Pittsburgh: Carnegie-Mellon University, 1971); Raymond A. Bauer and Dan H. Fenn, Jr., *The Corporate Social Audit* (New York: Russell Sage Foundation, 1972).

6 A good compendium dealing with a wide range of analytical and policy issues and containing a number of case studies, as well as references to other existing governmental studies, is provided in *The Analysis and Evaluation of Public Expenditures: The PPB System,* compendium of papers submitted to the Subcommittee on Economy in Government of the Joint Economic Committee, Congress of the United States, 91st Congress, 1st Session, 1969, Vols. 1, 2 and 3.

7 Richard M. Cyert and Charles L. Hendrick, "Theory of the Firm, Past, Present and Future: An Interpretation," *Journal of Economic Literature,* June 1972; Donald A. Schon, *Beyond the Stable State* (New York: Random House, 1971).

8 *Economic Fact and Antitrust Goals,* Tenth Conference on Antitrust Issues in Today's Economy (New York: The Conference Board, March 1971).

Finally, the relationship between the quantity, quality and cost of goods and services on the one hand and their actual capacity for satisfying consumer wants on the other is also being examined.[9]

Unifying these diverse efforts is a desire to find criteria that are more basic and permanent as well as more reflective of actual human wants and behavior than the conventional criteria now used which are typically defined by amounts of money, quantities of commodities or levels of activity of organizations.

The state of the art in all these fields is just being developed. Even though some major intellectual breakthroughs can be cited, the conceptual formulation as a whole, the orientation of questions, practical applications, and especially the data base that such work requires are still in an exceedingly primitive condition.[10]

The present work is related to this search and draws on its results. It, too, is experimental. It represents *an attempt to devise an analytical framework for systematically assessing existing possibilities for social change measured by a set of quantitative indicators.* More specifically, it focuses on the possible sources of change in specific social conditions that represent major aspects of the quality of life.

The first objective in the study is to develop a method for organizing existing knowledge about these interrelated social conditions into a coherent framework so that the possibilities for improvements in the conditions can be systematically assessed. In the language of economics, the objective is to find the "feasible set," and especially the "efficient set" (the "production possibilities frontier"), for desirable social change, as measured by selected statistical indicators. The second objective is to provide actual estimates of possible changes.

The analysis, to be manageable, had to be limited in scope regarding the subjects covered, the time horizon, and the detail used. The study is limited to domestic (as distinguished from international) social (as distinguished from purely personal or private) objectives. These objectives, such as improved health, personal safety and basic education, have recognizable expressions both in individual and in public behavior. The analysis is also limited to a 10-year period and to national aggregates, averages and comparisons (distinguished

---

9   This examination proceeds in a number of quite different ways and over a wide spectrum, including work by theoretical economists; see Gary S. Becker, "A Theory of the Allocation of Time," *The Economic Journal,* Vol. 75, No. 299, September 1965; Kelvin J. Lancaster, "A New Approach to Consumer Theory," *The Journal of Political Economy,* Vol. 74, No. 2, April 1966, and *Consumer Demand* (New York: Columbia University Press, 1971), on the one hand and consumer interest advocacy and public consumer protection literature, on the other.

10   How primitive the state of knowledge actually is in the various fields dealing with issues of prime social importance is apparent in the scarcity of and simplicity of the planning documents for public policy. For most policy fields, such documents do not even exist.

from regional, local and other group subaggregates). The empirical estimates
are limited by the amount and quality of the available data and the time available
for refining existing or for developing new information.

THE ELEMENTS OF THE SYSTEM

The analytical system for estimating possibilities for social change is based on
the following six elements.

(1) *Selection and definition of social concerns (such as health and public
safety) and identification of quantitative indicators (such as average life expectancy and the rate of violent crime) to measure the conditions that are the main
objects of the given concerns.* Because little work has yet been done regarding
actual identification and measurement of the goals represented by the concerns
and indicators, an experimental approach was necessary. Reliance had to be
placed on simple, reasonable assumptions.

One such assumption is that at least some important dimensions of the
major social concerns can, indeed, be identified and that sufficient information
and knowledge now exist to suggest that levels of achievement in these dimensions can be measured by specific indicators. Actually, the selection of concerns
is less complicated and requires fewer normative judgments than would be
required for a decision as to which concerns are, at which level of accomplishment, the more important. In any event, these latter questions are not approached in this study. The selection of the 18 concerns used in this study was
based on categorizations made in earlier research, public affairs discussions,
and existing budgetary and statistical definitions. (For a more detailed description, see Chapter 2.)

With the concerns identified, quantitative indicators that measure the level
or the quality of the major conditions for each concern were selected or developed. One or at most two indicators were chosen to represent a central
dimension of each concern, with a total of 21 indicators used.

These social indicators are taken as measures related to the well-being of
individuals rather than to the performance of institutions. In this sense, they are
measures of output rather than input of social production processes. For example, the objective of efforts and expenditures directed toward health is to
maintain or improve the state of health. Achievement of health goals within
society is thus better measured by such indicators as average life expectancy and
the occurrence of illnesses and disabilities than by outlays for health or work-
load items such as the number of doctor visits, of surgeries, of hospitalization
days, or of drugs and medicines consumed. Similarly, concern with education is
better measured by the knowledge of students (perhaps even in such comparatively basic and simple terms as language and mathematical skills as established
by existing tests) rather than by any organizational, fiscal or input indicators such

as class size, age of school buildings, academic degrees of teachers, or expenditure per pupil.

(2) *Projection of 10-year trends in both the conditions measured by the indicators and the resource use associated with the various concerns.* These projections define the base lines of resource use and of social conditions for the target date 10 years in the future, against which further changes can be analyzed. The projected base trend levels are those expected from ongoing activities and ongoing trends alone.

(3) *Distinction between fixed and discretionary activities and resources on the part of individuals, private institutions and governments.* Further changes in social conditions and increases in levels of achievement beyond the base trends are assumed to be feasible, contingent upon the occurrence of particular chains of events called here discretionary activities. These discretionary activities include not only new approaches but also expansions (not already under way or virtually certain to occur, which are to be considered to be part of the base) of those present activities that could significantly affect the conditions identified by the indicators. Thus, such discretionary activities as increases of pensions through social insurance systems and accelerated construction of housing represent extensions of already existing activities. In contrast, such activities as improvement in physical fitness habits, which is predicated on a very substantial investment in public recreation facilities, or the introduction of remedial tutoring by persons outside the school system represent departures from conventional systems.

It is such discretionary activities that hold the possibility for improvements above the levels expected by a continuation of the base trends. The base trends identified in this study are viewed as nondiscretionary. The activities that have the potential to effect further changes, on the other hand, are considered discretionary in the sense that there is no necessary and apparent reason why any of them should occur as a matter of high probability within the 10-year period.

The basic reason for a distinction between base trends and discretionary activities is to introduce realism into the analysis. The two are not symmetrical. Base activities are much less subject to redirection, and their discontinuance takes much more time and effort than the corresponding decisions to adopt or not to adopt a new activity. Also, in a 10-year time horizon, the base systems are not subject to total redirection. They are, in fact, to a substantial degree set on their course. Over 10-year intervals, many of the ongoing activities can be expected to continue at a reasonably high rate for a number of years. Quantitatively, the relative scope for undertaking discretionary activities increases with time since the momentum of ongoing activities is strongest in the earlier years.

Underlying the distinction between the base activities and the discretionary activities is the assumption of their different productivities. The set of discretionary activities contains by design only activities with substantial positive effects on social conditions. Included in it are also those extensions of the base activities which have a productive potential and are not already well under way and thus nondiscretionary.

In contrast, the base trends reflect nondiscretionary changes in resource use and in the social conditions associated with them. Any further large additions of resources to the base activities or their elements (beyond "normal growth" projected in the trend), are likely to be unproductive relative to their use for the discretionary activities (and perhaps absolutely).[11]

While the discretionary activities, which by definition include all the existing positive productive possibilities (those that may have negative effects on any of the indicators are not included), are not very numerous, there are many possibilities for unproductive uses of resources, including various possibilities for inflating the real cost of the base activities. It may therefore be argued that general expansion of resource use for the base activities beyond the levels which they will have achieved over the 10-year period will have little effect on output, especially when compared to the introduction of new approaches or increases of those specific activities which are still capable of generating substantial marginal products. This formulation of the possibilities of growth in social productivity is derived from the economic model of productivity growth,[12] which is based on a process of substitution of new technology and new production processes to replace or gradually supplant systems that have reached low productivity, saturation or negative marginal productivity levels.

(4) *Identification of discretionary activities, their cost and their effect on the conditions measured by the indicators.* A set of discretionary activities is presented in this report which was identified through a survey of the principal existing opportunities for increasing 1983 base trend levels of achievement of the conditions measured by the indicators. The activities have been drawn from various sources ranging from specific legislative proposals and scholarly studies to recommendations and expressions of need among experts and the public. Some were derived from the specification of a problem. All were designed with four attributes in common: (1) they would have at least one substantial positive effect; (2) they would not produce any negative effects on other goals; (3) they could be undertaken in a manner consistent with the broad social and political framework and would be historically and culturally believable; and (4) they would be economically feasible, that is, they would have the capacity to achieve

---

11   The present analysis deals only with the incremental or marginal productivity of resources in different types of activities. The questions of the total and average productivity of activities included in the base trends do not arise.

12   However, there may be an important structural difference regarding circumstances affecting growth of productivity: the incentives of competition which provide incentives for innovation in economic productivity change do not apply, or apply much less, to innovations for social productivity because generally there are no markets for social outputs.

their effects with the supply of resources available and at a total cost consistent with overall constraints. This collection of activities represents an attempt to arrange the different possibilities for social change in a common conceptual and quantitative framework in which output, timing and cost can be compared consistently.[13]

The discretionary activities identified are meant to represent the set of possibilities for effecting positive changes in the social conditions reflected in the indicators measuring these conditions. As such, they do not exhaust the full range of possibilities because the activities with mixed, i.e., positive and negative, effects on the various indicators were not considered.

While estimates of both the cost and the effect of activities can, of course, be improved, there is a limit to which specificity of activities can be usefully carried in an analytical and exploratory work such as this. A too detailed specification of activity components or of their scenarios which depend on what are necessarily uncertain and prospective events may needlessly limit the applicability of the underlying concepts and, by introducing superfluous constraints, may even lower the predictive quality of estimates.[14]

(5) *A 10-year projection of the resources available for discretionary activities by two subperiods (first 4 and later 6 years) and by public and private components.* These breakdowns are important because many activities possess specific requirements for either private or public financing. In many cases, they also need a minimum outlay in the early years to provide the necessary beginning.

The extent to which improvements in social conditions in the aggregate or in any single area of concern can be achieved depends on the availability of resources (public and private) as well as on the activities selected. Estimating available resources requires that a distinction be made between committed and discretionary resources, that is, between resources tied up in existing spending patterns and resources that can be allocated to new activities or to discretionary extensions of old ones. (Chapter 3 describes how this was done.)

The 10-year cost of all discretionary activities identified in this report is far more than the resources that are likely to be available for their undertaking. This clearly means that not all the activities that may be technically feasible will be economically feasible over the 10-year period. At most, only a part of the activities are economically as well as technically practical.

---

13   Since individual activities often affect more than one area of concern, and since more than one activity could be identified in support of any one goal, often with effects that are not additive, a matrix method of analysis was required. This method derives from those used in linear economic analysis and includes some nonlinear adaptations. As a rule, effects of two or more activities are not additive when taken together, and a special allowance was made in calculating the net effects of multiple activities.

14   Robert Ayres, *Technological Forecasting and Long-range Planning* (New York: McGraw-Hill, 1969).

Total resources available in the course of the 10-year period are not the only limitation. Resources for undertaking discretionary activities are likely to be much more limited in the early years than in the later years of the period. Therefore, the feasibility of the activities requiring considerable expenditures in the first few years to produce their results even in 10 years is further limited by the stringency of the resource supply in the early years of the period.

Also, expenditures with which to finance activities are specific in large measure as to their source (private or public). Virtually all of the transfers in support of elimination of poverty, for example, require public expenditures. On the other hand, considerable private outlays are likely to be the principal elements of financing such activities as construction and rehabilitation of housing, construction and maintenance of recreational facilities, and savings and insurance activities. Funds for components of these activities, though, particularly those aimed at research and development or institutional infrastructure, almost by necessity must come from public sources.

(6) *Calculation of the maximum feasible output of combinations of discretionary activities that can be undertaken within the estimated resource supply.* These are derived by making "least-cost" calculations for different combinations of output. They serve as benchmark estimates of the maximum potential for achieving social improvements that are both technically and economically feasible. However, in situations entailing large-scale noncompetitive and often even nonrepetitive choices and decisions, there is no automatic tendency toward a selection of activities that would bring about the optimum results. Consequently, the efficiency levels actually attained in the use of available resources may be much lower than those required for the least-cost outcomes, and the actual levels of achievement may be much lower than the least-cost benchmarks. The outcomes may even be no better than the base trends.[15]

This study, while abstract and selective, is intended to provide a methodological approach and a set of benchmark estimates for examining possible improvements in the quality of life and evaluating those improvements, not in isolation but in terms of their interactions. As a result, a number of interrelationships have been taken into account. They include: (1) the effect of activities on more than the objective toward which they may be primarily directed, since the means for influencing conditions in one area of concern usually affect those in others; (2) the interactions among the multiple and often alternative means of pursuing the same goals, the effects of which may either reinforce or cancel each other; (3) the relationships between the technical and

---

15   But, because activities with negative outputs are not considered in this study, the calculated outcomes can be no worse than the base trends. Possibilities of deterioration of social conditions *as a result of discretionary activites* constitute a valid subject of study, but a subject different from the one presently chosen. Deterioration of social conditions *as part of the base trend* can be readily included in the present analysis. Some of the base trend projections in this volume already imply deterioration of conditions.

economic feasibility of activities, the former depending on the state of knowledge and the latter on the availability of resources; (4) the interactions between the private and the public sectors, in both the effects of their distinct activities and in terms of organizing and channeling resources within the same activity; and (5) the relationships between the phasing of activities and the timing of the resource flows within a given time period.

Although various possibilities for discretionary social change are examined, no forecasts of actual outcomes are attempted. Nor are any attempts made at normative judgments regarding choices among different social objectives.

One specific class of normative conclusions has been made, however. Waste of human effort or of physical resources has been presumed to be undesirable and, to the extent that the cost of achieving the same level of improvement for some activities is less than for others, the less expensive activities have been judged preferable. If, as appears to be the case, substantial overlaps exist among the means for achieving different objectives, it may be possible to identify ways of achieving multiple goals that are not much more expensive in terms of real resources than the means for achieving a much more limited selection of goals.

THE ESTIMATES

The estimates used in this study result from an attempt to canvass the existing state of knowledge concerning social conditions that represent significant dimensions of the quality of life and to organize the most important elements of this knowledge into a coherent system of relationships. The data are not simply illustrative; they are based on existing knowledge and are intended to be as realistic as is possible given the limited state of that knowledge. Nevertheless, the estimates are highly tentative, primarily because the knowledge that would permit firmer estimates simply does not exist. To the extent possible in a research study of this scope, however, the best available information has been utilized.

The present estimates represent a third calculation of activities and resources. They were completed in the late summer of 1973 and are based on information available as of that time. Data that have appeared since that time have not been included in the calculations, but, when possible, important additions are noted in the text.

Each of the specific estimates lends itself to substantial elaboration in the future, for new knowledge, data and analysis can be easily incorporated in the analytical system. Thus far, the rate of progress between successive estimations has been considerable, indicating that continued attempts to develop such projections should provide increasingly better estimates of the technical relations between activities and social conditions, of the resource supply, and of the range of economically feasible social change. It is hoped that by frequent revision of such estimates, sufficient experience may be gained to produce materially less uncertain estimates in the future.

THE USES OF THE SYSTEM

The main use of an analytical system such as the one outlined here is as a general work of reference containing both methodology and data applicable to a variety of research uses. Since methodology is general and flexible, the system and much of the data can be applied to a variety of situations, including those with different sets of indicators or activities, a different time horizon, different geographical scope, or different formulations of resource cost.

The relationship of the system to decision making or policy development, whether public or private, is much less clear. The data and formulations can be useful as background information for policy decisions, but, for several reasons, the approach is not·directly applicable to decision making. For one thing, the model has been developed at a much more aggregated level regarding organizational units, time periods and the indicators of output than the level at which actual policy decisions are made.

The activities as defined here are relatively large-scale potential chains of events defined in terms of certain critical output and cost data, with the organizational details unspecified. Policy making in the public and private sectors concerns itself with outcomes and outputs that are much more specific and immediate than those identified in this analysis. Change in the output variables would require a major reformulation of the analysis. Also, considerable disaggregation of activities into organizational components and substantial shortening of the time horizon below 10 years would be required to approach the levels of decision making of even large programs of the federal government and of the multiplicity of independent consumer, business and local government units.

The most useful application of the system to policy making may thus be as an aid in identifying a larger environment within which policy implementation and effects take place. In this case, the analysis suggests: (1) consideration of multiple effects of activities and, in particular, "spillover" effects that go beyond the scope of a given area; (2) consideration of the longer-run effects of activities; and (3) explicit identification of varied activity components within the provinces of several decision makers, which may suggest possibilities for better coordination among activity components and among the policies of multiple decision makers.

One may visualize a role for such an analytical data system as a widely accessible medium of information that makes possible coordination of diverse plans and activities. The concept of *concerted planning* can help to explain this role. Concerted planning is a term which the late Gerhard Colm, for many years

Chief Economist of the National Planning Association, developed to describe the kind of planning which, in our pluralistic society, would combine the benefits of coordination of purpose and coordination of activity while preserving the necessary scope for individual freedom of choice and flexibility of organization.[16] His analogy was that of a chamber music concert in which the players have the score, know the music, and play without a conductor but in harmony.

An abundant flow of information about existing possibilities for improvements in a number of social fields could, by providing a common frame of reference and a rapid feedback, help to coordinate the activities of different levels of government (or even different agencies of the same government), of businesses, and of individuals and families, perhaps sufficiently to keep within tolerable limits the occurrence of cross purposes, loss of productivity and conflict while avoiding the need for a master control with its attendant risks and costs.

As a model of the uses of such information, consider the uses made of the bodies of macroeconomic analytical information on employment, price levels, aggregate production, aspects of distribution, and monetary phenomena organized by producing and consuming sectors of the economy. These data help focus policy considerations on such matters as inflation, unemployment and imbalances in international payments. This body of economic information, extensive and coherent, has been developed and perfected over many years. Although no one would suggest that this information is not highly useful, no one would maintain that recourse to such information alone does or could provide a clear guide for policies. The problem is not the quality of the information; rather, policy decisions involve trade-offs and choices that extend beyond the factual data and require normative judgments. This does not destroy the usefulness of the information; it simply places a limit on its uses. The same is obviously true of a social information system.

At present, the question of use relates only indirectly to the data and the analysis discussed here. Much more immediate is obtaining estimates that at least approach the degree of reliability of the macroeconomic data and developing a coherent framework into which the diverse and changing pieces of information can be integrated.

---

16   Gerhard Colm, "The Next Step: Concerted Planning," *State and Local Government Planning*, Proceedings of the Ninth Annual Conference of the Center for Economic Projections held October 24-25, 1968 (Washington, D.C.: National Planning Association, March 1969).

2

Basic estimates

The analysis of feasible social change begins with the identification of the social concerns. These concerns, such as health and public safety, are intended to represent social areas generally regarded as important for the quality of life in the United States. The selection of concerns was derived from a number of sources including national goals research work, social indicator analyses, public affairs discussions, public opinion surveys, and the classification used for consumer and governmental expenditures.[1]

The choice of concerns was based in part on a criterion of dependence on individual and collective activities, so that each concern by definition requires major public activities as well as those ordinarily provided by individuals or the private marketplace. The categories thus represent large expenditures of private and public energy and resources.

The social concerns selected for the study include:

Health	Economic Equality of Races
Public Safety	Economic Equality of Sexes
Basic Education	Housing and Neighborhoods
Higher Education	Pollution Control
General Level of Earnings	Outdoor Recreation
Ability to Earn	Preservation
Adequacy of Income	Discretionary Time
Continuity of Income	Science
General Economic Equality	The Arts

The selection is admittedly neither exhaustive nor unique. Many large and important classes of concerns were not included. Objectives dealing with international relations, trade and defense were excluded, as were the economic

---

1 Raymond A. Bauer, ed., *Social Indicators* (Cambridge: MIT Press, 1966); Albert D. Biderman, "Social Indicators and Goals," *Social Indicators;* Leonard A. Lecht, *Goals, Priorities and Dollars: The Next Decade* (New York: The Free Press, 1966); *Goals for Americans: The Report of the President's Commission on National Goals* (New York: Prentice-Hall, 1960); Kermit Gordon, ed., *Agenda for the Nation* (Washington, D.C.: The Brookings Institution, 1968); Bertram M. Gross, "The State of the Nation: Social Systems Accounting," *Social Indicators;* Eleanor Sheldon and Wilbert E. Moore, eds., *Indicators of Social Change: Concepts and Measurements* (New York: Russell Sage Foundation, 1968); U.S. Department of Health, Education, and Welfare, Social Security Administration, *Social Security Bulletin* (Washington, D.C.: U.S. Government Printing Office, 1969).

concerns of full employment and price stability. An attempt was made to include the areas of freedom, justice and social harmony, but the data have not been sufficiently developed to permit a quantitative approach.

Most of the concerns selected represent concerns which are also recognizable objects of behavior of individuals and households as could be observed from the patterns of allocation of their resources. But some are not directly relatable to the economic activity of households. These include concerns with economic distribution characteristics (the three dimensions of economic equality and perhaps adequacy of income) as well as such public goods concerns as science, the arts and perhaps preservation which, while directly and indirectly affecting the well-being of individuals, appear largely as given relative to the household allocation decisions.

Although many changes could no doubt be made in the selection and organization of concerns, no system can fully express all the important ones. The present analysis is limited to an open-ended selection of concerns, and emphasizes measurement of output and the estimation of cost of simultaneous achievement of multiple outputs. Extending the scope of the concerns covered, at this early stage of experimental development, in an attempt to be all-inclusive would simply make the system too cumbersome or too inattentive in detail to be useful at all.

The 18 concerns selected for this study embody a range of social conditions, many of which are interrelated. Together, the concerns represent a collection of recognizably important social objectives of sufficiently large scope, diversity and degree of interdependence that the feasibility of pursuing their multiple objectives simultaneously can be usefully studied. The questions of the criteria for a more systematic selection of the social concerns and the analytical treatment of the different types of concerns are being explored in the theoretical study by the author, now under way, which was mentioned earlier.

INDICATORS AND TRENDS

With the concerns identified, statistical indicators, deliberately limited in number, were selected to represent one or two central dimensions of each concern. These indicators directly measure levels of achievement for the major objectives embodied in the concerns.

The indicators have three characteristics.

First, they all are presumed to command a high degree of consensus as to the desirability of change in a given direction, as revealed by the behavior of individuals and of political bodies at national and local levels.

Second, they all have national attributes, as distinguished from purely personal or local ones.

Table 2-1.   A Summary List of Concerns and Corresponding Indicators

Concerns	Principal Indicators	Indicator Levels		
		1960	1973 Estimate	1983 Projection
I. Health and Safety				
Health	Average life expectancy at birth, years	69.7	71.3	72.7
	Percent of population with activity limiting disabilities	15.0	17.5	16.8
Public safety	Number of violent crimes per 100,000 persons per year	235	668	668
II. Education, Skills and Standard of Living				
Basic education	Index of performance in grade 12 based on standard tests, 1973=100	n.a.	100	105
	Percent of students 3 or more years behind 1973 average	n.a.	24	19
Higher education	Number of persons completing college, thousands	392	957	1,342
Ability to earn	Number of persons not in the mainstream of labor force, millions	n.a.	11.1	8.8
General level of earnings	Median annual wage and salary earnings of individuals, thousands 1973 dollars	4.8	5.9	7.8
III. Income				
Adequacy of income	Percent of population below present poverty standard	22.1	11.4	8.7
	Percent of population in near-poverty conditions	8.1	4.8	3.5
Continuity of income	Percent of population with living standard loss of over 30 percent	n.a.	8.6	8.7

Table 2.1. A Summary List of Concerns and Corresponding Indicators (continued)

Concerns	Principal Indicators	1960	Indicator Levels 1973 Estimate	1983 Projection
IV. Economic Equality				
General economic equality	Income ratio: 20th as percent of 90th percentile	20	25	25
Economic equality of races	Mean family income, blacks as a percent of whites	56	65	70
Economic equality of sexes	Hourly earnings of women as percent of earnings of men	n.a.	60	60
V. Human Habitat				
Housing	Percent of persons living in adequate houses	n.a.	88	92
Neighborhoods	Percent of persons living in satisfactory neighborhoods	n.a.	77	87
Pollution control	Percent of population exposed to bothersome pollution	n.a.	62	46
Outdoor recreation	Percent of persons 12 years and older regularly taking part in outdoor recreation	n.a.	21	54
Preservation	Index of preservation of life and natural forms	n.a.	100	110
VI. Art, Science and Free Time				
Discretionary time	Hours per person per year	n.a.	2,111	2,199
Science	Number of scientists active in basic science, thousands	n.a.	81	139
The arts	Number of active artists, thousands	206	265	323

n.a. = not applicable

Third, the conditions measured by the indicators require in most cases for their further improvement, or even for maintenance of present levels of achievement, joint or collective activities—a mix of individual, family and public activities. The latter may be in the form of providing research and development or regulatory support, direct program operation, or financing, either entirely or to supplement activities in the private sector.

Twenty-two indicators were identified for the 18 areas of concern. They are listed in Table 2-1, along with actual or estimated levels of indicators for the base year 1973 and trend projections of these levels to 1983 (as well as, where available, data for 1960 for historical reference).

The assumption underlying the projections is that some changes in the levels of achievement in the conditions measured by the indicators may be expected to result from the continuation of current or definitely foreseeable activities. The 1983 levels are thus identified as base trend levels beyond which further improvements can be achieved only as a result of certain specific developments called discretionary activities occurring during the period 1973-83.

By necessity, indicators vary in precision. Some, such as change in average life expectancy, are based on quite accurate existing data. For others, such as the number of persons affected by pollution, the measure was postulated and its levels estimated roughly since there is no firm data. For a number of concerns, the social situation to be measured is represented by a continuous phenomenon, as for adequacy of income or frequency of recreation. In these areas, the indicator had to be based upon a point that represents an "adequate" level, such as that at which income is considered to be minimally adequate or at which the recreational activities of people are sufficiently frequent to be considered "regular."

The indicators in this analysis thus range from those which are reasonably indicative of actual levels and magnitudes of change in social conditions to those which are merely suggestive of the kinds of analyses and measurements that must be undertaken to determine actual magnitudes. Throughout, the indicators have been treated as distinct entities, with no attempt to reduce them to a single measurement, such as a monetary valuation resulting in an adjusted GNP, or into a utility or decision function in which the individual indicators enter as weighted components or any other kind of index number. Aggregation was not attempted largely because the present limited state of the art makes such an aggregation of distinct social dimensions impossible.[2]

---

2   This type of research, much as it might be worthwhile on scientific grounds, would be far beyond the scope of the present study and would address itself to questions different from those addressed here. Such an approach would require a basic empirical utility analysis rather than an assessment of a range of possibilities. The present analysis can, in any event, be carried out as well with a nonaggregated function as with an aggregated function without raising a host of additional and highly controversial questions.

The selection and definition of the concerns and indicators are based on precedent and current emphasis, especially as revealed by amounts spent from personal and public resources for activities bearing on these concerns. This mode of selection was considered adequate for present purposes, especially since no feasible alternative is currently available.

Nevertheless, the concerns require validation and refinement to permit increasingly more sophisticated analysis. Specific objects of basic concerns and the extent of variation among individuals in the nature of these particular concerns need to be established more objectively. For example, what are the particular characteristics of health, such as longevity, risk of painful diseases, etc., that best reflect a concern with health? In addition, research is needed to help determine whether there is sufficient prevalence of a concern among individuals to consider it as a principal concern. Is, for example, flourishing of the arts a sufficiently strong and prevalent consideration to include it among some 20 major social goal categories selected for analysis? If so, is the extent of satisfaction of the concern with the arts best measured by the number of active artists?

Aside from some survey studies, however, no research has been done and no theory formulated that could provide guidance in specifying indicators as reflections of actual objectives of individuals. Perhaps the most promising approach lies in an extension of the research methods recently developed by economists for analysis of consumption and economic behavior of households. This research, including what are often called "Hedonic," "characteristics" and "household production" approaches, treats consumption as an active process in which various goods and services are obtained not for their own sake but for the sake of their various characteristics which, together with the consumers' time, work, skills, and other resources, are used as inputs in a "household production" process to produce the more fundamental outputs.[3] Quantities of these outputs are more closely related to the consumer's well-being than the quantities of the various commodities seen as (relatively) intermediate goods.

Application of such research techniques may help in distinguishing among alternative formulations of indicators for a given area of concern based on the degree to which they are in accord with the actual behavior of individuals, which in turn reveals their personal preferences. It may also suggest different classifications of the areas of concern and perhaps some new indicators of achievement. Such results would provide a test, and perhaps also a corrective, for the effects of obsolescence, idiosyncrasies or fashions among the producers of data or among the academic or official schools of thought, which can distort the

3   Zvi Griliches, ed., *Price Indexes and Quality Change* (Cambridge: Harvard University Press, 1971); Kelvin J. Lancaster, *Consumer Demand* (New York: Columbia University Press, 1971); Robert T. Michael and Gary S. Becker, "On the New Theory of Consumer Behavior," *The Swedish Journal of Economics*, Vol. 75, 1973.

Table 2-2. Discretionary Activities and Subactivities and Their Estimated Costs
at Full Capacity for the 10-Year Period, 1974-83

Activities	Total Cost 1974-83 (billions 1973 dollars)
1. Changes in health-related habits and patterns	$64
Smoking reduction	5
Fitness and diet improvements	35
Accident prevention	1
Alcoholism abatement	17
Drug abuse abatement	6
2. Extension of health services related to specific conditions	$66
Cancer: R&D, diagnosis and treatment	6
Mental health facilities	54
Arthritis prevention and treatment	6
3. Expansion of special health services for vulnerable population groups	$91
Services for the poor	73
Maternal and child services	18
4. Improvement of law enforcement systems	$26
Police	15
Courts	5
Correction	6
5. Employment and other opportunities for the young	$51
Schools	17
Jobs	26
Recreation	8
6. Expansion of remedial and augmenting educational inputs	$73
Remedial tutoring	25
Student counseling expansion	33
Parent counseling	5
Books for homes	10
7. Improved educational technology and new educational approaches	$183
New technologies	162
Training the very young	18
R&D and diffusion of innovation	3
8. General day care for children	$126
9. Universal access to higher education	$273

Table 2-2. Discretionary Activities and Subactivities and Their Estimated Costs at Full Capacity for the 10-Year Period, 1974-83 (continued)

Activities	Total Cost 1974-83 (billions 1973 dollars)
10. Structural improvements in higher education	**$70**
New institutions	27
Staff support	5
Technological change and systems	38
11. Maintenance, updating and improvement of job skills	**$342**
Skill maintenance and updating	232
Career development	100
Job inquiry service	10
12. Specialized training and facilities for those outside the mainstream of the labor force	**$94**
Training	32
Job placement system	8
Special workshops for handicapped	6
Child care	18
Capital investment	15
Operations subsidy	15
13. Private savings, insurance, pension plans	**$200**
14. Provisions for old age pensions at 40 percent of current median earnings	**$30**
15. Extension of welfare programs (tax and transfer to abolish poverty and near poverty)	**$76**
16. Aid to depressed communities	**$171**
Infrastructure	84
Human capital	42
Productive activities	45
17. Construction and maintenance of houses	**$108**
Construction	98
Maintenance and repair	5
R&D	5
18. Design and testing of new neighborhood, city and regional environments	**$202**
New towns and model cities	38
Development design	32
Apartment design	38
Neighborhood design	90
Research and development	4

Table 2-2. Discretionary Activities and Subactivities and Their Estimated Costs at Full Capacity for the 10-Year Period, 1974-83 (continued)

Activities	Total Cost 1974-83 (billions 1973 dollars)
19. Innovations in cars, roads and other transportation system components	$155
Improved design and repair of automobiles	26
Street and highway innovations	45
Efficient rapid transit in major cities	64
Taxi fleets	20
20. Pollution control	$171
Vehicle emission control	56
Industrial emission control	30
Municipal sewage systems	30
Industrial and energy plants	15
Solid waste disposal	30
Noise prevention and control	10
21. More basic environmental improvements	$332
Circulating waste disposal systems	60
Rehabilitation of bodies of water	150
Rehabilitation of damaged land	60
Protecting essential resource balances	40
Environmental R&D	10
Conservation R&D	12
22. Provision of recreation facilities in neighborhoods	$127
23. Creation of major parks and facilities	$80
24. Preservation of wilderness and scenery	$26
25. Increased support of pure science	$36
Education	2
Capital investment	26
Operations of scientific institutions	8
26. Increased support for the arts	$28
Communication with public	2
Institutional development	9
Subsidies	16
New forms	1
27. Reduction in working time	$107
28. Expanded use of time-saving innovations	$91
Capital and operating home innovations	58
Developing wider markets	26
R&D	7
Total cost of all activities	$3,399

usefulness of the indicators in the absence of some objective feedback. Such research belongs to the future, though, and much would need to be done before its results could be applied.

DISCRETIONARY ACTIVITIES

Twenty-eight discretionary activities have been identified in this study. They constitute a summary of the technically feasible possibilities for improving, over a 10-year period, specific aspects of the quality of life in the United States. Some have been derived from well-known proposals or analyses. Others were based upon less well-developed and even fragmentary information.

The discretionary activities have all been defined at the national level and in terms of their specific major components. Their output and cost have been measured at capacity level, the level up to which productive results can be obtained and beyond which the cost becomes very high in relation to results, which are increasingly uncertain.[4] All have been formulated primarily in terms of technical and economic feasibility without taking into consideration political constraints other than those already embodied in the construction of believable activity scenarios.

The selection of activities and of their levels of capacity (as well as their costs and outputs) constitutes approximations. Alternative designs or alternative selections (and aggregations) could be made and capacity levels might be placed differently. Nevertheless, not much is likely to be gained by attempting a more refined approach at this time. Rather, it is more important to reasonably approximate the nature of an activity in order to reasonably cover the possibilities for effecting social change and therefore to have a starting point for examining the costs and effects of the activities.

The discretionary activities and their principal components are listed in Table 2-2, which also shows their total 10-year costs for the period 1974-83 at full capacity levels of operation. Details of the rationale and calculations underlying these estimates are discussed in the respective chapters in Part II.

As a rule, in formulating the activities used in this report, generous allowances were made for costs. In particular, considerable expenditures beyond the points that might be judged to represent the "best technique" were assumed on the grounds that the best techniques are not likely to be generally employed and also that leakage of expenditures is a normal occurrence, especially in the political setting where the tendency to spread public outlays over large beneficiary populations is real and is likely to continue. Thus, the estimated costs of

---

4   The discretionary activities are viewed as linear approximations to the typical diminishing returns of production functions. Constant returns are assumed to prevail up to capacity level; zero marginal returns beyond it.

Table 2-3. Effect of Activities on Goal Output Indicators, 1974-83

Goal Output Indicators

Activity	Total cost: 1974-83 (billions 1973 dollars)	Health & Safety — 1. Average life expectancy at birth, years	2. Percent of population with major disabilities	3. Number of violent crimes per 100,000 persons per year	Education, Skills and Earnings — 4. Index of mean performance in grade 12 based on standard tests	5. Percent of students 3 or more years behind 1973 average	6. Number of persons completing college, thousands	7. Number of persons not in the mainstream of labor force, millions	8. Median earnings of individuals, thousands 1973 dollars	Adequacy and Continuity of Income — 9. Percent of population below poverty standard	10. Percent of population in near-poverty conditions	11. Percent of population with living standard loss of over 30 percent	Economic Equality — 12. Family income ratio: 20th to 90th percentile	13. Mean family income, blacks as a percent of whites	14. Hourly earnings of women as percent of earnings of men	Human Habitat — 15. Percent of persons living in adequate housing	16. Percent of persons living in adequate neighborhoods	17. Percent of population affected by bothersome pollution	18. Percent of persons regularly taking part in outdoor recreation	19. Index of preservation of life and natural forms	Arts, Science and Free Time — 20. Number of scientists active in basic science, thousands	21. Number of active artists, thousands	22. Discretionary time, hours per person per year	GNP — 23. GNP, billions 1973 dollars
Base 1973 / Base 1983	—	71.3 / 72.7	17.5 / 16.8	668 / 668	100 / 105	24 / 19	957 / 1342	11.1 / 8.8	5.9 / 7.8	11.4 / 8.7	4.8 / 3.5	8.6 / 8.7	25 / 25	65 / 70	60 / 60	88 / 92	77 / 87	62 / 46	21 / 54	100 / 110	81 / 139	265 / 323	2111 / 2199	1275 / 2033
1. Change in health-related habits and patterns	$64	5.3	-3.3	-129								-.9							25				57	
2. Health services related to specific conditions	66	1.7	-3.1	-69								-.4											53	
3. Special health services for vulnerable population groups	91	2.5	-1.0																					
4. Improvement of law enforcement systems	26			-180																				
5. Employment and other opportunities for the young	51			-240		.4		-1.5		-.9	-.4			2										
6. Remedial and augmenting educational inputs	73				16	-11	50		.1				2	1										44
7. Improved educational technology and approaches	183				21	-14	50		.2				1											60
8. General day care for children	126							-1.8		-1.7	-1.3		2		3								117	43
9. Universal access to higher education	273						1050		.2		-.4		1								20	32		29
10. Structural improvements in higher education	70						350		.1												20	11		10

Table 2-3. Effect of Activities on Goal Output Indicators, 1974-83 (continued)

11. Maintenance, updating and improvement of job skills	342						650	-3.4	.2	-.9	-.9	-.9	6							10	16			34
12. Specialized training for those outside mainstream of labor force	94							-5.0	-1.3	-.4	-.4		2	4	3									21
13. Private savings, insurance, pension plans	200								-.9	-.6	-4.3		1	1										
14. Old age pensions at 40 percent of current median earnings	30								-1.7	-.6	-2.6		1	1										
15. Extended welfare program: tax and transfer to abolish poverty and near-poverty	76								-8.7	-3.5	-1.3			3	3									
16. Aid to depressed communities	171						-1.8		.2	-.9	-.9		1	2		4	5	-.2	5					17
17. Construction and maintenance of houses	108								-.4	-.4			1	8			5	-.2	5					
18. Design and testing of new neighborhood, city and regional environments	202									2	10	10						-.9	3					
19. Innovations in cars, roads and other transportation system components	155										-.4												71	
20. Pollution control	171												5			5		-29						
21. More basic environmental improvements	332	1.1	-.4															-17	4					
22. Recreation facilities in neighborhoods	127														5		12		5					
23. Major parks and facilities	80																	5	10					
24. Preservation of wilderness and scenery	26																		50					
25. Pure science—institutions, education, communication	36																				51			
26. The arts—institutions, education, subsidies, new forms	28																					300		
27. Reduction in working time	107																						60	
28. Time-saving innovations	91												1		2				4				319	50
TOTAL LISTED (output not additive)	(3,399)	(8.9)	(-6.8)	(-448)	(27)	(-16)	(1300)	(-7.2)	(1.4)	(-8.7)	(-3.5)	(-6.9)	(9)	(12)	(11)	(8)	(13)	(-37)	(28)	(60)	(81)	(315)	(677)	(160)

activities exceed the expenditures that might be most cost-effective in a strict sense, but as a practical matter, and especially in the aggregate, the theoretically low-cost figures imply greater ability to control expenditures than experience has shown to exist.

PRODUCTIVE RELATIONSHIPS

Estimates of the productive effects of discretionary activities on the conditions measured by the indicators have been combined into a matrix, shown in Table 2-3. (The corresponding set of activity-cost relationships is shown in Table 2-5.)

The entries in Table 2-3 show how much a given activity may contribute to a gain in the given indicator. Thus, for the first entry, activity number one (change in health-related habits and patterns) is estimated to possess a potential to improve health by increasing life expectancy (the first indicator) by as much as 5.3 years beyond the change expected from the continuation of current trends. The actual 1973 level of 71.3 years and the trend projection to 72.7 years in 1983 are shown immediately below the indicator titles at the top of the table.

This activity represents a futuristic scenario of events comprising reductions in the occurrence of smoking and obesity, abatement of alcohol and drug abuse, and widespread improvements in physical fitness that are considered techni-cally feasible provided such changes become widely accepted objectives of individuals and government agencies. The calculations of the effects of such changes on health are based on presently available knowledge of statistical connections between these various habits and conditions and the occurrence of specific diseases and losses of life expectancy connected with them. The activity scenario also includes estimates of the resource requirements and the timing and fiscal incidence of these requirements based on a series of direct and supporting activities needed to make these changes practical.[5]

In most cases, the effects of multiple activities on the given indicator are not additive. When undertaken at the same time, the different activities may either interfere with each other or achieve the maximum possible effect on the given indicator at levels lower than their full capacity. Therefore, the possible com-bined effect of more than one activity directed toward the same social area is, as a rule, less than the sum of the individual effects of each activity taken sepa-rately. The nonadditive effects were calculated by an approximative method of applying linear programming analysis which was developed in the course of the present study. The method consists of developing different sets of estimates of the effects of activities on indicators for different levels of output. In Table 2-4, the matrix has been expanded to include alternate columns for specified ranges

---

5   The activities and the calculations of their effects and costs are described in detail in Chapters 5-22.

of output. The column applicable to each output range represents productive possibilities approximately along the least-cost expansion path which are available at this level of output given the interference effects among the activities. The higher the output level the greater are these interference effects. For each column, the activity-output coefficients for each indicator are based on the particular interactions among the effects of activities on the given indicator at the given range of output. These interactions are discussed in the concluding sections of Chapters 5 to 22 dealing with the respective indicators. For each indicator, the first column shows the activity-output coefficients applicable in the absence of any offsetting effects which is always the case if the activities are taken singly. These columns form the matrix in Table 2-3. For some output indicators, the interactions among activities were judged to be sufficiently small to be ignored. In such cases, only one column appears for the indicator in Table 2-4, the same as in Table 2-3. A detailed discussion of the way in which the stage columns for the matrix were derived and of the manner in which the linear stage method approximates the nonlinear relationships may be found in an NPA technical staff paper.[6]

The maximum effect of all activities relevant to a particular indicator, if pursued together, is shown on the bottom lines in Tables 2-3 and 2-4. For the life expectancy indicator, for example, this effect is an additional 8.9 years of life compared to the sum of individual effects of 10.6 years. To a considerable extent, multiple activities were identified because there exist alternative approaches for achieving a particular social change.

Table 2-5 contains the activity-cost matrix. It gives the total cost of activities in the first column and the breakdown of total cost into public and private outlays by two subperiods in subsequent columns. As an addendum, the last two columns show (1) the percent of total cost which must be provided for within the first 4 years of the 10-year period in order to implement the nonpostponable early phases of the activities, and (2) public outlays as percent of total cost.[7] For activity one, the cost differences of the components as estimated happen to average out, resulting in overall even divisions, but for other activities very different cost breakdowns occur.

Differences in the financing requirements of the various activities are considerable. Funding requirements for the early phases may reflect either a need to complete the introduction of an activity with a long phasing-in period dictated either by the scale of the activity or by a long production period, such as in the

---

6   Neil J. McMullen, "A Piecewise Linear Adaptation of Linear Programming for the Estimation of the Costs of Achieving National Goals," A Technical Staff Paper (Washington, D.C.: National Planning Association, December 1974).

7   Some activities—for example, reductions in working time—may reduce the gross national product. Such reductions are treated as costs.

Table 2-4 (Part 1). Effect of Activities on Goal Output Indicators, 1974-83, At Different Levels of Output Requirement

Goal Output Indicators (dollar amounts in 1973 prices)

Activities	Total Cost: 1974-83, billions 1973 dollars	Health & Safety													Index of mean performance in grade 12 based on standard tests		
		1. Average life expectancy at birth, years				2. Percent of population with major disabilities					3. Number of violent crimes per 100,000 persons per year				4.		
		0 to 2.5	2.5 to 4.1	4.1 to 6.8	6.8 to 8.9	0 to 1.0	1.0 to 3.3	3.3 to 4.1	4.1 to 5.9	5.9 to 6.8	0 to 129	129 to 309	309 to 334	334 to 448	0 to 16	16 to 25	25 to 27
1. Change in health-related habits and patterns	$64	5.3	5.3	5.3	5.3	-3.3	-3.3	-3.1	-3.0	-2.9	-129	-129	-129	-78			
2. Health services related to specific conditions	66	1.7	1.6	1.5	1.4	-3.1	-3.1	-2.9	-2.9	-2.8	-69	-34	-25	-14			
3. Special health services for vulnerable population groups	91	2.5	2.5	2.0	2.0	-1.0	-1.0	-1.0	-1.0	-1.0							
4. Improvement of law enforcement systems	26										-180	-180	-180	-170			
5. Employment and other opportunities for the young	51										-240	-240	-192	-186	5	4	1
6. Remedial and augmenting educational inputs	73														16	13	10
7. Improved educational technology and approaches	183														21	21	16
8. General day care for children	126																
9. Universal access to higher education	273																
10. Structural improvements in higher education	70																
11. Maintenance, updating and improvement of job skills	342																
12. Specialized training for those outside mainstream of labor force	94																
13. Private savings, insurance, pension plans	200																
14. Old age pensions at 40 percent of current median earnings	30																
15. Extended welfare program: tax and transfer to abolish poverty and near-poverty	76																
16. Aid to depressed communities	171																
17. Construction and maintenance of houses	108																
18. Design and testing of new neighborhood, city and regional environments	202																
19. Innovations in cars, roads and other transportation system components	155																
20. Pollution control	171																
21. More basic environmental improvements	332																
22. Recreation facilities in neighborhoods	127	1.1	1.0	.2	.2	-.4	-.3	-.3	-.3	-.1							
23. Major parks and facilities	80																
24. Preservation of wilderness and scenery	26																
25. Pure science—institutions, education, communication	36																
26. The arts—institutions, education, subsidies, new forms	28																
27. Reduction in working time	107																
28. Time-saving innovations	91																
MAXIMUM POSSIBLE	3,399	8.9				-6.8					-448				27		

Table 2-4 (Part 1 continued)

Education, Skills and Earnings													Adequacy and Continuity of Income											
5. Percent of students 3 or more years behind 1973 average			6. Number of persons completing college, thousands			7. Number of persons not in the mainstream of labor force, millions						8. Median earnings of individuals, thousands 1973 dollars	9. Percent of population below poverty standard				10. Percent of population in near-poverty conditions				11. Percent of population with living standard loss of over 30 percent			
0 to 11	11 to 14	14 to 16	0 to 650	650 to 1050	1050 to 1300	0 to 1.8	1.8 to 3.4	3.4 to 4.0	4.0 to 5.0	5.0 to 5.7	5.7 to 7.2	0 to 1.4	0 to 0.9	0.9 to 1.7	1.7 to 3.0	3.0 to 8.7	0 to 0.6	0.6 to 1.1	1.1 to 2.2	2.2 to 3.5	0 to 0.9	0.9 to 1.3	1.3 to 4.3	4.3 to 6.9
																					-.9	-.7	-.7	-.4
																					-.4	-.4	-.3	-.2
-4	-3	-1				-1.5	-1.5	-1.4	-1.4	-1.4	-.5		-.9	-.9	-.9	-.6	-.4	-.4	-.2	-.2				
-11	-9	-1	50	50	50							.1												
-14	-14	-14	50	50	50							.2												
						-1.8	-1.8	-1.8	-1.2	-1.2	-.3		-1.7	-1.7	-1.3	-1.0	-1.3	-1.3	-1.3	-0.8				
			1050	1050	1050							.2					-.4	-.4	-.4	-.2				
			350	225	100							.1												
			650	525	50	-3.4	-3.4	-3.4	-3.4	-2.8		.2	-.9	-.4	-.4	-.4	-.9	-.9	-.9	-.5				
						-5.0	-5.0	-5.0	-5.0	-4.0	-3.3		-1.3	-1.3	-.9	-.8	-.4	-.2	-.2	-.2	-.4	-.4	-.4	-.2
													-.9	-.9	-.5	-.4	-.6	-.3	-.3	-.3	-4.3	-4.3	-4.3	-4.3
													-1.7	-1.7	-1.7	-1.7	-.6	-.6	-.6	-.6	-2.6	-2.6	-2.6	-.9
													-8.7	-8.7	-8.7	-8.7	-3.5	-3.5	-3.5	-3.5	-1.3	-1.3	-.9	-.9
						-1.8	-1.2	-.6	-.6	-.3	-.3	.2	-.9	-.7	-.5	-.5	-.9	-.9	-.7	-.5				
													-.4	-.4	-.3	-.2	-.4	-.2	-.2	-.2				
												0.4												
-16			1,300			-7.2						1.4	-8.7				-3.5				-6.9			

Table 2-4 (Part 2). Effect of Activities on Goal Output Indicators, 1974-83, At Different Levels of Output Requirement

Goal Output Indicators (dollar amounts in 1973 prices)

Activities	Total Cost: 1974-83, billions 1973 dollars	Economic Equality										
		12. Family income ratio: 20th to 90th percentile				13. Mean family income, blacks as a percent of whites				14. Hourly earnings of women as percent of earnings of men	15. Percent of persons living in adequate housing	
		0 to 2	2 to 2.8	2.8 to 5.2	5.2 to 9.0	0 to 1	1 to 3	3 to 7	7 to 12	0 to 11	0 to 4	4 to 8
1. Change in health-related habits and patterns	$64											
2. Health services related to specific conditions	66											
3. Special health services for vulnerable population groups	91											
4. Improvement of law enforcement systems	26											
5. Employment and other opportunities for the young	51					2	2	1	1			
6. Remedial and augmenting educational inputs	73	2.0	1.6	1.6	1.6	1	0	0	0			
7. Improved educational technology and approaches	183	1.0	.8	.8	.8							
8. General day care for children	126	2.0	2.0	2.0	1.6					3		
9. Universal access to higher education	273	1.0	1.0	.9	.7							
10. Structural improvements in higher education	70											
11. Maintenance, updating and improvement of job skills	342	2.0	1.8	1.2	1.2	4	4	4	4	6		
12. Specialized training for those outside mainstream of labor force	94					3	3	1	1			
13. Private savings, insurance, pension plans	200	1.0	1.0	1.0	1.0	1	1	1	1			
14. Old age pensions at 40 percent of current median earnings	30	1.0	1.0	1.0	1.0	1	1	1	1			
15. Extended welfare program: tax and transfer to abolish poverty and near-poverty	76					3	3	3	2			
16. Aid to depressed communities	171	1.0	.8	.8	.7	2	2	1	1		4	3
17. Construction and maintenance of houses	108					1	1	1	1		8	8
18. Design and testing of new neighborhood, city and regional environments	202										2	2
19. Innovations in cars, roads and other transportation system components	155											
20. Pollution control	171											
21. More basic environmental improvements	332											
22. Recreation facilities in neighborhoods	127											
23. Major parks and facilities	80											
24. Preservation of wilderness and scenery	26											
25. Pure science—institutions, education, communication	36											
26. The arts—institutions, education, subsidies, new forms	28											
27. Reduction in working time	107											
28. Time-saving innovations	91	1.0	.8	.8	.4					2		
MAXIMUM POSSIBLE	3,399	9.0				12				11	8	

Table 2-4 (Part 2 continued)

Human Habitat													Arts, Science and Free Time							
16. Percent of persons living in adequate neighborhoods				17. Percent of population affected by bothersome pollution				18. Percent of persons regularly taking part in outdoor recreation				19. Index of preservation of life and natural forms	20. Number of scientists active in basic science, thousands				21. Number of active artists, thousands			22. Discretionary time, hours per person per year
0 to 5	5 to 10	10 to 12	12 to 13	0 to 8.7	8.7 to 30.3	30.3 to 34.6	34.6 to 36.8	0 to 12	12 to 25	25 to 27	27 to 28	0 to 60	0 to 20	20 to 30	30 to 51	51 to 81	0 to 32	32 to 300	300 to 315	0 to 677
								25	25	22	22									57
																				53
																				117
													20	15	15	13	32	25	11	
													20	15	15	13	11	9	3	
													10	10	5	4	16	4	1	
5	3	2	2	-2.2	-2.2	-2.2	-.8	5	1	0	0									
5	3	2	2	-2.2	-2.2	-1.7	-1.7													
10	10	9	8	-8.7	-7.8	-4.5	-4.5	3	1	0	0									
				-4.3	-1.7	-1.7	-.5													71
5	3	1	1	-28.6	-28.6	-25.0	-21.0													
				-17.3	-17.3	-9.6	-8.3	4	1	0	0									
5	5	3	2					12	12	4	3									
								5	2	1	1	10								
												50								
													51	51	51	51				
																	300	300	300	
																				60
								4	4	4	2									319
13				-36.8				28				60	81				315			677

**Table 2-5. Estimated Cost of Discretionary Activities: 1974-83, Total
Distribution by Subperiod and Private and Public Financing Requirements**

Activities	Total Cost: 1974-83, billions 1973 dollars	Components of Total				As Percent of Total Cost	
		Public Outlays, 1974-77	Private Outlays, 1974-77	Public Outlays, 1978-83	Private Outlays, 1978-83	All Outlays, 1974-77	All Public Outlays
1. Change in health-related habits and patterns	64	17	16	15	16	52%	50%
2. Health services related to specific conditions	66	11	6	33	16	26	66
3. Special health services for vulnerable population groups	91	30	0	61	0	33	100
4. Improvement of law enforcement systems	26	10	1	15	0	41	96
5. Employment and other opportunities for the young	51	7	2	34	8	17	80
6. Remedial and augmenting educational imputs	73	11	1	55	6	17	90
7. Improved educational technology and approaches	183	7	0	158	18	4	90
8. General day care for children	126	17	4	84	21	17	80
9. Universal access to higher education	273	5	0	268	0	2	100
10. Structural improvements in higher education	70	11	2	53	4	18	91
11. Maintenance, updating and improvement of job skills	342	46	22	183	91	20	67
12. Specialized training for those outside mainstream of labor force	94	9	0	85	0	10	100
13. Private savings, insurance, pension plans	200	16	64	24	96	40	20
14. Old age pensions at 40 percent of current median earnings	30	0	0	30	0	0	100
15. Extended welfare program: tax and transfer to abolish poverty and near-poverty	76	0	0	76	0	0	100

Table 2-5. Estimated Cost of Discretionary Activities: 1974-83, Total (continued)
Distribution by Subperiod and Private and Public Financing Requirements

Activities	Total Cost: 1974-83, billions 1973 dollars	Components of Total				As Percent of Total Cost	
		Public Outlays, 1974-77	Private Outlays, 1974-77	Public Outlays, 1978-83	Private Outlays, 1978-83	All Outlays, 1974-77	All Public Outlays
16. Aid to depressed communities	171	18	3	136	14	12%	90%
17. Construction and maintenance of houses	108	14	17	36	41	29	46
18. Design and testing of new neighborhood, city and regional environments	202	16	16	85	85	16	50
19. Innovation in cars, roads and other transportation system components	155	1	7	27	120	5	18
20. Pollution control	171	12	12	76	71	14	51
21. More basic environmental improvements	332	75	8	224	25	25	90
22. Recreation facilities in neighborhoods	127	15	10	61	41	20	60
23. Major parks and facilities	80	13	3	51	13	20	80
24. Preservation of wilderness and scenery	26	6	0	18	2	25	92
25. Pure science—institutions, education, communication	36	4	1	24	7	15	79
26. The arts—institutions, education, subsidies, new forms	28	3	1	16	8	15	69
27. Reduction in working time	107	0	0	21	86	0	20
28. Time-saving innovations	91	1	6	17	67	8	20
TOTAL LISTED	3,399	375	202	1,966	856	17%	69%

construction of houses, if results are to be achieved by the target date or a need to provide the necessary research and development, as in the case of basic environmental improvements. On the other hand, activities involving a transfer of funds, e.g., transfers to eliminate poverty and near-poverty by 1983, do not require any major lead-time for early phasing-in once the decision to undertake such an activity has been made. Note that this results as of a specific date, here 10 years in the future. Nothing is said about either relative values of different goals or the relative urgency of achieving them.

In order to take into account these differences in the timing of resource use, the activity cost and also the resource projections are shown in detail for the two subperiods. There are several reasons for choosing only two subperiods and of these particular lengths. The scope of the present study could accommodate very few subperiods. Little would be gained by attempting a year-by-year analysis; the data clearly did not permit that fine a resolution. In fact, the empirical data made it very difficult to distinguish even among three sub-periods; two of them invariably got blurred. And yet, one period would not be enough because the time shape of resources availability is highly unequal between the early and later years of the 10-year period. The disparity in the estimated amounts available, say, in the third year and in the eighth year is enormous. Because the activities do have different time cost profiles, the time shape of the availability of resources is an important dimension of the economic constraint. Using aggregates for two subperiods as distinct inputs was virtually the only available choice consistent with making some allowance for the differ-ences in the early resource requirements among the activities, on the one hand, and the tremendous differences over time in the supply of the discretionary resources, on the other.

The length of four and six years was chosen by first reviewing the activity time profiles. It was decided that the initiation phase should be shorter than the implementation phase but should be longer than two years since a short initial period would be vulnerable to the uncertainties in the actual estimation of the early resource requirements. Also, the very small size of the discretionary resources in the public sector available over such periods could easily be lost within the margin of fiscal fluctuations. The same problem but in lesser degree applies to the three years. For that reason, a four-year initial period was chosen. The design of the analysis in matrix form is both flexible and general and can easily accommodate redefinition of indicators, activities and costs. Indicators for new areas and additional indicators for identical categories can be readily included, while indicators of a concern receding from public prominence can be deleted. Additions, deletions, aggregations, and disaggregations of activities can be made with equal ease. Cost categories can also be changed to reflect changed conditions.

The activities included in this study were intended to represent the main opportunities available (other than those already well under way and therefore treated as part of the nondiscretionary trend) for improving particular social conditions. Since each activity entails some departure from past patterns, it is therefore inherently uncertain as to its effect and cost. Short of actual attempts to implement the activities, at least through development and testing on a small scale, there are no methods to measure, *a priori,* their effectiveness. Only more or less uncertain forecasts are possible. Because existing knowledge regarding the cost of the activities, their effect and the level up to which they could reasonably be productive is incomplete and uncertain, working all these diverse pieces of information into a consistent time, cost and effect framework required a substantial amount of interpolation and filling in of information gaps.

The activities could be more disaggregated, but at that point the difficult technical problem would arise of dealing simultaneously with positive and negative interactions. More important, the uncertainties as to their effect would cumulate but the level of practicality probably would not be raised much. Therefore, it is left for later research, perhaps even research with more direct intent toward application in a given field, to develop more detailed and more specific estimates of activities. Also, the question of possibly breaking up activities into more and less productive segments depending on the scale of result intended is similarly left for future research. The main objective of this study has been to develop the analytical framework and within it to identify the principal existing opportunities and to make approximate benchmark estimates of their productivity and cost.

It should be noted that the discretionary activities defined here are not recommendations for government programs or for general social adoption. Rather, they should be viewed as technical estimates of possible alternative trends. Taken together, they may serve as a vehicle for coordinating knowledge about possible large-scale change within a 10-year national framework that encompasses activities of both private and public sectors.

3

Availability of resources

The availability of resources places definite limits on the extent to which discretionary activities can be undertaken. The resources under consideration in this chapter are formulated in terms of real dollar resources, i.e., as generalized future purchasing power expressed in 1973 prices which can command real resources needed to launch and support every discretionary activity. Nonmonetary resources, such as manpower and specialized forms of human capital, the capacity for information processing and policy making, and substitutability among resources, have been taken into consideration in the estimates of the capacity of discretionary activities to produce outputs, the productivity of the activities (embodied in the output coefficients), and the interactions among activities.

Because resources available in the economy over a future period cannot be freely substituted for each other within the total, two major constraints are placed on the total resources available for discretionary activities—the source of financing, that is, whether it is public or private, and the time of availability, that is, whether the resources are available early or late in the 10-year period.

To determine where the resource availability lies, the projections of total resources available for discretionary activities over the 10-year period 1974-83 were made in detail of four components reflecting two two-fold divisions, first into the public and the private sector components, and then their distribution by subperiods, one encompassing the first 4 years of the period (1974-77) and the other the last 6 (1978-83).

DETERMINANTS OF THE RESOURCE SUPPLY

The total resources available for discretionary activities over the 10-year period are determined by three principal factors: (1) the rate of economic growth; (2) the share of GNP (and selected resource transfers) used for expenditures in social categories; and (3) the degree to which those resources are *de facto* committed to financing ongoing base activities.

Economic growth

A 4.8 percent rate of growth in real GNP per year, the projection of the

National Planning Association current as of this writing,[1] has been used for the base projection of GNP. To consider a range of possible rates of economic growth and resulting variations in the availability of resources, a lower figure of 4 percent and a higher figure of 5.5 percent growth per annum have been considered as well.

Some of the discretionary activities have a positive effect on the rate of economic growth and thus could be at least in part self-financing. The effects of discretionary activities on economic growth are discussed in Chapter 23, but the feedback between discretionary activities and economic growth is not explored here.[2] One reason is that it would increase the complexity of the analysis; another, that the present results would not be affected to any extent because little additional resources could be generated through such increases in economic growth in the critical early years of the period. Such an extension of the analysis will become more important in future work, especially in dealing with periods longer than 10 years, and in formulating rigorous analytical models.

Share of resources allocated to social areas

Since social objectives, as defined in this analysis, absorb only a part of the nation's resources, and presumably constitute only a part of a broader system of individual and national objectives, the share of resources directed toward social goals needs to be estimated specifically to determine the resource base for discretionary activities. For convenience, such resources are called "social resources."

The base year level of social resources has been determined approximately by aggregating selected categories from the national income accounts. Such an arrangement of the 1972 expenditure data is shown in Table 3-1.

In the table, expenditures for health care, research and training in the health professions and for police, fire protection and corrections are included under health and safety. Consumer expenditure items relating to personal safety, such as the costs of locks, alarm systems, guards, etc., were not broken out of personal consumption expenditure because the data were not available at this level of detail. Education includes only direct outlays. Elements consistent with a broader and perhaps more relevant concept of learning—for example,

---

1 Since that time, the NPA projection of the rate of economic growth has been revised substantially downward to *3.9 percent*. See Robert Dennis, *Clambering into the Eighties* (Washington, D.C.: National Planning Association, 1974), p. 1. This lower rate is sufficiently close to the 4 percent lower variant assumption discussed next to have its implications apply to it as well.

2 William Cooper has suggested to me how the present system could be generalized to include this feedback effect of discretionary activities on economic growth.

Table 3-1. Allocation of National Expenditures by Social Areas, 1972

(money amounts in billions of dollars)

Social Areas	Total	Percent of Grand Total	Personal Savings and Consumption[1]	Private Investment[2]	State and Local Expenditures	Federal Expenditures
Health and Safety	**$93.7**	**6.9%**				
Health & hospital services (including health insurance)	78.9		$57.4	$3.2	$13.9	$4.4
Veterans' hospital care	2.4					2.4
Correction	2.5				2.3	0.2
Police	6.9				6.7	0.2
Fire protection	3.0				2.0	
Education	**87.6**	**6.5**				
Education, public	72.1				65.6	6.5
Education, private	12.9		12.0	0.9		
Education, veterans	2.6					2.6
Income Security and Maintenance	**179.0**	**13.2**				
Social security & social welfare services (Old age, unemployment benefits, etc.)	63.0					63.0
Personal savings	49.7		49.7			
Agriculture price & income support	4.2					4.2
Personal insurance (life & car)	13.5		13.5			
Public assistance & relief	37.3				22.6	14.7
Other payments to veterans	7.1					7.1
Private welfare[3]	2.5		2.5			
Regulation of business	1.7				1.5	0.2
Human Habitat	**395.5**	**29.1**				
Rental value & new residential construction	164.0		105.5	53.1	0.9	4.5
Transportation	147.8		95.6	25.9	18.5	7.8
Communication (including postal)	15.9		14.3			1.6
Agricultural conservation	1.9				1.4	0.5
Conservation & development of resources	4.4				1.5	2.9
Sanitation	4.1				3.1	1.0
Personal recreation	47.8		47.8			
Public recreation	2.8				2.3	0.5
Foreign travel	6.8		6.8			
Total for Social Goals	**$755.8**	**55.6%**	**$405.1**	**$83.1**	**$143.3**	**$124.3**
Mostly Private Expenditure for Other than Social Goals	**461.7**	**34.0**	**371.1**	**90.6**		
Food and clothing	230.6		230.6			
Other consumption	140.5		140.5			
Other investments	90.6			90.6		
Mostly Public Expenditure for Other than Social Goals	**141.0**	**10.4**			**20.7**	**120.3**
Grand Total	**$1,358.5**	**100**	**$776.2**	**$173.7**	**$164.0**	**$244.6**
Less transfers & personal saving	203.4	15.0	49.7		13.5	140.2
GNP	**$1,155.1**	**85.0%**	**$726.5**	**$173.7**	**$150.5**	**$104.4**

Note: This arrangement of expenditures is based on published detail of objects of expenditures and consequently certain categories which would logically correspond to other items included under various headings were not identified.   Detail may not add to totals due to rounding.

[1]   Includes purchases of goods and services by nonprofit institutions.

[2]   Includes net exports.

[3]   Assumed that out of $10.1 billion spent for religious and welfare activities in the consumer sector, 25 percent is for philanthropy.

Source: U. S. Department of Commerce, Bureau of Economic Analysis, *Survey of Current Business,* July 1973, pp. 18, 27, 29, 35, 39. All the numbers are from this source except where otherwise noted.

the cost incurred by parents for teaching their children within the home—were not allocated.

In addition to income transfers, income maintenance includes personal savings, on the ground that they are directed toward the protection of income and the preservation of living standards, and expenditures for the regulation of business, since ultimately they are directed toward the protection of income and living standards by eliminating losses resulting from monopolistic prices or unfair business practices.

National expenditures in the various categories have been broken down into private (consumer expenditure and savings, private investment) and public (state and local spending, federal spending) components, following the categorizations of data in the national income accounts. Intergovernmental transfers have been netted out, but transfers through the government sector to individuals are counted twice, first as public and then as consumer expenditures. The amount of personal savings, classified explicitly under income maintenance, is also counted twice: once as the income maintenance item and again as various investment expenditures. The double counting in these instances is necessary because transfers of resources through the tax system and private savings accumulation constitute important resource allocations toward some of the particular social goals, thus representing distributional concerns.

This formulation of the resource cost concept has the advantage of permitting an analysis of the cost of achieving different goals in terms of consumer and governmental expenditures and is compatible with the respective budgetary data. But it has the disadvantage of double counting. Potentially, the levels of transfers could be arbitrary. In this work, the level of transfers was constrained by the amount of transfers anticipated in the NPA economic projections data used to derive resource estimates. At present, the resource cost of activities includes real resources as well as certain transfer payments. The individual cost coefficients do not specify the distribution between real resources and transfers except indirectly through the distinction between private and public sector resources. Use of this mixed resource cost concept is unsatisfactory for a longer range. It was not practical within the scope of the present study to develop an approach which would make a consistent distinction between real economic production and transfers of resources, for example, in the form of separate matrixes for real resources and for transfer payments. Such development, however, seems to be a very desirable direction for future work because it could help to relate the goals accounting system directly to both national income accounting and to fiscal analysis.[3]

The "mostly private" spending not related to the social areas identified here consists primarily of consumer expenditure for food and clothing and of busi-

---

3 Development of such links is being explored in the ongoing theoretical work by the author mentioned earlier.

ness investment in plant and equipment.[4] The "mostly public" group comprises essentially general government and defense activities. In the "mostly private" group are largely activities in support of the objectives of individuals and households and of businesses which are satisfied largely or completely through the private market system. In the "mostly public" group are the categories requiring primarily the support of expenditures and activities of the public sector alone. The social goals categories, on the other hand, are affected for the most part by inputs from both the private sector (markets and households) and the public programs.

The grand total in Table 3-1 consists of GNP plus selected transfers and savings. In 1972, expenditures for social areas represented about 56 percent of the grand total of national expenditures and were 65 percent of GNP (technically .65 relative to GNP, because some of the resources essential in these expenditures are not a part of GNP).

To determine the relationship between social resources and GNP over time, an examination of national expenditures by social areas was made for the 20-year period 1952-72. Then, the 10-year projections of social resources were made —including a "standard" projection, a high alternative and a low alternative. These social resource trends and projections appear in Chart 3-1.

As the chart shows, social resources increased from about 47 percent of GNP in 1952 to 55 percent in 1966 and 65 percent in 1971 and 1972. As the chart also shows, the public component of those resources rose from about 23 percent in 1952 to about 32 percent in 1965 to just over 35 percent in 1972.

The projections of future social resources were based on these 20-year trends and assumptions about the next 10 years. The high alternative roughly corresponds to growth rates over past periods. These rates appear to be upper limits since their continued growth would result in social resources preempting a share of total resources larger than seems feasible. The standard projection assumes a more moderate rate of growth, particularly of the public share. The low alternative assumes constant or slightly decreased percentages of social resources. This alternative seems less probable than the standard projection since the momentum created by recent social expenditures seems likely to generate a positive rate of growth in this proportion.

In the standard projection, the ratio of social resources to GNP was estimated to rise to 69 percent in 1983 while the ratio of public social expenditure to total social expenditure was estimated to rise to 39 percent. This assumes annual growth rates of 5.3 percent for total social resources, 6.4 percent for public social resources, and 4.7 percent for private social resources.

The high alternative is estimated at 72 percent of 1983 GNP (annual growth

---

4   Because it is not an object of the present analysis, international trade was not analyzed in detail, and net surplus was included with investment.

Chart 3-1. Social Resource Trends and Projections*

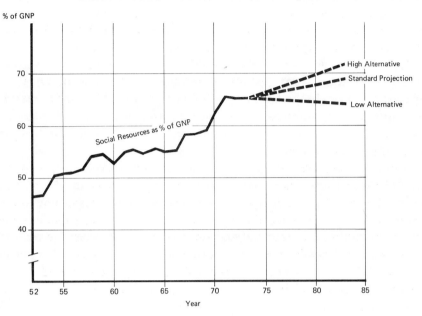

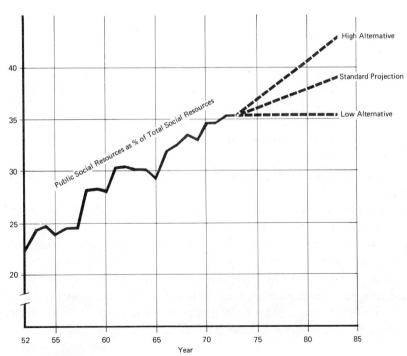

* Based on current dollars.

Source:　Department of Commerce, Bureau of Economic Analysis, *Survey of Current Business,*
July issue, approximate years.

rate: 5.8 percent), with 43 percent of the resources coming from the public sector (annual growth rate: 7.4 percent). The low alternative is estimated at 64 percent of 1983 GNP (annual growth rate: 4.5 percent), with the public share at 35.4 percent (annual growth rate: 5.4 percent).

Table 3-2 presents an estimate of 1973 resources and, using the standard projection, a projection of 1983 resources in 1973 dollars. Resources for social concerns, as shown in the table, are estimated at $834 billion in 1973 and $1,403 billion in 1983, with the total 10-year flow aggregating to approximately $11.2 trillion. The 10-year cost of the discretionary activities described in this analysis is estimated at $3.4 trillion.

At first glance, then, it might seem that all the discretionary activities are economically feasible since their total cost is well under the 10-year supply presumed to be allocated to social areas. This is not the case, however, since most social expenditures are already committed to ongoing activities expected to be continued throughout the decade, perhaps at diminishing rates of implementation, but nevertheless at important levels. In any case, they will not be below the levels necessary for supporting the ongoing base trends. To determine the resources available for discretionary activities, it is necessary to determine the proportion of social resources committed to base trend activities.

Base trend commitments

Since resources are limited, discretionary activities must compete for funds with existing activities. Discretionary funds cannot be viewed as a residual after the claims of ongoing uses have been satisfied, since ongoing uses are capable of absorbing resources at increasing rates that tend to eliminate any residual.[5] Therefore, the amount of resources that can be diverted to discretionary activities is predicated on constraining and/or phasing out expenditures for ongoing activities, though without impairing the output they have been producing in the process of substitution.

A certain amount of resources, depending largely on population growth, is required to maintain the output of activities. In many cases, this amount probably consists of a constant absolute or a constant per capita level of resources for the 10-year period. In some fields, maybe in pollution control, for example, maintaining projected trends may require increased real spending per capita at certain minimum rates to maintain current levels of environmental quality. On the other hand, the amount required to produce a constant level of output may be expected to diminish with time, at least in some fields, as the productivity of

---

5   The historical record has not been studied but it would probably show that *ex post* the discretionary margin was established through new activities introduced under various pressures rather than through an allocation of an unused residual "in a vacuum."

Table 3-2. Estimated Resource Allocations, 1973 and 1983
(billions of 1973 dollars)

	1973			1983			Average Annual Rate of Change, 1973-83		
	Total	Public	Private	Total	Public	Private	Total	Public	Private
Grand Total	$1,497	$448	$1,049	n.e.	n.e.	n.e.	n.e.	n.e.	n.e.
Expenditures:[1]									
Social expenditure	834	295	539	$1,403	$547	$856	5.3	6.4	4.7
Other government[2]	153	153	n.a.	n.e.	n.e.	n.a.	n.e.	6.4	n.a.
Other private[3]	510	n.a.	510	n.e.	n.a.	n.e.	n.e.	n.a.	n.e.
Type of Expenditure:									
GNP	1,275	281	994	2,033	n.e.	n.e.	4.8	n.e.	n.e.
Transfers and savings[4]	222	167	55	n.e.	n.e.	n.e.	n.e.	n.e.	n.e.

n.e. = not estimated

n.a. = not applicable

[1] The expenditures were deflated by the implicit GNP deflator uniformly on the grounds that ex ante they are free generalized resources rather than the result of a specific activity or output configuration.

[2] Mostly defense, international and interest payments.

[3] Mostly consumption of food and clothing, net exports, and business investments.

[4] "Transfers and savings" are partial duplication items from GNP which are included in the resource total because some social objectives involve specific transfer or savings activity regardless of the production of GNP.

Note: GNP figures are based on NPA projections in real dollars. The percentage distribution for the components in 1972 (Table 3-1) is maintained for 1973. Only the components directly related to the resource projections made here were estimated for 1983.

the producing organization grows and knowledge bearing on its activities accumulates. In the present analysis, it has been assumed that these two opposing tendencies cancel each other and that continued use of resources in constant amounts is both necessary and sufficient to maintain the productivity of base trend activities. The assumption that constant absolute amounts of resources are necessary to support the base output trend consists of assuming that population growth, which in the absence of productivity changes would require constant per capita amounts of expenditure, is offset by productivity growth, which proceeds at the same rate.

Analysis of actual experience should provide useful guides to the degree of flexibility in resource use that can be expected in the future. Unfortunately, there exists very little analysis of past or current patterns of resource reallocation or their effects on output.[6] Therefore, the attempt to estimate discretionary resources has to rely on such scattered fragments of empirical evidence as are available now. To determine the amount of discretionary resources available and the deceleration rate of base trend expenditures thus requires a fairly lengthy analysis, which follows.

Sources of discretionary resources

Discretionary and nondiscretionary social resources exist in both the private and public sectors. Because of the different expenditure patterns, the two sectors are examined separately.

Public sector resources

There are three prime sources for discretionary public funds: (1) the fiscal dividend of federal, state and local governments; (2) a shifting of funds among programs, which is dependent upon the flexibility of existing programs; and (3) changes in institutional arrangements, such as levying of additional taxes. In addition to these basic sources of discretionary funds in the public sector, government revenues, and with them discretionary resources, can increase also through two other developments. One is inflation which because of the progressive tax structure results in a transfer of real resources to the government, and the other is increases in real product resulting from reduction of unem-

---

6   Until quite recently, the question of flexibility in resource reallocation received little attention from analysts and economists. Consequently, the concept of what constitutes a discretionary resource has not been well-defined. The importance of the issue, however, has now been recognized. See Michael E. Levy, "The New Federal Budget," *Conference Board Record* (New York: The Conference Board, April 1972); Charles Schultze et al., *Setting National Priorities: The 1974 Budget* (Washington, D.C.: The Brookings Institution, 1973); and Murray L. Weidenbaum and Daniel Larkins, *The Federal Budget for 1973* (Washington, D.C.: American Enterprise Institute, 1972). See also reviews of later federal budgets by these authors.

ployment of existing resources or improvements in the efficiency of their utilization. These latter possibilities are discussed in Chapter 4.

The fiscal dividend. During most of the country's history, economic growth tended to generate increases in federal revenues that exceeded the expenditures needed to carry out federal programs. This fiscal dividend could be used either to implement new programs or to lower taxes. But that situation changed in the 1960s. As a result of the tax cuts of 1964, 1969 and 1971, and the growth of new domestic programs in the 1960s, it became evident that, for at least the next decade, the fiscal dividend could not be relied upon to finance new programs. In fact, commitments involved in existing programs suggested substantial budgetary deficits, even on a full-employment basis, for four to five years. The fiscal 1974 U.S. budget, for example, projected no discretionary margin for 1974 and a fiscal dividend margin of 0.7 percent ($2 billion) in 1975 and 10.7 percent ($35 billion) in 1978, provided a series of proposed budget cuts are enacted.[7] Comparable Brookings Institution projections predicted a fiscal dividend of 6.3 percent in 1978, claiming that many of the expenditure cuts listed in the official budget do not represent actual reductions in the level of federal spending.[8]

We have assumed a 1978 fiscal dividend (year five for this study) that lies between these two estimates. The average of the two gives an 8.5 percent fiscal dividend for the federal budget for 1978. We have reduced this average by 20 percent, to 6.8 percent, since past estimates of fiscal dividends have shown a decrease over time even when they were not based on budget cuts.

State and local finances have changed in recent years, too. In 1970 and 1971, there appeared to be a crisis in state-local finances since tax bases did not seem to be expanding fast enough to meet higher costs. However, improved general economic conditions, reduced birth rates and federal assistance changed the picture. By the end of fiscal 1972, almost one-third of the state governments expected to have substantial surpluses. In 1973, the fiscal situation of state and local governments eased further as pressure for expenditures began to abate with decline in school enrollments and as additional funds became available through the revenue sharing system. The 1973 Brookings study projected for state and local resources a fiscal dividend equivalent to 5.3 percent in 1975 and 3.5 percent in 1978.[9] NPA projections suggest a fiscal dividend of 4.1 percent in

7   Executive Office of the President, Office of Management and Budget, *The Budget of the United States, Fiscal Year 1974* (Washington, D.C.: U.S. Government Printing Office, 1973), p. 46. The budget for fiscal 1975 projects no margin through 1978, a budget margin of 0.1 percent in 1979, and a margin of 5.0 percent in 1980. See ibid., *Fiscal Year 1975,* p. 44.

8   Schultze et al., *National Priorities: 1974 Budget,* p. 444.

9   Ibid., p. 271.

the 1977-81 period in the aggregate.[10] The average of the Brookings and NPA projections gives a fiscal dividend of 3.8 percent in 1978, which we have used for this study.

To determine discretionary social resources for the government sector as a whole in 1978, we determined the share of the fiscal dividend available for social expenditure. In 1972, state and local social spending was 54 percent of total spending; federal social spending was 46 percent of total spending. We projected a slight increase in the state and local share for 1978. Assuming that 55 percent of the state and local fiscal dividend and 45 percent of the federal fiscal dividend could be used for social areas, discretionary social resources thus come to 5.2 percent of total government revenues in 1978.

Shifting expenditures. The shifting of expenditures among programs is a second source of discretionary funds. Past experience has shown that the amount of funds that can be derived from this source is limited by such factors as the influence of the clientele benefiting by the various programs and the importance of budgetary allocations in the balance of power between the legislatures and the executives at all levels of government. We have assumed, therefore, that the rate at which public social expenditures are subject to such internal reprogramming would not cummulate to more than 1 percent over a five-year period. The 1.0 percent of the total government spending is consequently added to the discretionary margin in the fifth year.

Changing institutional arrangements. The third source of discretionary funds results from cutting the expenditures for existing programs identifiable with the base and/or increasing taxation through new legislation.

Experience has shown that the repeal or reduction of existing programs, even those which appear to have outlived their usefulness, are very difficult and involve high political costs. Increasing the level of taxation, whether through new taxes or increases in existing schedules, on a large scale also seems improbable at present (with the possible exception of the social security taxes, in the short run) in view of the evidence of more than usual antipathy toward tax increases and the apparent lack of confidence in the performance capability of the public sector.

For these reasons, no additional discretionary resources were assumed to become available through tax increases or expenditure reductions other than those allowed for under the fiscal dividend.

Private sector resources
Fiscal flexibility in the private sector is much more difficult to determine

---

10   National Planning Association, *U.S. Economic and Demographic Projections: 1972-81,* Report No. 72-N-2 (Washington, D.C., January 1973), p. 28.

than in the public sector since even fewer studies on private resource flexibility have been made. It appears, however, that private sector expenditures are more flexible than those of the public sector but the degree of flexibility is difficult to determine.

One indication of this flexibility appears in a study concerned with the division of disposable income into a component required to purchase necessities and to meet fixed financial obligations and a component that is discretionary.[11] The resulting estimates, which have subsequently been revised to correspond with the concept of purchasing power rather than income,[12] are maintained on a current basis by the Conference Board. They show that, for the period 1967-72, discretionary income made up 41 percent of consumers' disposable income. This estimate is not comparable with the discretionary component as defined here, either in concept or in time dimension, and can be used only as a point of reference.

In the absence of any data with a direct bearing on the flexibility of private social expenditures, a lower bound of flexibility in consumer spending for the categories considered is simply postulated (business spending is relatively small and does not require a separate assumption) until more direct estimates become practical through future research. As it turns out, this expedient does not affect the results of the present analysis in a substantive way because even a low assumption about spending flexibility in the private sector yields comparatively large estimates of discretionary resources.

We assumed that, by the year 1980, the discretionary component of total resources projected to be available in the private sector for social objectives would be 25 percent. In other words, consumers could, after seven years, redirect one-fourth of their expenditures to social areas without disrupting their lives, breaking commitments or suffering losses in the current trends in their quality of life. (As described below, an explicit constraint reflecting the resource requirements of the base trends is introduced.)

Determining discretionary social resources

Estimates of discretionary social resources are based on a formula developed during the present study in which discretion in the use of resources is very small initially and increases progressively throughout the period. In the formula, the level of discretionary resources available at a given time is depen-

---

11   William Franklin, "Discretionary Income," A Technical Paper (New York: National Industrial Conference Board, 1957).

12   Morton Ehrlich, "Discretionary Spending," Technical Paper No. 17 (New York: The Conference Board, 1966).

dent upon the number of years elapsed from the beginning of the period, total social resources available at the beginning of the period, the rate of growth in these resources, and the "rate of deceleration" for base trend expenditures. (See Chart 3-2.) The formula is sufficiently flexible to accommodate any foreseeable pattern of spending within a 10-year, or shorter, period.[13]

It is realistic to assume that in the first year all expenditures are committed to existing programs. However, as time passes, fewer expenditures will be committed so the amount of available discretionary resources will increase with time. The rate of deceleration represents the proportion of resources that each year are no longer committed to base trend activities, seen *ex ante* from a fixed initial point in time.

The mathematical formula representing these assumptions, and embodying the presently projected rate of growth of 5.3 percent of all social resources, is:

$$FR_t = B_0(1.053)^t - B_0 \prod^t [1.053 - \alpha(t-1)]; \ t > 0, \ \alpha \geqslant 0,$$

where FR represents free resources, B_0 the level of base trend resource use in year 0, and α represents the rate of deceleration of base trend expenditure.

The formula for free resources, which is expressed in constant dollars, consists of two terms. The first, $B_0(1.053)^t$, simply represents the total social resources, i.e., resources directed toward social concerns at time t. The initial amount in the base year grows at a constant rate shown here as 5.3 percent a year, which is the projected growth rate in all social resources in the economy including private and public sectors.

The second term, $B_0 \prod^t [1.053 - \alpha(t-1)]$, preceded by the minus sign represents the committed resources. It consists of the initial amount of resources times the cumulated product compounded for the periods from 0 to t, as indicated by the symbol $\prod^t$ of a decreasing function of time which includes the rate, represented by the parameter α, at which the committed resources become released per unit of time. The structure of the formula was dictated by the need to work with the annual data.

The most crucial variable in the formula is the rate of deceleration. In Chart 3-2, a wide range of deceleration rates (α) are graphed, illustrating the dependence of discretionary resources upon the rate. At one extreme, there is a deceleration rate of 0, which leaves no free resources over the 10-year period. At the other extreme is a deceleration rate of .053, equal to the rate of growth of

---

13   For longer periods of estimation and for theoretical generality, a continuous function which approaches zero asymptotically or the limit representing the amount of resources necessary for the support of the base trends is more desirable. However, for present purposes, adopting such a formula was not necessary.

Chart 3-2. Hypothetical Growth of Nondiscretionary Expenditure Resulting at Different Rates of Deceleration of Growth of Fixed Commitments

(Total social resources in year 0 equal 1.0; 5.3% growth in total social resources)

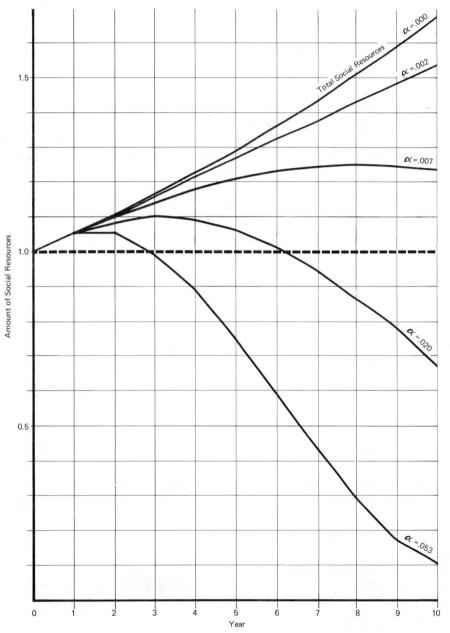

Note: For discussion of the underlying formula, see pages 47-50

resources. In this case, the amount of committed resources increases in the first year (and equals total social resources), remains constant in year two, and decreases rapidly thereafter, releasing many resources for discretionary activities. What, then, are the expected deceleration rates of base trend expenditures in the public and private sectors?

Separate projections made for the public sector and for the private sector give very different estimates of the critical deceleration parameter (alpha) based on the knowledge which could be gathered regarding the flexibility of expenditure over five- to seven-year time horizons. In both cases, the alphas were estimated from a proportion of discretionary resources given for one particular year. These estimates were derived as follows.

In fiscal year 1978, year five, federal, state and local discretionary social resources have been calculated at 5.2 percent of total public social resources. Using this figure, the deceleration rate of base trend expenditures can be calculated from the formula and then used to compute estimates of discretionary resources for other years. The deceleration rate derived is .006.

A deceleration rate of .006 suggests that new social activities would be difficult to finance through the public sector. For the first four fiscal years, the total amount of public discretionary resources is estimated at only $19 billion. Not until the seventh year does the absolute level of free public resources exceed $50 billion annually. (See Chart 3-3.)

In the private sector, we have assumed a 25 percent redirection of private expenditures to social areas by 1980, or year seven. The rate of deceleration of fixed private expenditures implied by this assumption is .014. Consequently, there is estimated to be available $82 billion of private social discretionary resources in the first four years. By year nine, there would be over $300 billion of private discretionary resources available according to the formula. (See Chart 3-3.)

However, the estimate of the nondiscretionary resources given by the formula for the private sector has to be raised somewhat to satisfy the minimum resource requirement. This maintains the base trends in the indicator output which was assumed to equal the total social resources in the base year.

Unlike the case with the public sector, a significant level of private social expenditures can, by all indications, be allocated toward new activities. Even with the private sector discretionary amounts reduced to satisfy the resource requirements of the social output trends, it appears these resources would still not become a binding constraint.

RESOURCE AVAILABILITY

To examine the flow of resources over the 10-year period, the separate annual estimates developed for private and public sectors were aggregated by sector

Chart 3-3. Discretionary and Nondiscretionary Resources for Social Purposes

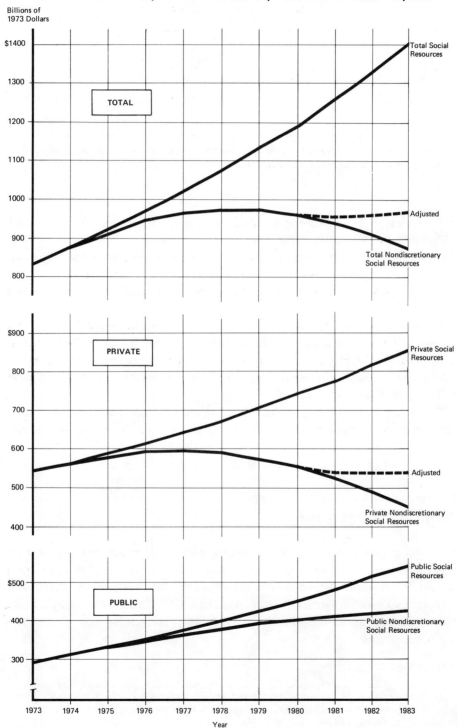

Table 3-3. Resources Available for Discretionary Activities,
1974-83, by Subperiod and Sector
(billions 1973 dollars)

Period	Available in the Private Sector	Available in the Public Sector	Total
Available in 1974-77	$ 82	$ 19	$ 101
Available in 1978-83	1,208	399	1,607
Total for 1974-83	1,290	418	1,708

Note: Estimates made from the formula adjusted to satisfy the resource requirements
of maintaining the base trends in the indicator levels.

and subperiod.[14] The resulting available resources adjusted for base trend
requirements are shown in Table 3-3.

As in the case of estimates of productive relationships, estimates of available resources constitute first-time approximations. Nevertheless, they reflect
the knowledge available at the present and provide a starting point for further
research.

As Chart 3-3 shows, for the first four years, only $101 billion of discretionary
social resources are available, with 61 percent of that becoming available in year
four. After year four, there is a considerable increase in discretionary resources
as growth in the absolute level of nondiscretionary resources tapers off. By year
ten, over $400 billion are available.

It thus appears that the availability of resources constitutes a major constraint upon the initiation of any new social activities in the first four years.
Moreover, those activities which are to be financed through public funds will be
extremely hard pressed to find available resources.

ALTERNATIVE PROJECTIONS

Clearly the availability of public resources, especially those in the first subperiod, is the most severe constraint on the implementation of discretionary
activities. What, then, would be the effect on the first subperiod activities of
alternative assumptions about the rate of growth of GNP and of the availability of
social resources (assuming that the availability of private resources is not a
binding constraint)?

---

14   It is recognized that certain inconsistencies in the projection might arise from adding the results
of two multiplicative formulas, yet the discrepancy is numerically small (4 percent discrepancy over 4
years, and 2.3 percent over 10).

Table 3-4. Effects of Variations in the Economic Growth and Allocation Assumptions on the Availability of Discretionary Resources in the Public Sector

Projection Assumptions	Discretionary Public Sector Resource (in billions of 1973 dollars)	
	1974-77	1974-83
Standard Projection		
GNP growth: 4.8%/year; Total social resources: 69% of 1983 GNP; Public social resources: 39% of 1983 total social resources	$19	$418
GNP Growth Variations		
GNP growth: 5.5%/year	21	441
GNP growth: 4.0%/year	17	398
Total Social Resource Variations		
Total social resources: 72% of 1983 GNP	21	433
Total social resources: 64% of 1983 GNP	17	398
Public Social Resource Variations		
Public social resources: 43% of total resources	23	455
Public social resources: 35.4% of total social resources	19	391

The standard projection assumes that GNP grows at an annual rate of 4.8 percent, that total social resources equal 69 percent of 1983 GNP, and that public social resources equal 39 percent of 1983 total social resources. Alternative assumptions for growth in GNP are 5.5 percent and 4.0 percent; for total social resources, 72 percent and 64 percent of 1983 GNP; for public social resources, 43 percent and 35 percent of total social resources in 1983. Public funds in the first subperiod and for the entire decade under these alternative assumptions are shown in Table 3-4. In calculating the alternatives, only the variable under consideration was changed.

As can be seen, the alternative assumptions have virtually no effect on the availability of public resources in the first subperiod and little effect overall. The reason is that the deceleration rate of base trend expenditure, α, in the projection formula remains unchanged. Thus, the alternative assumptions about GNP, social resources and public social resources, which were considered to provide reasonable limits in both directions, are not important in determining the availability of public discretionary funds. Discretionary resources are sensitive to the rate of deceleration only. (An earlier calculation using an α of 0.004, for example, based on the 1972 Brookings analysis and the U.S. budget for fiscal year 1973, resulted in public discretionary resources available in the first sub-period of $10 billion compared with the $19 billion estimated in the present analysis. (The difference arises from the larger fiscal dividends being projected in the later year.)

Because of the uncertainties involved in estimating deceleration rates for public funds, alternative rates were not considered for this analysis. Rather, a maximum estimate of discretionary public resources is developed in Chapter 4, and its implications for the achievement of improvements in the different areas of social goals are discussed in the light of efficiency of use of resources which are available. Since the activities differ in the efficiency (or unit cost) with which they may produce outputs, the actual effect of the availability of resources on achieving social change is not predetermined. It entails complex relationships which are discussed next.

4

The range of feasible improvements

Economic constraints limit the extent to which the 28 discretionary activities can be undertaken. The projected discretionary social resources for the 10-year period would cover only 50 percent of the estimated cost of all activities. However, as seen in Table 4-1, the supply of resources, specified as to subperiod and sector, covers even smaller proportions of activity costs, except for private sector resources in the second subperiod. Projected resources would cover 18 percent of the first subperiod costs of all activities and 57 percent of the second subperiod costs. More importantly, projected resources would cover only 5 percent of the public outlays needed in the first four years.

The share of public outlays in the cost of activities is high, constituting 69 percent of the total cost of the discretionary activities compared to 35 percent in the 1973 base of social resources. A possible explanation for this difference is that the inventive efforts in the social field, which determine the nature of the

Table 4-1. A Comparison of the Cost of 28 Discretionary Activities with the Projected Resource Supply
(dollar amounts in billions of 1973 dollars)

	Cost of 28 Activities	Projected Resource Supply	Supply as Percent of Cost
The entire period, 1974-83	$3,399	$1,708	50%
Public Resources	2,341	418	18
Private Resources	1,058	1,290	122
The first subperiod, 1974-77	577	101	18
Public Resources	375	19	5
Private Resources	202	82	41
The second subperiod, 1978-83	2,822	1,607	57
Public Resources	1,966	399	20
Private Resources	856	1,208	141

Source: Tables 2-5 and 3-3.

discretionary activities, have been directed to public resource intensive rather than public resource saving innovations. This difference may also explain some of the recent rapid growth trends in governmental spending.

Since activities differ in the proportion of output that can be achieved per unit of resources, activities with a high return can be substituted for those with a low return, thus raising the proportion of attainable output potential. For any level and combination of output, there exists a combination, or combinations, of activity levels which would produce that output at a cost lower than any other combination of activities.

LEAST-COST ANALYSIS

The ratios of resources to activity costs shown in Table 4-1 are based on implementing all 28 activities. The maximum output that is economically feasible then can be determined by using least-cost assumptions, that is, that the given supply of resources will be used for activities that are most efficient in reaching the chosen objectives.

One may thus select any set of objectives for the 1983 levels of the respective indicators and then calculate the least-cost combination of activities for achieving these levels. The only restriction is that the levels selected fall between the trend projections for 1983, which are taken as a fixed base, and the maximum level attainable by means of all discretionary activities, i.e., the maximum level which is *technically* feasible. The extent of *economically* feasible change can then be determined by comparing the calculated least-cost of different levels of improvements with estimates of the supply of resources available for discretionary activities.

The least-cost of achieving uniform proportions—10, 30, 50, 70, 90, and 100 percent—of the technically feasible change in the conditions measured by the indicators was calculated and cost curves of the lowest cost at which the given level of output can be produced were drawn. The least-cost derived in this manner was computed first in terms of total 10-year costs, then in terms of costs incurred within the first 4 years, and finally in terms of governmental expenditure for the entire period and in the first 4 years. After performing these calculations for the different levels of output of all the indicators taken together, comparable estimates were made for groupings of selected indicators, in which output requirements were limited to indicators within the given group.

This method for selecting output benchmarks, though rather mechanical, permits one to calculate the cost of a wide range of possible output levels and combinations (corresponding to different types of change to be achieved) and to identify the major trade-offs that may exist between two or more competing combinations of objectives, which may be mutually incompatible at the given level of resource supply.[1]

It was not practical to postulate *a priori* distinct sets of historically realistic output requirements, because there is no basis at the present state of knowledge to make realistic specifications which would be any more structured than those derived by the method adopted. Most political debates and public discussions are conducted at a level which, in this analysis, corresponds to choices among activities rather than among the output indicators, and they involve shorter time horizons than 10 years.

LEAST-COST ESTIMATES

The four panels in Chart 4-1 show the least-cost curves for attaining given levels of output together with the corresponding resource projections for discretionary social resources. As the chart shows, the "standard projection" of discretionary resources would permit achievement of a minimum of 75 percent of the output potential for all indicators over the 10-year period if only the most efficient activities were funded. Public resources for the first subperiod, the most limiting constraint, would permit achievement of 16 percent of the output potential. Since maximum feasible level of attainment is determined by the most stringent of the constraints, it appears that only 16 percent of the technical potential for change is possible with the projected resources.

SUBSTITUTION OF RESOURCES

The extent to which substitution of resources between subperiods and between sources (public and private) can occur, though, would change these results. Complete substitutability of resources is required if the total 10-year supply of resources is to be regarded as the only economic constraint. Under such extreme assumptions, 75 percent of the technical potential for change would be feasible. At the other extreme—if no substitutions are possible and hence the

---

1   These calculations were made by solving linear program problems with the given proportions of the output potential specified as minimum inequality requirements to be met while the objective function to be minimized was the resource cost. The calculations were also subject to the limitation that the activity levels not exceed their capacity and were carried out with a special mode of calculation designed to reflect the existence of nonadditive interaction effects of activities on outputs. This method is described in Neil J. McMullen, "A Piecewise Linear Adaptation of Linear Programming for the Estimation of the Costs of Achieving National Goals," A Technical Staff Paper (Washington, D.C.: National Planning Association, December 1974). Because joint products are prevalent, for some outputs percentages higher than those required are obtained as a byproduct of satisfying the given output requirement for other outputs.

Chart 4-1. Least Cost Estimates for the Different Levels of Output and Different Formulations of Resource Cost Compared with Resource Projections
(in billions of 1973 dollars)

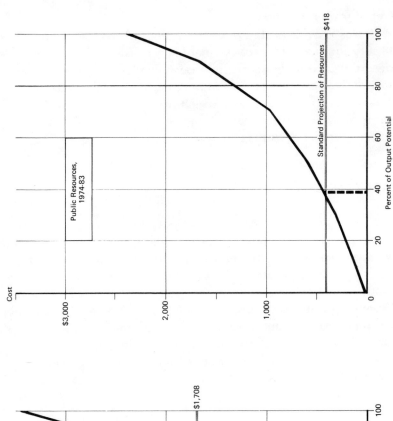

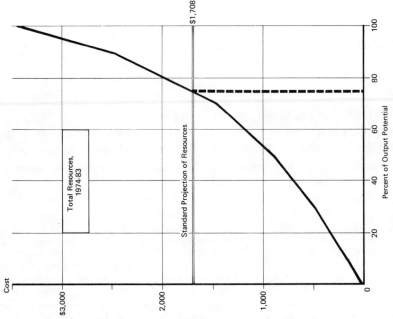

Chart 4-1. Least Cost Estimates for the Different Levels of Output and
Different Formulations of Resource Cost Compared with Resource Projections (continued)
(in billions of 1973 dollars)

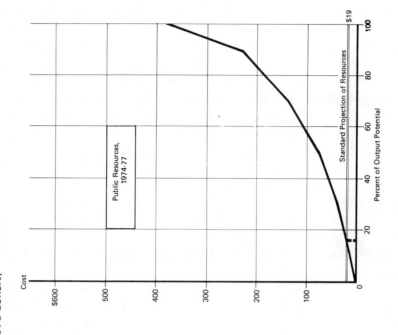

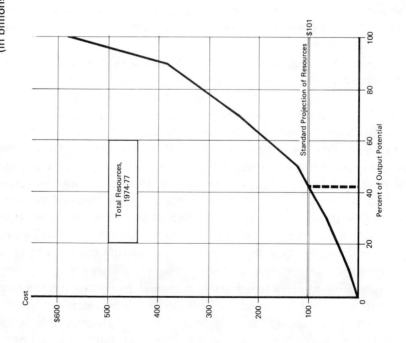

amount of public resources available during the first four years is the effective constraint—the maximum feasible achievement is limited to 16 percent. With a complete substitution between sources but not between periods (i.e., re-sources for the first subperiod are treated as the constraint regardless of whether they are private or public), the maximum feasible change is estimated at 42 percent. With complete substitutability of resources over time but not by source, so that total public resources are the constraint, the maximum feasible change is estimated at 39 percent.

Possibilities for substitutions between subperiods and sources, though, do exist. Substitutions between private and public sectors can be affected by governmental borrowing or taxation, which increase the public sector share of the total, and by retirement of the public debt or by tax reductions, which raise the private share. At this stage of analysis, the distinction between federal, state and local government is ignored and the public sector is treated as a whole, thus implicitly assuming perfect substitutability of discretionary resources within the public sector.

Resource substitutions between earlier and later years to increase the supply of resources in the critical first subperiod may occur through borrowing from, or impositions on, the categories of objectives outside the social areas and by borrowing from or sale of assets to the rest of the world. Within the constraint of maintaining the expenditures necessary to support the base trends, and given the share of social resources in total resources, the feasible amount of taxation or borrowing is limited by the amount estimated as the discretionary margin in the private sector.

It is unlikely that all the discretionary resources could be freely substituted for each other. Therefore, a level much lower than 75 percent of the technical potential is likely to constitute a realistic upper limit on the amount of feasible change. On the other hand, the low estimate of only 16 percent based on no substitutability is probably too low. The amount of discretionary public re-sources on which it is based does not allow for substitutions within existing governmental programs that would increase the more productive elements of the programs, for increases in taxes, for inflation, for more than a few selected expenditure cuts, for any improvements in productivity of the public sector (other than those which may be implicit in the estimates of the discretionary margins), or for increases in the level or in the efficiency of employment of resources. Where, then, does the level of maximum feasible change fall within this range?

To establish such a benchmark, one must determine the amount by which first subperiod public resources could be increased since this constraint is the most critical. In making this judgment, it is to be assumed that serious efforts would be made to increase public resources but that no major changes would occur in the functioning of the economy, the role of the public sector, or the nature of the tax system. The augmentation of first subperiod public resources is also limited by the amount of discretionary resources that can be transferred between sectors and subperiods without depleting either the private sector resources in the first subperiod or the public sector resources in the second below the levels necessary for supporting the expansion in output permitted by the increases in the public sector resources in the first subperiod.

Keeping these constraints in mind, discretionary public resources could be augmented in a number of ways.

Taxation. A 5 percent increase in the tax rate is taken as feasible (10 percent is judged too high). It is assumed that 90 percent of new revenue would be directed toward social concerns (compared with 66 percent in 1973) and that 70 percent of the additional revenues (compared to only 1 percent in the standard projection for 1974-77) would actually become available for discretionary ac- tivities, with 30 percent going to base activities through relaxation of controls over the base as a result of fiscal ease. This scenario would generate in the first subperiod $16 billion of additional public discretionary funds available for social objectives.

Borrowing. An additional $10 billion a year can be borrowed by govern- ments from the private sector, transferring the discretionary resources. Assum- ing the same rates of allocation of additional resources to social areas and discretionary activities (90 percent and 70 percent) as for taxation gives $25 billion in four years.

Program effectiveness. Substitutions of programs or program components within the same general categories could increase the effectiveness of public programs. Experience, including that obtained in the course of efforts to install Planning-Programming-Budgeting systems in government, has shown that the cost-reducing potential of intraprogram substitutions is limited. While no direct estimates exist, a rate of cost reduction through increased program effective- ness of 0.5 percent per annum is postulated here. Applied to the present estimates of all public social resources, this rate would yield $7 billion in four years.

Government productivity. Studies of governmental productivity based on direct measurement of physical production units suggests that the productivity growth rate in the public sector has been much slower than in the private sector.[2] Labor productivity has been increasing on the average by some 1.5

---

2 Executive Office of the President, Bureau of the Budget, *Measuring Productivity of Federal Government Organizations* (Washington, D.C.: U.S. Government Printing Office, 1964); and *Measuring and Enhancing Productivity in the Federal Sector,* Report of a Joint Project conducted by the Civil Service Commission, General Accounting Office, Office of Management and Budget and 17 participating agencies, June 1972.

percent a year in the measured federal agencies and by 3.5 percent in the measured private sectors. Studies of productivity over long periods suggest that substantial accelerations in productivity growth have occurred historically in whole industries or economic sectors.[3] Based on that evidence, one may postulate that a serious effort to raise productivity in the public sector may accelerate productivity growth by 2 percentage points over a number of years. However, in the course of the initial four-year period, many local governments and perhaps many agencies of federal and state governments may not have sufficient flexibility to implement the necessary changes. In the short term, therefore, a 1 percent acceleration appears more believable. Such an acceleration, given the amount of total public social resources in the base year, would in the course of four years release $14 billion, all or some of which could be used for discretionary activities.

New activity development. The discretionary activities identified in the present study use public resources very intensively. Presumably, activities could be invented that would conserve public resources either by being more productive than the activities identified or by substituting private resources for public resources. Such activities would require considerable time for development and considerable lead time for implementation. For that reason it is doubtful that large savings of public resources could be realized in four years. The amount of public discretionary resources that could be replaced by private discretionary resources in the first subperiod is therefore postulated at $10 billion, and even that may be high.

Inflation and full employment. Discretionary governmental revenue would also rise with increases in the rate of inflation, as has occurred in recent years. But increasing inflation is not a desirable policy for generating discretionary governmental resources and no estimate is made here of such an effect. Depending on the short-term cyclical condition or the longer-term structural situation, increases in the employment level would generate different amounts of additional production and government receipts. For each percentage increase of output, the governmental receipts would grow by about 1.1 percent. Thus, a permanent 1 percent increase in the national product, in the course of four years, would result in an increase of about 4.5 percent of the base year revenue. Given the present division between social and other goals, such an increase would raise public social resources by $13 billion, most of which could be discretionary.

---

3   John W. Kendrick, *Productivity Trends in the United States,* NBER General Series 71 (Princeton: Princeton University Press, 1961), and *Postwar Productivity Trends in the United States, 1948-1969,* NBER General Series 98 (New York: National Bureau of Economic Research, 1973).

Table 4-2. Output Achievement: Maximum 1983 Levels
(Set at 30 percent of Technical Potential)
Consistent with Maximum Resource Supply of the Limiting Resources

Indicators	1973 Base Estimate	1974-83 Base Increment	1983 Trend Projection	Maximum 1983 Level Assuming Achievement of a Minimum of 30% of the Technical Potential	
				Increment over Trend Projection	Total
1. Average life expectancy at birth, years	71.3	+1.4	72.7	+2.7	75.4
2. Percent of persons with major disabilities	17.5	-1.1	16.4	-2.0	14.4
3. Number of violent crimes per 100,000 persons per year	668.0	0	668.0	-134.4	533.6
4. Index of mean performance in grade 12 based on standard tests	100.0	+5.0	105.0	+8.1	113.1
5. Percent of students 3 or more years behind 1973 average	24.0	-5.0	19.0	-4.8	14.2
6. Number of persons completing college, thousands	957.0	+385.0	1,342.0	+390.0	1,732.0
7. Number of persons not in mainstream of labor force, millions	11.1	-2.3	8.8	-2.2	6.6
8. Median earnings of individuals, thousands 1973 dollars	5.9	+1.9	7.8	+0.4	8.2
9. Percent of population below poverty standard	11.4	-2.7	8.7	-2.6	6.1
10. Percent of population in near-poverty conditions	4.8	-1.3	3.5	-1.0	2.5
11. Percent of population with living standard loss of over 30 percent	8.6	+0.1	8.7	-2.1	6.6
12. Family income ratio: 20th to 90th percentile	25.0	0	25.0	+2.7	27.7
13. Mean family income, blacks as a percent of whites	65.0	+6.0	71.0	+3.6	74.6
14. Hourly earnings of women as percent of earnings of men	60.0	0	60.0	+3.3	63.3
15. Percent of persons living in adequate housing	88.0	+4.0	92.0	+2.4	94.4
16. Percent of persons living in adequate neighborhoods	77.0	+10.0	87.0	+3.9	90.9
17. Percent of population affected by bothersome pollution	62.0	-16.0	46.0	-11.1	35.1
18. Percent of persons regularly taking part in recreation	21.0	+33.0	54.0	+8.4	62.4
19. Index of preservation of life and natural forms	100.0	+10.0	110.0	+18.0	128.0
20. Number of scientists active in basic science, thousands	81.0	+58.0	139.0	+24.3	163.3
21. Number of active artists, thousands	265.0	+58.0	323.0	+94.5	417.5
22. Discretionary time, hours per person per year	2,111.0	+88.0	2,199.0	+203.1	2,402.1

Realizing all these possibilities for expanding first subperiod public resources would add $85 billion to discretionary public funds. It is highly improbable, though, that all these possibilities would be realized, so the total amount is very unlikely.[4] Rather, a fraction of this total is a more realistic maximum amount. It is postulated that $20 billion, approximately the same amount that is available under the standard projection of resources, could be derived from these other sources. That $20 billion added to the standard projection of $19 billion gives a total of $39 billion available for discretionary activities within the public sector during the first subperiod.

MAXIMUM FEASIBLE CHANGE FOR ALL OUTPUTS

With $39 billion available in first subperiod public funds, a minimum of 30 percent of the output potential for all the indicators could be achieved during the 10-year period. As Table 4-2 shows, the 30 percent level of achievement would provide substantial improvements over the base trends. Because the activities have multiple outputs, more than 30 percent is actually achieved for several indicators when a minimum of 30 percent is reached for all, but these additional gains are not shown in the table.

The estimates in Table 4-2 represent a more realistic, though still quite uncertain, benchmark of maximum feasible change than either the 75 percent calculation based on the complete substitutability of resources or the 16 percent calculation that assumes no flexibility in the supply of governmental resources within the initial subperiod.

MAXIMUM FEASIBLE CHANGE
FOR SPECIFIC OUTPUT COMBINATIONS

In addition to estimating feasible change in all areas of concern at once, comparable calculations were made for groupings of concerns. The indicators were combined into the following categories:

HEALTH AND SAFETY
1. Average life expectancy
2. Percent of population with major disabilities
3. Rate of violent crime

---

4   The present analysis is predicated on realizing the output within 10 years. Extending the time horizon is not legitimate analytically. However, if realization of output were to be postponed by 2 years, the projected discretionary public resources of year 5 and year 6 would add $55 billion.

EDUCATION AND SKILLS
  Education
      4. Index of Performance in grade 12
      5. Percent of students 3 or more years behind 1973 average
      6. Number of persons completing college
  Skills
      7. Number of persons not in mainstream of labor force
      8. Median earnings of individuals

INCOME DISTRIBUTION
  Adequacy and Continuity of Income
      9. Percent of population below poverty
      10. Percent of population in near-poverty conditions
      11. Percent of population with living standard loss of over 30 percent
  Equality of Income
      12. Family income ratio: 20th to 90th percentile
      13. Black/white mean family income ratio
      14. Mean hourly earnings of women as percent of hourly earnings of men

HUMAN HABITAT
      15. Percent of persons living in adequate housing
      16. Percent of persons living in satisfactory neighborhoods
      17. Percent of population affected by bothersome pollution
      18. Percent of persons regularly participating in recreation
      19. Index of conservation

ART, SCIENCE AND FREE TIME
      20. Number of scientists active in basic science
      21. Number of active actists
      22. Discretionary time

    As was the case when considering all indicators at once, public resources available in the first four years impose the binding constraint in achieving output potential within each category.
    To determine maximum feasible change for specific output combinations, first subperiod public costs of activities were matched against first subperiod public resources. Least-cost estimates for the various categories were calculated, with the activity levels constrained not to exceed their capacity and with an allowance for the interaction among activities so that duplication of output would be eliminated. The results are given in Table 4-3 and, for the aggregate groupings also diagrammatically, in Chart 4-2. The percentages of output potential that are attainable for the various categories under the standard projection of

Table 4-3. Minimum First Subperiod Public Costs
for Attaining 30, 70 and 100 Percent of the
Output Potential of Selected Output Combinations
(in billions of 1973 dollars)

Output Combinations	Percent of Output Potential		
	30%	70%	100%
All Outputs (indicators 1-22)	$39	$139	$375
Health and Safety (1-3)	12	30	90
Education, Skills and Income Distribution (4-14)	15	85	190
Education (4-6)	4	10	87
Skills (7-8)	5	42	132
Income distribution (9-14)	9	85	179
Adequacy and continuity of income (9-11)	0*	11	53
Equality of income (12-14)	9	85	151
Human Habitat (15-19)	15	40	188
Art, Science and Free Time (20-22)	3	14	116

* The entire cost of the activities required to produce the output is expended in the second subperiod.

public resources for the first four years and the projected maximum of such resources, rounded to $40 billion, are given in Table 4-4.

A number of observations and conclusions may be drawn from these results for specific output combinations.

(1) Initially, high percentages of output can be obtained at relatively low cost, while the last 30 percent of the output is much more expensive.

(2) For any *one* major combination of activities, a minimum of 44 percent of the output potential (education, skills and income) is feasible with the projection of $40 billion in first subperiod discretionary public resources.

(3) Achievement of 91 percent of the output potential for adequacy and continuity of income is feasible under the $40 billion projection because much of the cost of output to be achieved in 10 years in these categories is postponable until the second subperiod.

(4) The prevalence of joint products suggests that diversified output requirements are not much more difficult to satisfy than requirements oriented exclusively to one or few outputs since much output is produced "free" as a byproduct. The prevalence of these joint products may be gauged by comparing, in Table 4-3, the cost of achieving the components of a combination separately with the cost of the entire combination. Thus, the income distribution objectives have a high joint-product correlation with education and skill objectives.

THE RANGE OF POSSIBILITIES

Estimated maximum feasible change is, of course, just that. Actual outcomes may result in no change whatsoever or in much less change than the theoretical

Table 4-4. Percent of Output Potential Attainable for Categories of Concern Under Two Resource Projections

Output Combinations	First Subperiod Public Resources of:	
	$19 billion	$40 billion
All Areas of Concern	16%	30%
Health and Safety	45	75
Education, Skills and Income Distribution	32	44
Education	74	82
Skills	45	68
Income distribution	35	46
Adequacy and continuity of income	76	91
Equality of income	35	46
Human Habitat	36	70
Art, Science and Free Time	71	78

maximum.[5] For example, unrestrained growth of base activities, inefficient choice of activities, or inefficient conduct of activities could reduce or even eliminate the potential for improvement.

Indeed, an efficient outcome near the theoretical maximum is a very special possibility. Productive outcomes require minimum levels of understanding, commitment, competence, and coordination at numerous critical decision-making points of the private and public sectors.

Realizing high output potential by chance is wildly improbable because of the succession of conditions that must be met for successful accomplishment of any one of the activities. In fact, chance alone would probably lead to a zero or near-zero output increment.

It is equally unrealistic to expect an efficient outcome to result automatically either from the play of market forces in a situation approaching "perfect competition" or from the effectiveness of governmental control in a situation of "perfect planning."

This study deals with the productive possibilities in their general outlines while the whole mass of particulars including organizational arrangements is left unspecified. It is not possible, however, to consider such specifics here.

For example, in order to make any useful distinctions between productive and less productive implementation possibilities of particular activities it would be necessary to perform highly technical and detailed analyses and major R&D and monitoring efforts, or at least substantial simulations. Such studies can be

---

5   The present analysis is limited to a discussion of possibilities for change above base trends. Deteriorations in the base conditions are, of course, possible but are not discussed here. As trends for such deterioration become apparent, they can be accommodated within the present analytical framework by appropriate changes in the projections of indicator trends and of resource supply. Discretionary activities with negative outputs cannot be accommodated.

Chart 4-2. Minimum First Subperiod Public Cost of Obtaining 30, 70 and 100 Percent of Output Potential of Selected Activity Combinations

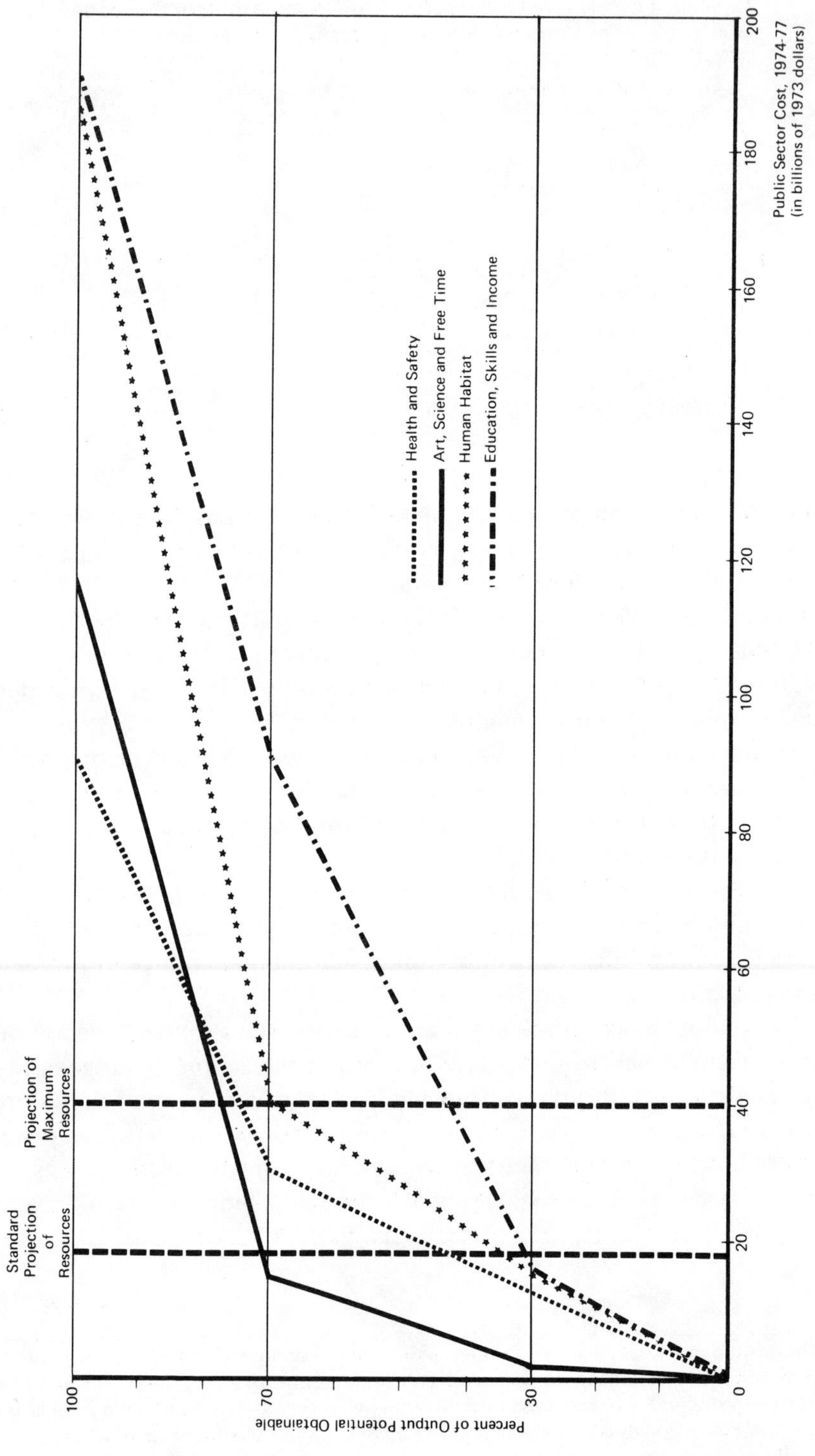

.... Health and Safety

——— Art, Science and Free Time

✶✶✶✶✶ Human Habitat

—·—· Education, Skills and Income

Standard Projection of Resources

Projection of Maximum Resources

Percent of Output Potential Obtainable

Public Sector Cost, 1974-77 (in billions of 1973 dollars)

undertaken effectively only in a more immediate programmatic setting and probably for a rather limited set of objectives and activities at a time.

It would be pointless, and perhaps even misleading, because of a spurious appearance of realism, to even consider here any practical implementation scenarios for the activities discussed in this work and the efficiency and equity considerations or organizational arrangements involved in their implementation alternatives.

It is possible, however, to take note of some events and influences which may likely affect, favorably or adversely, the level of output potential actually achieved. Some of these potential events were already discussed, including increases in taxes or government borrowing, increase in the effectiveness of the use of governmental resources, and development of social innovations that would substitute private sector outlays for public expenditure.

To these, one may add possibilities of discovery of activities with shorter lead times and innovations to improve the ability to reallocate expenditures by governments, and perhaps also by businesses and families, in line with changing opportunities. Such developments may include for the private sector primarily improvements in the consumer and job information systems and improvements in the functioning of the important markets. Most important is the functioning of the job market with respect to mobility, freedom of entry, divisibility and flexibility of working time, and an effective range of choices regarding retirement. In the public sector, the time lags entailed in the achievement of outputs may be reduced through improvements in the budgetary processes and in the development and evaluation of public programs, especially regarding feedback relationships between the executives and the legislatures and between the governments and the public.

Developments opposite to those identified as favorable would depress the level of output achievement. They include reduction in taxes and in borrowing, reduced efficiency of government, and the absence of innovations to conserve public resources or to reduce the time lags.

EFFECTS OF SOCIAL ENVIRONMENT

In addition to such more or less specific developments, certain characteristics of the general social environment would also influence the level of social outputs actually achieved.

A general *interest in and understanding of goals* is probably essential to their achievement. Widespread apathy and inertia without any attempt to identify goals would make improvements unlikely. Without some reasonably deliberate corrective mechanisms and a more or less generally recognized realization of what the objectives are, and the effective means of pursuing them, it may be technically impossible to reach them.

Technical competence and its application also appear very important. Even if the goals are reasonably well and widely perceived and the potential of activities for social improvements is well understood, potential for improvement may be lost through incompetence. Because of the lack of actual technical competence and organizational capability to follow through, the allocation and decision systems simply may not be up to the technical level needed for pursuing the activities. The technical demands of implementing decisions implied by the discretionary activities are quite considerable. In terms of the probability of achieving results, at least insofar as the principal public goods components of the activities are concerned, the model of space navigation may be more applicable here than the model of perfect markets as if guided by an invisible hand. In space navigation, many successive and difficult steps have to be successfully completed in order to achieve the desired result. Major failure at any one of these steps may result in complete failure of the entire undertaking. There is comparatively little scope for trial and error and for correction of mistakes. Perhaps some of the risks could be reduced by innovations which could substitute activity components based on recurrent learning processes for components dependent on large-scale management.

Organizational competence providing the ability to pursue decisions effectively is also important both in the public and private sectors. Such ability may be injured by bureaucratization or decline of competition. The number of participants and the layers of authority required to reach a decision or the numbers holding veto power over decisions may be such that the decisions necessary for accomplishment cannot be completed within the time interval necessary for minimum success.

Finally, just as economic productivity and growth depend on the level of *voluntary cooperation and trust prevalent in the society,* the quality of things that are taken for granted in the culture and embedded in the individual behavior would influence the level of achievement of social improvements.

In short, regardless of the technical and economic feasibility of a potential maximum level of output, actual output can be anywhere from zero to maximum, and the high output possibilities are comparatively very rare within the universe of all possible outcomes.

PART II

ESTIMATES FOR SINGLE GOALS

5

Health

OBJECTIVES

   Long life.

   Life characterized by physical and mental well-being.

INDICATORS

   Average life expectancy at birth (a measure of the length of life).

   Percent of population with disabling conditions (a measure of the health quality of that length of life.

Life expectancy is based on actual rates of mortality by age as of a given period. The rates are taken to represent probabilities of survival until the next year. Thus, a statement that life expectancy at birth in the United States was 71.3 in 1973 means that, according to actual counts of deaths of persons at different ages in 1973, a newborn would have a mathematical mean expectation of living until the age of 71.3. The measure is not a forecast of his individual longevity. It reflects the state of health in 1973 as determined by events of 1973 and up to 1973. Disability is defined as the level at which persons suffer from a chronic condition that imposes some limitation on their major activities.

   These two indicators together tell us how long one lives and how free that life is of disability. Because the indicators are aggregated national measures, they do not reveal distributions. For example, increases in life expectancy may come about as a result of reductions in mortality in infancy, in childhood, in the prime of life, or in old age. The indicator shows only that a change has occurred. So, too, differences in average life expectancy between specific groups, such as between men and women and whites and nonwhites, do not appear. No analysis of the composition of national totals and averages has been undertaken. (The activities discussed in the following pages probably would have a considerable effect on reducing the health differentials by race and a smaller but discernible effect on the differentials by sex, but this inference is speculative. Clearly, the subject requires further study.)

BASE TRENDS

Indicators	1973	1983 Projection	Projected Change
Average life expectancy at birth (years)	71.3	72.7	+1.4
Percent of population disabled	17.5%	16.8%	−1.1%

Life expectancy increased 26.9 years between 1900 and 1950. In comparison, recent gains have been quite modest. Life expectancy was 68.2 years in 1950, 69.7 years in 1960, and 71.2 years in 1972.[1] The projection of average life expectancy at birth for 1983 was derived by extrapolating the average annual rate of gain in life expectancy from 1950 to 1972. Although this gain is larger than would be projected by extrapolating a more recent trend, the higher estimate was chosen as realistic because of existing public health programs and an increased awareness of preventive measures among individuals, as well as the declining infant mortality expected to accompany a declining birth rate.[2]

The number of persons with chronic disabling conditions in 1973 was projected from 1971 data derived from several sources.[3] Estimates for the number of disabled persons living in households were taken from the National Center for Health Statistics Interview Surveys. The latest data available cover the survey conducted in 1971.[4] (Of the different degrees of disability identified in the survey, the one denoted as having "chronic conditions causing activity

1   U.S. Department of Commerce, Bureau of the Census, *Statistical Abstract of the United States: 1972,* 93rd edition (Washington, D.C.: U.S. Government Printing Office, 1972), Table 74, p. 55; U.S. Department of Health, Education, and Welfare, National Center for Health Statistics, "Provisional Statistics, Annual Summary for the United States, 1972," *Monthly Vital Statistics Report,* HSM-73-1121, No. 13 (Washington, D.C.: U.S. Government Printing Office, June 27, 1973).

2   The population totals used here are 210,501,000 estimated for 1973, and 231,044,000 projected for 1983 from U.S. Department of Commerce, Bureau of the Census, "Projections of the Population of the United States, by Age and Sex: 1972 to 2020," *Current Population Reports,* Series P-25, No. 493 (Washington, D.C.: U.S. Government Printing Office, December 1972).

3   The projection was judgmental and was based primarily on trends in affected population groups.

4   U.S. Department of Health, Education, and Welfare, Public Health Service, "Current Estimates from the Health Interview Survey—United States (1971)," *Vital and Health Statistics,* HSM-73-1505, NCHS Series 10, No. 79 (Washington, D.C.: U.S. Government Printing Office, February 1973).

limitations'' was used.)[5] To this number was added the number of mental patients in institutions, the number of persons in long-term institutions other than mental,[6] and the number of alcoholics[7] and of drug addicts[8] (which the survey identifies only in a small part). The latest estimates for all these categories were simply added together, with no adjustment for overlap or time trends between the date of information and 1973 because of uncertainty about the data and the magnitude of work involved. The estimates obtained were judged sufficiently indicative of actual magnitudes to be serviceable in the present analysis.

The 1983 projection of the disabled was made by first projecting to 1983 the number of persons chronically disabled in households, based on the 1969-70 disability rates by age groups and the 1983 population projection for these groups. The resulting projection was reduced by 2 percent to allow for a trend of improvement in health. The 1983 figure is 26.7 million compared to 25.2 million in 1973, an increase of 6 percent. For consistency, we assume the same increase for the total disabled population in long-term institutions, from 1.9 million (0.3 million in mental and 1.6 in other institutions in 1973) to 2.0 million in 1983. Disabilities due to addiction to alcohol were assumed to remain constant at 9.0 million. No growth was projected because of the increased public awareness of the problem and a stepping up of the efforts to cope with it. The number of persons abusing drugs to a disabling degree was projected to rise from 0.7 million in 1973 to 1.2 million in 1983, assuming continued rapid growth of drug addiction, but not as rapid as in recent years. (The last two projections are obviously highly uncertain, but they appear to be reasonably in accord with ongoing trends and prospective limits on the growth of both types of abuses.)

CAUSES OF MORTALITY AND DISABILITY

A summary of the major causes of mortality and disability is shown in Table 5-1.

---

5   This refers to the data on specific conditions, other than alcohol and drug abuse, for persons in households from U.S. Department of Health, Education, and Welfare, Public Health Service, "Limitation of Activity Due to Chronic Conditions—United States (1969 and 1970)," *Vital and Health Statistics*, NCHS Series 10, No. 80 (Washington, D.C.: U.S. Government Printing Office, April 1973).

6   U.S. Department of Health, Education, and Welfare, Public Health Service, *Health Resources Statistics in Brief*, a summary of *Health Resources Statistics*, HSM-73-1509 (Washington, D.C.: U.S. Government Printing Office, April 1973).

7   National Health Education Committee, Inc., *Facts on the Major Killing and Crippling Diseases in the United States Today* (New York: National Health Education Committee, Inc., 1971).

8   "Drug Abuse Now Epidemic and What's Being Done about It," an interview with Special Assistant Attorney General Myles J. Ambrose, *U.S. News and World Report*, April 3, 1972, pp. 38-45.

Table 5-1. Principal Causes of Life Expectancy Loss
and of Chronic Disability in the United States

Causes	Years of Mean Life Expectancy at Birth Lost[1] 1959-61	Number of Persons with Serious Disabilities (millions)[2] 1969-71
Total	n.a.	36.3
Heart disease	5.9	3.6
Hypertension without heart involvement	0.1	1.1
Stroke	1.3	0.6
Cancer	2.3	0.4
Mental and nervous disorders (including persons in institutions)	n.a.	1.3
Homicide, suicide	0.4	0
Arthritis	0	3.3
Allergies	0	1.0
Accidents	1.2	n.a.
Visual impairments	0	1.1
Spine impairments	n.a.	1.6
Diseases of early infancy	1.1	n.a.
Persons in long-term institutions (except mental)	n.a.	1.6
Alcohol abuse	n.a.	9.0
Drug abuse	n.a.	0.7

[1] U.S. Department of Health, Education, and Welfare, Public Health Service, National Center for Health Statistics, *Life Tables: 1959-61*, Vol. 1, No. 6 (Washington, D.C.: U.S. Government Printing Office, May 1968). p. 8. Losses of life expectancy have been calculated actuarially on the assumption that if the individual causes of death were eliminated one at a time the relative incidence of all other causes would remain unchanged. No calculation has been made for all the listed causes combined.

[2] Number of persons disabled is the sum of disabled persons in households, persons in long-term care institutions, alcoholics, and drug addicts. See U.S. Department of Health, Education, and Welfare, Public Health Service, Health Services and Mental Health Administration, "Current Estimates from the Health Interview Survey-United States (1971)," *Vital and Health Statistics* (HSM 73-1505), NCHS Series 10, No. 79 (Washington, D.C.: U.S. Government Printing Office, February 1973); data on the specific conditions, other than alcohol and drug abuse, for persons in households is from U.S. Department of Health, Education, and Welfare, Public Health Service, Health Services and Mental Health Administration, "Limitation of Activity Due to Chronic Conditions-United States (1969 and 1970)," *Vital and Health Statistics,* NCHS Series 10, No. 80 (Washington, D.C.: U.S. Government Printing Office, April 1973); the number of persons in long-term care institutions in 1971 (preliminary) from U.S. Department of Health, Education, and Welfare, Public Health Service, National Center for Health Statistics, *Health Resources Statistics in Brief,* a summary of *Health Resources Statistics* (HSM 73-1509), (Washington, D.C.: U.S. Government Printing Office, April 1973); and the number of alcoholics and drug addicts in 1971 and 1972, respectively, from National Health Education Committee, Inc., *Facts on the Major Killing and Crippling Diseases in the United States Today* (New York: National Health Education Committee, Inc., 1971); and "Drug Abuse Now Epidemic and What's Being Done about It," an interview with Special Assistant Attorney General Myles J. Ambrose, *U.S. News and World Report,* April 3, 1972, pp. 38-45.

For loss of life, the chief causes are heart diseases, cancer and strokes; for disabilities, the chief causes are mental conditions (including alcoholism and drug addiction), heart diseases and arthritis. These major threats to life and health were the targets of various programmatic analyses and recommendations which were used in formulating the discretionary activities that follow.

DISCRETIONARY ACTIVITIES TO EXTEND LIFE AND REDUCE DISABILITY

The activities discussed below describe ways in which health can be improved, as measured by the indicators, beyond the level of change expected by a continuation of current trends. The major components, or subactivities, of each discretionary activity are defined at a level representing full capacity operation, leaving out that segment which, even under optimistic assumptions, does not appear feasible because of technical or scientific limits, unduly high costs, or encroachment on other goals or on values such as individual freedom.

CHANGES IN HEALTH-RELATED HABITS AND PATTERNS

Changes in health-related habits encompass five subactivities: reduction in smoking, improvement of nutrition and fitness, prevention of accidents, reduction of alcoholism, and reduction of drug abuse. The estimated outputs and costs are summed up below:

Activity and Maximum Percent of Relevant Population Affected	Average Life Expectancy (years)	Percent of Population Disabled	Total 10-Year Cost (billions of 1973 dollars)
Reduction of smoking (90%)	+1.8	−0.4%	$ 5
Improvement of nutrition and fitness (70%)	+3.8	−1.6	35
Prevention of accidents (50%)	+0.6	−0.2	1
Reduction of alcoholism and alcohol abuse (33%)	+0.3	−1.3	17
Reduction of drug abuse (90%)	+0.1	−0.5	6
Total output (adjusted for overlap)	+5.3	−3.3	64

Reduction of smoking

Reduction of the smoking habit would reduce mortality and disabilities from the two diseases most closely linked to smoking: arteriosclerotic heart disease and cancer of the respiratory system.[9] We estimate that the elimination of all smoking by 1983 would:

- reduce the number of deaths due to arteriosclerotic disease of the heart by 43 percent, adding 1.71 years of life expectancy at birth;[10]
- reduce the number of deaths from cancer of the respiratory system by 85 percent, thus increasing life expectancy by 0.23 years;[11] and
- reduce the number of disabilities from both diseases in the same proportions as the reductions in mortality.

Assuming a 90 percent rate of success (a theoretical maximum) in eliminating smoking gives a gain in life expectancy of 1.75 years and a decrease in the percent of the population disabled by 0.4.

The component parts of this subactivity include:

- an effort to reduce smoking by encouraging members of the medical profession to advise patients to change their smoking habits and an increase in mass media coverage concerning the effects of smoking on health was estimated to cost $30 million a year for five years and to have the capacity to reduce by approximately one-fourth the deaths caused by smoking.[12] The extension of such a program over 10 years would probably cost $300 million and may reduce deaths caused by smoking by one-half. An additional increment of $180 million per year is estimated as needed to intensify and expand the program to reach 90 percent of the smoking population;
- a program of clinical and pharmacological research at an estimated cost of $60 million per year;

---

9   U.S. Department of Health, Education, and Welfare, Public Health Service, "Mortality from Diseases Associated with Smoking: United States, 1950-64," *Vital and Health Statistics*, NCHS Series 20, No. 4 (Washington, D.C.: U.S. Government Printing Office, October 1966); cancer of the bronchus, trachea and lung; neoplasm of the larynx, lip and pharynx, bronchitis, and emphysema. (The age adjusted death rate per 100,000 population was about 34 in 1964.) U.S. Department of Health, Education, and Welfare, Public Health Service, National Institutes of Health, *National Cancer Program*, "Report of the National Cancer Advisory Board," January 1973, p. 8.

10   Gains in life expectancy are derived as reductions in the life expectancy lost from the given cause calculated as proportional to the reduction in mortality from the same cause.

11   The 85 percent is derived from summing the first four causes of death associated with smoking in U.S. department of Health, Education, and Welfare, Public Health Service, *Smoking and Health*, PHS Publication No. 1103, Report of the Advisory Committee to the Surgeon General of the Public Health Service (Washington, D.C.: U.S. Government Printing Office, January 1964), p. 29, Table 2, and comparing expected and observed deaths.

12   Derived from U.S. Department of Health, Education, and Welfare, Office of Program Coordination, *Cancer*, Program Analysis 1966-3, Disease Control Programs (Washington, D.C., October 1966), pp. 76-80, Tables 1 and 5.

● transition subsidies to tobacco farmers and processors, which would probably be involved, at an estimated cost of $240 million per year.

The total cost of eliminating smoking among 90 percent of smokers is thus estimated at $510 million per year, or $5.1 billion for 10 years. Virtually 100 percent of that cost would require financing from public sources, almost all at the federal level.

Improvement of nutrition and fitness

This subactivity is concerned with thręe health-related conditions: obesity, lack of physical fitness and malnutrition.

Obesity

Eliminating obesity among all adults[13] by 1983 is estimated to:

● decrease deaths from cardiovascular diseases by 20 percent (The mortality rate for all cardiovascular diseases among the obese is approximately 40 percent higher than that for the nonobese.[14] We have assumed that elimination of obesity in adults could decrease deaths from cardiovascular diseases by one-half the observed differential.);

● decrease deaths from diabetes, nephritis and diseases of the digestive system by 50 percent.[15]

A 70 percent success rate in eliminating obesity, a more likely maximum rate than 100 percent, would add 1.51 years to mean life expectancy from the decrease in cardiovascular diseases and 0.14 years from the decrease in diseases of the endocrine and digestive systems, a total effect of 1.65 years.

Physical fitness[16]

There are indications that physical fitness may be associated with lower heart disease mortality apart from the effects of diet and other factors.[17] Improving the physical fitness of 70 percent of the population not physically fit (80 percent of Americans[18]) is assumed to:

---

13   In 1960, 50 percent of all Americans aged 20 to 70 were classified as obese (their average weight was at least 10 percent above the norm) and 30 percent of the population was overweight by 20 percent or more. U.S. Department of Health, Education, and Welfare, Public Health Service, *Obesity and Health,* A Source Book of Current Information for Professional Health Personnel, PHS Publication No. 1485 (Washington, D.C.: U.S. Government Printing Office, 1966), p. 20, Table 1.

14   Ibid., pp. 28-29, Figures 2 and 3.

15   Ibid., p. 20, Table 1.

16   Here defined as the ability to run 1.5 miles in 12 minutes. See Kenneth H. Cooper, *The New Aerobics* (New York: Bantam Books, May 1970), pp. 31-33.

17   W.J. Zukel et al., "A Short-term Community Study of the Epidomiology of Coronary Heart Disease," *American Journal of Public Health,* Vol. 49, No. 12, December 1959, p. 1637.

18   Kenneth H. Cooper, "The Art of Aerobics," *Time,* March 8, 1971, p. 60.

• reduce mortality from the cardiovascular diseases and from the diseases of the endocrine and digestive systems by the same magnitude as the 70 percent success rate in the reduction of obesity.

Reduction in disability from 70 percent reduction in obesity and 70 percent improvement in physical fitness of the total population is calculated at 1.4 percent based on the ratio of life expectancy losses from deaths from cardiovascular diseases to the percentage of population disabled by heart diseases, hypertension not involving heart diseases, and strokes.

Malnutrition

Eliminating undernourishment entirely and reducing malnutrition by 70 percent are arbitrarily[19] estimated to:
• increase life expectancy by 0.5 years;
• decrease the percent disabled by 0.2.[20]

The combined effects of reducing obesity and improving nutrition and physical fitness are therefore estimated to increase life expectancy by 3.8 years and reduce the disabled population by 1.6 percent.

The components of these subactivities include:
• an intensified research program dealing with physical fitness and nutrition, at a cost of $120 million per year above trend spending;
• the development and introduction of a method that would allow individuals to monitor their physical activity and its effects on their health, at an estimated total cost of $0.6 billion;
• widespread adoption of personal physical fitness programs, involving, for example, three episodes of one hour each for the first two weeks and a minimum of 30 minutes per week thereafter;[21]
• investment and operating outlays for recreational facilities.[22] Since the population served by recreational facilities would in all likelihood be more than doubled, as would the cost of staffing and maintaining new and old facilities, we estimate combined investment and operation costs for additional recreational facilities at $26 billion for the period;
• provision of adequate food for all Americans, estimated to cost $500 million a year;

---

19   Foregoing these arbitrary judgmental assumptions would amount to automatic arbitrary assumptions of zero effects, which we consider too extreme.

20   U.S. Department of Agriculture, unpublished, 1973.

21   George V. Mann et al., "Exercise to Prevent Coronary Heart Disease," *American Journal of Medicine*, Vol. 46, January 1969, p. 25.

22   Since it would be pointless, as well as infeasible, to develop such recreation facilities solely for their therapeutic effect, the activity would have to be developed for a joint health and recreation objective.

• a program for informing people about wholesome eating, including curriculum revisions in home economics and physical education classes, estimated to cost $200 million a year.

The total 10-year cost of the subactivity is calculated at $35 billion.

Prevention of accidents

Improving the safety of motor vehicles and household, job and recreational items is estimated to reduce mortality and disabilities from accidents by 50 percent,[23] thus adding 0.6 years to mean life expectancy and reducing the percent disabled by 0.2.

This subactivity would consist of a motor vehicle safety program and R&D for design of safe articles for household, job and recreational use and for motor vehicle systems. The estimated cost is $1 billion over the 10-year period.

Reduction of alcoholism and alcohol abuse

There are now approximately 9 million alcoholics in the United States.[24] It is assumed that the alcoholic population would remain constant (at 9 million) to 1983, with offsetting inflows and outflows. Although Alcoholics Anonymous reports a cure rate of close to 80 percent once an alcoholic confronts his problem, the recovery potential varies among drinkers and their conditions,[25] so we have assumed a 33 percent cure rate as a technically feasible maximum.

A 33 percent reduction in the number of alcohol abusers and alcoholics by 1983 is estimated to:

• reduce homicides by 20 percent (60 percent of homicides are associated with alcohol abuse),[26] thus adding 0.03 years to life expectancy;

• reduce traffic deaths by 16 percent (nearly one-half of the 58,000 traffic deaths per year are linked to problem drinking),[27] thus adding 0.09 years to life expectancy;

---

23 U.S. Department of Health, Education, and Welfare, Office of Program Coordination, *Motor Vehicle Injury Prevention Program,* Program Analysis 1966-1, Disease Control Programs (Washington, D.C., August 1966).

24 *Facts on Major Killing and Crippling Diseases.*

25 Alcoholics Anonymous, unpublished data; U.S. Department of Health, Education, and Welfare, Public Health Service, *Alcohol & Health* (Washington, D.C.: U.S. Government Printing Office, June 1974), p. 154.

26 The President's Commission on Law Enforcement and Administration of Justice, *Task Force Report: Drunkenness* (Washington, D.C.: U.S. Government Printing Office, 1967), p. 40.

27 "The Drinking Killer Problem," an article by James E. Clayton in *The Washington Post,* August 21, 1970, p. A-22; and U.S. Department of Transportation, National Highway Traffic Safety Administration, "Alcohol—Safety Countermeasures Program," April 1971 and November 1972.

- reduce the 100,000 annual accidental deaths other than traffic deaths[28] by 16 percent (assuming the same correlation as between alcohol abuse and traffic deaths), adding 0.1 years to life expectancy;
- decrease deaths from cirrhosis of the liver by 33 percent, adding 0.06 years to life expectancy;
- decrease the number of suicides[29] by 20 percent (assuming the same correlation as between alcohol abuse and homicide),[30] thus adding 0.04 years to life expectancy.

Reducing the number of alcoholics by 33 percent is thus estimated to increase life expectancy by 0.3 (rounded) years and reduce the percent of the population disabled by 1.3.

Components of this subactivity include:

- treatment for alcoholics. Hypothetical treatment elements and their cost, in rounded figures based upon the methods of treatment given by Alcoholics Anonymous, would consist of the following:

Two weeks hospitalization	$1,300
Twenty visits at $25 a visit	500
Group therapy	400
Drugs	300
Total per case treated	$2,500

In order to cure the 3 million, all of the 9 million alcoholics would need to be approached. It is assumed that 6 million would participate in treatment. Treatment for alcoholics is thus estimated to cost $15 billion.

- related research and education are assumed to cost $2.0 billion.

The estimated total cost of this subactivity is therefore $17 billion.

Reduction of drug abuse

Curing 90 percent of those addicted to drugs in 1983 (projected at 1.2 million[31]) is estimated to:

---

28   *Task Force Report: Drunkenness*, p. 39.

29   In 1965, an estimated 23,000 people committed suicide. See U.S. Department of Commerce, Bureau of the Census, *Pocket Data Book* (Washington, D.C.: U.S. Government Printing Office, 1967), p. 63.

30   *Task Force Report: Drunkenness*, p. 36.

31   An estimated 600,000 people are addicted to drugs at present. (These figures are based on discussion and estimates from several sources. Special Assistant Attorney General Myles Ambrose estimated the number of addicts to be between 500,000 and one million in an interview in *U.S. News and World Report*, April 3, 1972, and the number is assumed to double by 1983. Such projections are extremely uncertain, but by all evidence, the growth in drug addiction continues, and a doubling of the addict population in 10 years does not seem improbable.)

- raise life expectancy by 0.1 year (assuming that, on average, a drug addict loses 10 years of life expectancy);
- decrease the percent disabled by 0.5.

This subactivity would include developing and implementing treatment programs, supporting research into the medical and health problems of drug addiction and into the influence of drugs on criminal behavior, and obtaining a commitment on the part of institutions, voluntary organizations and governments to accept drug addiction as a disease and to develop ways of treating it. Such a comprehensive program is estimated to cost $3,000 per addict per year for an average of 1 2/3 years or a total of $5,000 per addict.[32] Total cost for the decade for reaching all addicts would come to $6 billion.

Of the total cost of all the subactivities combined, 50 percent is projected as public outlays and 52 percent is estimated as needed in the first four years of the 10-year period.

IMPROVEMENTS IN HEALTH SERVICES RELATED TO SPECIFIC CONDITIONS

This major activity comprises three subactivities: treatment of cancer, mental illness and arthritis. Estimates of the effects and costs are presented in the following table:

Activity and Maximum Percent of Relevant Population Affected	Average Life Expectancy (years)	Percent of Population Disabled	Total 10-Year Cost (billions of 1973 dollars)
Cancer diagnosis and treatment (50%)	+1.0	−0.1%	$ 6
Mental health treatment (30%)	+0.7	−1.9	54
Arthritis treatment (70%)	0	−1.1	6
Total	+1.7	−3.1	$66

---

32 Based on estimates in Robert Dupont, "The District of Columbia Experience Treating Heroin Addicts," *Public Management,* March 1972, p. 8.

Diagnosis and treatment of cancer

According to the American Cancer Society, about one-half of the cancer deaths now occurring are avoidable, and a World Health Organization Committee estimates that 75 percent or more of all human cancers will prove to be preventable.[33] Assuming this proportion to be the technically feasible maximum for the 10-year period, a 50 percent decrease in the number of deaths from all forms of cancer (other than respiratory, which is treated under smoking)[34] by 1983 can be calculated to:
- increase life expectancy by 1.0 year;
- decrease the proportion of disabled by 0.1 percent.

The components of such an activity would include:
- a research program at an estimated cost of $3 billion;
- a diagnostic and treatment program (more extensive than the earlier HEW design for early detection and treatment of cancer at four sites, head and neck, breasts, uterus, rectum and colon)[35] at an estimated cost of $3 billion.

The total cost for the subactivity over the 10-year period is us calculated at $6 billion.

Mental health care

Successfully treating 30 percent of the mentally ill[36] is estimated to:
- cut mortality from homicides, suicides and accidents by 44 percent (including a 50 percent addition for avoidance of indirect loss of life), adding 0.7 years to life expectancy;
- decrease the number disabled due to mental disorders, alcoholism and drug use by 1.9 percent.

The components[37] of this activity include:

---

33   American Cancer Society, '73 Cancer Facts and Figures, New York, 1972; National Cancer Program, "The Strategic Plan," January 1973, pp. 11-15.

34   Michael B. Shimkin (HEW National Cancer Institute), Science and Cancer (Washington, D.C.: U.S. Government Printing Office, 1969).

35   '73 Cancer Facts and Figures, p. 13; National Cancer Program, "Report to the Director," January 1973, pp. 13-15.

36   Limitations in the supply of qualified professionals and of the legal and institutional infrastructure in communities make a higher percentage of coverage appear unlikely within 10 years. The estimated output includes alcoholics and drug addicts as well as persons disabled by mental conditions, as determined by the National Health Survey.

37   Many of these elements have been taken from the proposals of the National Committee Against Mental Illness, Inc., What Are the Facts about Mental Illness in the United States? (Washington, D.C., 1966), pp. 4, 15, 47.

● 2,000 new treatment centers (one center for each 50,000 persons), at an estimated cost of $26 billion;

● 10,000 additional psychiatrists and psychologists, at an estimated cost of $6.5 billion;

● 25,000 additional trained nurses and teachers, estimated to cost $6 billion;

● 10,000 specialized teachers and other trained personnel, at an estimated cost of $13 billion;

● an expanded research program, at a cost of $240 million above the trend level.

Total cost: $54 billion.

Treatment of arthritis

According to a judgment by the National Health Education Committee,[38] substantial reductions in the disabilities resulting from arthritis may be possible for 70 percent of arthritis sufferers. Using this figure as the maximum, we calculate that a 70 percent reduction in disabilities due to arthritis would lower the total percent of population disabled in 1983 by 1.1 percentage points.[39]

This estimate is based upon the institution of a comprehensive treatment program along the lines of, but more intensive than, that proposed in the 1966 HEW arthritis study.[40] Such a program is estimated to cost an average of $633 million a year, or $6 billion (rounded) over the 10-year period.

Of the total cost for all the subactivities, 60 percent is estimated as public financing, with 26 percent of the cost assumed to occur in the first four years and 74 percent in the last six years.

SPECIAL HEALTH SERVICES FOR VULNERABLE POPULATION GROUPS

This activity would provide special health services for vulnerable population groups for whom current programs are inadequate or nonexistent. The estimated outputs and costs of this activity are summarized below:

---

38 *Facts on the Major Killing and Crippling Diseases,* p.3.

39 According to the National Health Interview Survey, 3.3 million persons in 1971 were limited in their activities because of arthritis, *Vital and Health Statistics,* April 1973.

40 U.S. Department of Health, Education, and Welfare, Office of Program Coordination, *Arthritis,* Program Analysis 1966-4, Disease Control Programs (Washington, D.C., September 1966).

Activity and Maximum Percent of Relevant Population Affected	Average Life Expectancy (years)	Percent of Population Disabled	Total 10-Year Cost (billions of 1973 dollars)
Expanded services for the poor (100%)	+2.2	−1.0%	$73
Expanded maternal and child services (100%)	+0.6	—	18
Total	+2.5	−1.0	91

Expanded services for the poor

A simple, naive calculation using two simultaneous equations with figures for life expectancy and poverty among whites and nonwhites yields a life expectancy differential between poor and nonpoor of 19 years.[41] It is assumed arbitrarily that one-half of this difference reflects the effects of poor health on income. We assume, then, that if adequate comprehensive health care would be provided to all of the poor and the near-poor:
- half of this spread in life expectancy could be eliminated and average life expectancy would be increased by 2.2 years;
- the proportion of disabled would decrease by 1.0 percent.

The extended services for the poor are based on three related approaches at the following levels of operation:[42]
- comprehensive health-care centers and outpatient clinics to serve 16.8 million poor and near-poor;
- outpatient clinics attached to public or private nonprofit hospitals or health departments to serve the 14.6 million metropolitan and rural poor and near-poor;

---

41   In 1966, there were 29.7 million poor ($3,335 income for a nonfarm family of 4), of which 20.3 million were white; 15.2 million near-poor ($4,345 income for a nonfarm family of 4), of which 12.3 million were white. See Mollie Orshansky (HEW Social Security Administration), *Social Security Bulletin* (Washington, D.C.: U.S. Government Printing Office, March 1968), p. 5. Therefore, 22.8 percent of the U.S. population, comprising 19 percent of the white population and 56 percent of the nonwhite population, were considered poor or near-poor by HEW standards. The average difference in life expectancy between white (71.7) and nonwhite (64.6) was 7.1 years in 1970 (preliminary). See *Statistical Abstract: 1972,* Table 74, p. 55.

42   Extrapolated from U.S. Department of Health, Education, and Welfare, Office of Program Coordination, *Delivery of Health Services for the Poor,* Program Analysis 1967-12 (Washington, D.C., December 1967), Table 4, p. 100.

• extended traditional medical practice to serve the remaining 13.6 million poor and near-poor.

The cost of these approaches is estimated to be $7.8 billion per year, or $78 billion for the 10-year period.

Expanded maternal and child services

Based on comparisons of the average infant mortality rate in the United States and the rates prevailing in certain large parts of the nation or in some foreign countries, a 40 percent reduction in the U.S. average infant mortality rate appears feasible over the 10-year period.[43] Achieving this, it is estimated, would:

• avoid 41,000 deaths, thus adding 0.6 years to life expectancy;

• reduce the disabled population by 0.05 percent.

The components[44] of this activity would include:

• improved and expanded family planning services, at an estimated annual cost of $115 million;

• comprehensive care to 500,000 poor mothers and their children, at an estimated annual cost of $965 million;

• intensive-care units for high-risk newborns, at an estimated cost of $734 million per year.

The total cost is assumed to be publicly financed, with one-third of the funds needed in the first subperiod.

RECREATIONAL FACILITIES IN NEIGHBORHOODS

The establishment of additional recreational facilities in neighborhoods has already been discussed in relation to nutrition and fitness. Here, it is treated as a separate activity designed to encourage recreation and at the same time to enhance physical and mental well-being. This activity includes extending and upgrading present recreational facilities plus developing natural environmental features, such as beaches or ski slopes, available in a locality. In addition to improving the quality of neighborhoods, this activity is assumed to encourage regular recreational activity.

---

43   For a later analysis of the international differentials in infant mortality, see Helen C. Chase, "The Position of the United States in International Comparisons of Health Status," *American Journal of Public Health,* Vol. 62, No. 4, 1972.

44   These estimates are from the HEW Program Analysis; *Delivery of Health Services for the Poor,* Sec. IV, 10.

Expanding recreational facilities is assumed to increase life expectancy by
1.1 years[45] and decrease the percent of the population disabled by 0.4. The
total cost for the activity is estimated at $127 billion, most of which would be
incurred at the end of the 10-year period. For a more detailed discussion, see
Chapter 18.

Table 5-2. Effects of Activities on Average Life Expectancy and the Number of Persons Disabled

Activity* and Percent of Relevant Population Affected	Total Cost 1974-83 (billions of 1973 dollars)	Average Life Expectancy (years)	Percent of Population Disabled
Base 1973	—	71.3	17.5%
Base 1983	—	72.7	16.8%
1. Changes in health-related habits & patterns	$ 64	+5.3	-3.3%
(a) Elimination of smoking (90%)	5	+1.8	-0.4
(b) Improvement of nutrition & fitness (70%)	35	+3.8	-1.6
(c) Prevention of accidents (50%)	1	+0.6	-0.2
(d) Reduction of alcoholism and alcohol abuse (33%)	17	+0.3	-1.3
(e) Reduction of drug abuse (90%)	6	+0.1	-0.5
2. Health services related to specific conditions	66	+1.7	-3.1
(a) Cancer: R&D, diagnostic and treatment expansion (50%)	6	+1.0	-0.1
(b) Mental health treatment (30%)	54	+0.7	-1.9
(c) Arthritis prevention & treatment (70%)	6	+0.0	-1.1
3. Special health services for vulnerable population groups	91	+2.5	-1.0
(a) The poor (100%)	73	+2.2	-1.0
(b) Maternal and child services (100%)	18	+0.6	—
22. Recreation facilities in neighborhoods	127	+1.1	-0.4
Combined Effects			
1,22. Health-related habits; Recreational facilities	191	+5.5	-3.4
1,2. Health-related habits; Health services	130	+6.8	-5.9
1,3. Health-related habits; Special health services	155	+7.3	-4.1
2,3. Health services; Special health services	157	+4.1	-3.9
3,23. Special health services; Recreational facilities	218	+3.5	-1.3
1,2,3. Health-related habits; Health services; Special health services	221	+8.7	-6.7
Total, all activities	**$348**	**+8.9**	**-6.8%**

*The numbers preceding the activities refer to their order in the matrix, Table 2-4.

---

45 For comparison, it may be noted that this is 15 percent of mortality from heart disease,
hypertension and stroke. It is 50 percent of mortality from coronary heart disease.

INTERACTIONS AMONG ACTIVITIES

In estimating combined effects, outputs from activities are treated as interdependent but costs are considered additive. The gains from combined discretionary activities are less than the sum of the individual gains, as shown in Table 5-2, because of offsetting interactions among the effects of the activities.

The most important offsets are between:

— changes in health-related habits and patterns (which include physical fitness) and recreational facilities in neighborhoods;

— abatement of drug abuse and alcoholism and the development of a network of diversified mental health facilities. These two activities, if maintained concurrently at full capacity levels, would be reaching overlapping population components;

— activities improving specialized services for the poor and those improving the general health status of the entire population. Offsets occur where the conditions that are the objects of general health improvement are more prevalent among the poor. However, these offsets are not complete, and it is possible that special outlets for reaching the poor would make the other health activities more effective in the long run.

No adjustment for less important offsetting effects has been made here. For example, alcoholism and smoking interact, but only in a limited way since most alcoholics also are heavy smokers but most smokers are not alcoholics. There is no functional overlap between the populations served for cancer, mental health and arthritis.

The result of all the activities as shown in Table 5-2 is estimated to be an overall gain in life expectancy of 8.9 years above the trend projected and a 6.8 percent decrease in the population that is chronically disabled. The total cost of all activities is calculated at $348 billion.

6

Public safety

OBJECTIVE

> *Freedom from violence, most specifically from violent crime, and the fear of violence.*

INDICATOR

> *The number of violent crimes per 100,000 persons per year.*

Violent crime, as defined in official statistics, includes murder, forcible rape, aggravated assault, and robbery. These four categories of crime differ fundamentally in seriousness, but in the aggregate they represent a basic level of concern for public safety. Obviously, the indicator does not cover all types of crime. To some extent, changes in many types of crimes against property probably would correlate with changes in violent crimes.

BASE TRENDS

Indicator	1973	1983 Projection	Projected Change
Number of violent crimes per 100,000 persons per year	668	668	0

The object of national concern is not simply reported crime but actual crime. To estimate the actual level of violent crime, the national crime statistics published by the FBI were adjusted to account for unreported crime. The adjustment was based on the findings of the National Opinion Research Center (NORC) that only 59 percent of violent crimes were reported to the police in

Table 6-1. Violent Crime, 1966*

Type of Violent Crime	Estimated Actual Crime		Crime Reported to Police		Crime Cleared	
	Number, thousand	Percent of Total	Number, thousand	Percent of Actual Crime	Percent of Crime Reported	Percent of Actual Crime
Murder	11	2%	11	100%	88%	88%
Forcible rape	85	12	25	29	61	18
Aggravated assault	437	61	232	53	69	37
Robbery	188	26	157	83	30	25
Total	720	100	425	60	52	31
Rate per 100,000 population	358		217			

*Actual number of crimes used here are the figures from the NORC Survey of Crime Victims, 1965-66, as reported in the President's Commission on Law Enforcement and Administration of Justice, *The Challenge of Crime in a Free Society* (Washington, D.C., February 1967). Data on reported and cleared crime are from Federal Bureau of Investiation, *Crime in the United States, Uniform Crime Reports—1967.* The number of murders is assumed to be the same as reported.

1966.[1] Table 6-1 gives the 1966 base year figures for actual, reported and cleared violent crime.

There has been a significant increase in the reported rate of violent crime in the United States in recent years. In 1960, the rate of reported violent crimes was 159 per 100,000 population; by 1969, that rate had increased by 104 percent to 325 per 100,000. In 1970, it was 359; in 1971, 393; and by 1972, it was an estimated 397 per 100,000. Based on the 1971-72 change and preliminary data for 1973, the rate would be 401 per 100,000 in 1973.[2] There are indications that the reporting rates for violent crime on the whole (except for rape) may not have changed much since 1966. Recently published results of a victimization survey for 1972 for the five largest cities show the rates of victimization to the number of crimes reported to the police of magnitudes comparable to those

---

1   The President's Commission on Law Enforcement and Administration of Justice, *The Challenge of Crime in a Free Society,* a survey conducted by the National Opinion Research Center (Washington, D.C.: U.S. Government Printing Office, February 1967), p. 21.

2   Data used in this chapter were taken from Federal Bureau of Investigation, *Crime in the United States, Uniform Crime Reports,* for 1966, 1967, 1968, 1971, and 1973, unless otherwise indicated.

   According to the final data for 1973 which became available after this chapter was completed, this rate was 414 in 1973; the rate of increase reported for the nine-month period of 1974 would yield 447 in 1974 when projected for the whole year.

found in the 1966 survey.[3] We assume, therefore, that the proportion of reported crime to actual crime in 1973 has remained at about 60 percent. The
actual crime rate in 1973 is thus estimated at 668 per 100,000.

Over the last three years of actually reported rates, i.e., 1969-72, the rate of
violent crime grew by 22 percent, or by 6.9 percent per year. However, by
examining a longer period (from 1933 to 1963), the growth rate of reported
violent crime is so small as to be insignificant. Because the growth of crime is
such a fluctuating variable, future growth between 1973 and 1983 can be assumed to lie between a minimum of no growth and a maximum of 6.9 percent
per year. It might even lie outside this range—for example, between 1969 and
1971, it grew at 10.0 percent; on the other hand, demographic trends in the
violent crime-prone population age groups suggest that a decline in crime is
possible by the end of the decade. In light of these conflicting alternatives, we
have projected no change from the 1973 violent crime rate, in spite of the still
rising crime rates. The rate of violent crime in 1983 is thus assumed to remain at
668 per 100,000 population.

THE CHARACTERISTICS OF VIOLENT CRIME

Identifying circumstances in which violent crimes occurred and characteristics
of the offenders helps in defining discretionary activities that would seem to
hold the promise of reducing crime. Even though the data in the field of public
safety is quite fragmentary (and often speculative), certain observations can be
made. In general, violent crime may be divided into crimes relating to
pecuniary motives, including robbery and some murders, and "crimes of pas-
sion," including rape, aggravated assault and murder. Drug addiction is associated with violent crime, since addicts often steal and sometimes kill to
obtain money with which to buy drugs. Drunkenness and abuse of alcohol are
also associated with the occurrence of crime.

Most violent crimes are committed by persons who have previously committed violent or nonviolent offenses.[4] An entry into a "career of crime" typically occurs early in life.[5] There may also be an important association between
mental and emotional disturbances and violent crime.

Indicators of the association of some of these conditions and violent crime
are shown in Table 6-2. No attempt has been made to systematize these data by

---

3   U.S. Department of Justice, Law Enforcement Assistance Administration, *Crime in the Nation's
Five Largest Cities,* National Crime Panel Surveys, Advance Report, Washington, D.C., April 1974,
p. 28.

4   *Uniform Crime Reports,* 1970, pp. 37 and 38.

5   *Uniform Crime Reports,* 1966, p. 39, and *The Challenge of Crime in a Free Society,* p. 46.

Table 6-2. Factors Associated with Violent Crime

	Percent Indicator of Association
(1) Percent of arrests for violent crime of persons with prior arrest for same offense, 1967-68	28%
(2) Percent of arrests for violent crime of persons with prior arrest for any offense, 1967-68	89
(3) Percent of arrests for violent crime of persons under 18, 1971	24
(4) Percent of offenses committed by drug addicts, 1971 estimate:	
robberies	25
all violent crimes	10
(5) Percent of violent crimes associated with abuse of alcohol, 1967:	
rape	35
murder, homicide	60
aggravated assault	60
all violent crimes	49

Sources: For (1) and (2): FBI, *Uniform Crime Reports—1968,* p. 36; for (3): FBI, *Uniform Crime Reports—1971,* p. 118; for (4): see p. 100 of this chapter; for (5): President's Commission on Law Enforcement and Administration of Justice, *Task Force Report: Drunkenness,* 1967, pp. 40-41. Proportion of murders is derived from information from a number of studies reported in this source.

direct and indirect or immediate and remote chains of interdependence. These indicators of association, however, may suggest the maximum ceiling on the reduction in crime that could be achieved by removing the contributing causes (assuming the existence of exclusive causal relationships reflected in these associations).

While highly speculative, the magnitudes of the numbers in Table 6-2 suggest the magnitudes of possible improvements. Replacing entry into a crime career with entry into some other career would, it appears, prevent the development of a chain of multiple repeat offenses. This might be accomplished by developing effective opportunities early in life. Considerable reduction in crime might also result from breaking such chains by means of removal from society through increased effectiveness of the police and court systems or through effective rehabilitation programs. Other opportunities for reducing violent crime may lie in abatement of alcohol abuse and drug addiction. An assessment of the possible results of activities based on these and other possibilities follows.

DISCRETIONARY ACTIVITIES TO REDUCE VIOLENT CRIME

Improvement of the law enforcement system

In the subactivities that follow, we have identified some of the major possibilities for change within the law enforcement system that appear to offer the opportunity for reducing violent crime. These changes focus on separate institutions—the police, the courts and the jails—but their effects overlap. A summary of the effects and costs is given below:

Activity	Number of Violent Crimes per 100,000 Persons per Year	Total 10-Year Cost (billions of 1973 dollars)
Improving effectiveness of police	− 94	$15
Improving court efficiency	− 67	5
Improving rehabilitation	− 40	6
Total	−180	$26

Improving effectiveness of police

This subactivity consists of modernization and technological improvements aimed at improved communications systems—from the public as well as within the police system—reduction in police response time to calls, and improved data processing and laboratory techniques, along the lines of the improvements suggested in the Report by the President's Commission on Law Enforcement and Administration of Justice.[6] Since there is a definite correlation between response time and arrest rates[7] (although the relationship may not be directly cause-and-effect) and since a rise in arrest rates appears to have a definite effect on preventing crime,[8] increasing the visibility of police patrols and the risk of apprehension by decreasing patrol response time, together with the other improvements in police efficiency, is estimated to:

6   *The Challenge of Crime in a Free Society,* pp. 245-257.

7   Ibid., p. 248, Table 1.

8   State of California, *Deterrent Effects of Criminal Sanctions,* Progress Report of the Assembly Committee on Criminal Procedure, May 1968, p. 30; see also Gary S. Becker, "Crime and Punishment: An Economic Approach," *Journal of Political Economy,* April 1968.

• reduce the violent crime rate by 14 percent—7 percent as a result of apprehension and hence removal from opportunity for crime, and 7 percent as a result of indirect deterrence—thus reducing the number of violent crimes per 100,000 persons per year in 1983 by 94.[9]

The cost of these improvements is calculated by extrapolating the $4,494 million 1970 outlay for police protection[10] to $6 billion by 1973, and assuming an additional 25 percent of that base or $1.5 billion per year to finance these improvements. This would amount to a cost of $15 billion for the decade.

Increasing court efficiency

Based on two studies done by the Washington, D.C., Police Department,[11] we calculated that 17 percent of the robberies committed in the Washington, D.C., area in an average year were committed by men under indictment for a previous robbery and out on bail. Assuming that conditions similar to those in Washington, D.C., exist in other large metropolitan area court systems, we estimate that reducing the average time within the court system by 40 percent (from five to three months)[12] would:

• reduce violent crime committed by those on bail by half. This would result in a 9 percent reduction in robberies (giving a 3 percent reduction in the overall rate of violent crime by 1983).[13] Adding those released on bail to await trial for forcible rape and aggravated assault, assumed to number relatively more in proportion to the number of those crimes, gives a decrease in the rate

---

9   The District of Columbia Crime Commission found that close to 40 percent of violent crimes occur on the streets. Based on estimates given in James V. DeLong, "Deterrence and Crime Prevention," mimeographed (Washington, D.C.: U.S. Bureau of the Budget, 1968), p. 33, the doubling of patrol forces would reduce street crime by 25 percent by 1980. The number of police is calculated at 200 times the D.C. effort and the cost at twice the current national expenditure, or roughly 230,000 more policemen at a cost of $3 billion per year. Assuming that increased police protection also has a 40 percent indirect deterrent effect, a total of 14 percent of violent crime in 1983 would be prevented.

10   U.S. Department of Commerce, Bureau of the Census, *Statistical Abstract of the United States: 1972,* 93d edition (Washington, D.C.: U.S. Government Printing Office, 1972), p. 415.

11   Robert E. Reiver, "Survey of the Apparent Abuse of the Bail Release System," mimeographed (Washington, D.C.: Police Department, 1968); The President's Commission on Law Enforcement and Administration of Justice, *Task Force Report: Science and Technology* (Washington, D.C.: U.S. Government Printing Office, 1967), p. 40, Figure 13.

12   *The Challenge of Crime in a Free Society,* pp. 258-259.

13   The estimated 3 percent reduction in violent crime is probably a conservative estimate. In the Washington, D.C., study, the same men were indicted again for eight other violent crimes while on bail.

of violent crime of 10 percent by 1983, or a decrease of 67 in the number of violent crimes per 100,000 persons.[14]

This subactivity would consist of the addition to the capabilities of the prosecution, judges and defense counsels, implementation of new court management procedures,[15] and increased upgrading and specialization for court personnel, at an estimated cost of $1 million per court per year for 500 courts (about one for every 500,000 persons). The total cost is thus approximately $500 million per year, or $5 billion for the decade.

Improving rehabilitation

We assume that, at present rates of actual crime, arrest and conviction, by 1983, 70 percent of violently criminal offenders will serve sentence for one of their offenses. We also estimate that, based on fragmentary data for successful programs[16] and assuming their replication on a wide scale, improved rehabilitation programs could prevent one-fourth of repeat crimes.

We estimate that improved rehabilitation would:

● reduce the rate of violent crime by 6 percent (one-fourth of the 70 percent of the 35 percent who would normally return to prison),[17] or a decrease of 40 in the number of violent crimes per 100,000 persons per year.

The cost of adopting effective measures to reduce recidivism by one-half is estimated at $2,000 per prisoner per year, over and above the $7,000 now being spent. An additional $1,000 for each of the 100,000 prisoners being released each year is included as the cost of gradual reentry into society. The total cost for this activity is assumed at approximately $6 billion for the 10-year period.

We estimate that implementation of this entire activity, including all three subactivities, would reduce the annual number of violent crimes per 100,000 persons in 1983 by 180 at a cost of $26 billion, with 96 percent coming from public funds and 41 percent needed in the first subperiod.

---

14 While increasing the sentences of all those convicted of violent crime would reduce the rate of violent crime in the short run, this approach places the burden of deterrence on the length of the sentence, which affects only a small part of the universe of committed offenses. By all indications, the price of crime could be raised more effectively by increasing the rates of apprehension, prosecution, conviction, and sentencing than by increasing the terms of those sentenced, which would also be inequitable.

15 Committee for Economic Development, Research and Policy Committee, *Reducing Crime and Assuring Justice,* A Statement on National Policy, June 1972, pp. 19, 27.

16 The President's Commission on Law Enforcement and Administration of Justice, *Task Force Report: Corrections* (Washington, D.C.: U.S. Government Printing Office, 1967), p. 28.

17 Daniel Glaser, *The Effectiveness of a Prison and Parole System* (Indianapolis: The Bobbs-Merrill Co., 1964), p. 19.

Employment and other opportunities for the young

The statistics about crime and youth are compelling. Persons under age 25 commit more crimes than any other segment of the population.[18] In 1966, approximately half of those arrested for violent crimes were under age 25; in 1971, this percentage rose to 59.3 percent.[19] Of those with a federal crime record, 44 percent are first arrested before the age of 20 and 75 percent before the age of 25.[20] Young offenders have the highest rate of recidivism.[21] The estimated effect and cost of providing employment and other opportunities for the young to direct them away from entering a crime career are summarized below:

Activity	Number of Violent Crimes per 100,000 Persons	Total 10-Year Cost (billion of 1973 dollars)
Employment and other opportunities for youth	−240	$51

This activity, it is assumed, would avoid both first arrests and subsequent rearrests annually for half the young people who would otherwise have become first offenders. Thus, by 1983, the tenth year, it would:

• reduce the rate of violent crime by 36 percent, and the number of violent crimes per 100,000 persons by 240.[22]

This subactivity consists of three main components providing educational, job and recreational opportunities:

• a program designed to keep young people in school, estimated to cost $17 billion for the decade;

18 *Uniform Crime Reports*, 1971, p. 124; and 1966, p. 116.

19 Ibid.; and 1967, pp. 34-35, Table A.

20 Ibid.

21 *Uniform Crime Reports*, 1971, p. 36.

22 Total arrests are assumed a function of first arrests; also, this analysis assumes a constant proportion of crime to arrest.

• a job training program[23] for one-half of the youth population not in school (assuming that one-half of those out of school can be trained for employment) at a cost, including administration, training and living allowances, of $26 billion for the decade;

• recreation and community activities for young people, at an estimated cost per person of $2,000 and a 10-year cost of approximately $8 billion.

The total cost is thus estimated at $51 billion. As in the case of other activities with effects on more than one area of social concern, it is unlikely that the events of which these activities consist would actually occur and the underlying decisions would be made with respect to only one of their consequences. This activity consists primarily of enhancement of education and human skills and, as in the case of recreational activities with physical fitness and health effects, it is unlikely to be implemented simply for the sake of one outcome, here the reduction of crime. Because its primary orientation appears to be educational, this activity is described in more detail in Chapter 7.

Changing health-related habits and patterns

This discussion deals with alcoholism and drug abuse in relation to criminal behavior. Since the activity is primarily oriented toward improved health, it is discussed at greater length in Chapter 5. A summary of the effects on crime and cost of the activity appears below:

Activity	Number of Violent Crimes per 100,000 Persons	Total 10-Year Cost (billions of 1973 dollars)
Reduction of alcoholism	− 67	$17
Abatement of drug addiction	− 62	6
Total	−129	$64*

*Total includes other subactivities discussed in Chapter 5.

With 49 percent of all violent crime associated with alcohol abuse, as shown in Table 6-2, curing 33 percent of the estimated 9 million alcoholics in 1983, aiming the activity especially at the problem drinker is estimated to:

---

23 Evidence suggesting that the effect of unemployment on juvenile delinquency is positive is found, for example, in Belton M. Fleisher, "The Effect of Unemployment on Juvenile Delinquency," *Journal of Political Economy*, December 1963, p. 543.

• reduce the number of dangerous cases of alcoholism by 40 percent. Assuming that one-half of the crimes associated with alcohol abuse would not occur if alcoholism were eliminated, the rate of violent crime would thus be reduced by 10 percent, decreasing the number of violent crimes per 100,000 persons by 67.

Curing 33 percent of the 9 million alcoholics is estimated to cost $17 billion over the 10-year period. The activity components are described in Chapter 5.

We assume that crime related to drug addiction is primarily associated with the acquisition of money rather than that drug addiction in itself inclines the addict to violent behavior. We have projected the number of drug addicts in the United States in 1983 at 1.2 million. It is assumed that one-fourth of drug addicts maintain their addiction at least partly by crime, and that each criminal addict commits an average of 20 robberies, burglaries or larcenies per year to support his habit.

Eliminating 90 percent of drug abuse by 1983 is estimated to:

• eliminate 90 percent of the robberies attributable to drug addiction, reducing the rate of violent crime by 9 percent and decreasing the number of violent crimes per 100,000 persons by 62.

The estimated cost of curing 90 percent of drug addicts is $6 billion. The activity is presented in detail in Chapter 5.

Health services related to specific conditions

The specific conditions related to public safety toward which this activity is directed are mental health problems, especially those related to the abuse of alcohol and drugs. A summary of the effect and cost of the activity is given below:

Activity	Number of Violent Crimes per 100,000 Persons	Total 10-Year Cost (billions of 1973 dollars)
Mental health facilities	−69	$66*

*The total activity cost (which includes cancer and arthritis treatment as well).

Assuming, largely on the basis of the correlation between drug and alcohol abuse and violent crime, that 70 percent of violent crimes result from some mental or emotional disturbance, successfully treating 30 percent of those with mental or emotional problems is estimated to:

- reduce the violent crime rate by just over 10 percent, about one-half the expected correlation because some of those cured would not cease their criminal activity, with a resulting decrease in the number of violent crimes per 100,000 of 69.

The development of mental health diagnostic and treatment facilities capable of reaching 30 percent of those with mental health problems is estimated to cost $54 billion over the decade. A more detailed description of the activity is provided in Chapter 5.

INTERACTIONS AMONG ACTIVITIES

If the different activities discussed here were implemented at the same time, there would obviously be overlapping effects, although the level of the overlap would depend on the crime population affected and on the interaction of the components of the activities. Table 6-3 provides a summary of the interactions.

Within the health-related habits activity (1) and the health services activity (2), there is considerable overlap. It is assumed that the combined effect of these activities reduces the effect of the second activity by one-half, resulting in a reduction in the violent crime rate of 24 percent, or a decrease in the number of violent crimes per 100,000 a year of 163.

All the other effects of activities are calculated as successive reductions of the universe in which they operate. For example, the interaction between improved law enforcement (4) and employment for the young (5) is calculated first by estimating a 36 percent reduction resulting from the full-employment activity. The 27 percent reduction due to improved law enforcement is then applied to the reduced total (64 percent). Therefore, the combined effects result in a 53 percent reduction in the rate of violent crime.

Combining the health-related habits activity (1) with employment for the young (5) is estimated to reduce violent crime by 48 percent, or by 321 crimes per 100,000 per year. If improved law enforcement (4) were substituted for employment for the young (5) in the above combination, output is estimated to decline by 2 percent while the cost would decrease by $25 billion.

The same method was used to calculate effects of multiple combinations. Thus, combining the health-related habits activity (1), health services (2) and improved law enforcement (4) is estimated to reduce violent crime by 50 percent at a cost of $156 billion. Substituting employment for the young (5) for the health services activity (2) in the above group is estimated to increase output by 15 percentage points to an effective reduction in violent crime of 65 percent, while the cost would decline to $141 billion.

Combining all four activities results in the calculated maximum total reduction of violent crime by 67 percent at an estimated cost of $207 billion over 10 years.

Table 6-3. Effects of Activities on Violent Crime

Activity*	Total Cost 1974-83 (billions of 1973 dollars)	Percent Change in Rate of Violent Crime	No. of Violent Crimes per 100,000 Persons per Year
Base 1973	—	—	668
Base 1983	—	—	668
1. Changes in health-related habits and patterns	$ 64**	-19%	-129
(a) Abatement of drug addiction	6	- 9	- 62
(b) Reduction of alcoholism and alcohol abuse	17	-10	- 67
2. Health services related to specific conditions	66**	-10	- 69
(a) Mental health facilities	54	-10	- 69
4. Improvement of law enforcement	26	-27	-180
(a) Improved effectiveness of police	15	-14	- 94
(b) Increased effectiveness of case processing	5	-10	- 67
(c) Improved rehabilitation	6	- 6	- 40
5. Employment and other opportunities for the young	51**	-36	-240
Combined Effects			
1,2. Health-related habits; Health services	130	-24	-163
4,5. Improved law enforcement; Employment for the young	77	-53	-356
1,5. Health-related habits; Employment for the young	115	-48	-321
1,4. Health-related habits; Improved law enforcement	90	-46	-309
1,2,4. Health-related habits; Health services; Improved law enforcement	156	-50	-334
1,4,5. Health-related habits; Improved law enforcement; Employment for the young	141	-65	-434
Total, all activities	**$207**	**-67%**	**-448**

*The numbers preceding the activities refer to their order in the matrix, Table 2-4

**These totals include subactivity components not related to the reduction in crime. See Chapters 5 and 7.

7

Basic education

OBJECTIVES

Providing young people with basic skills and abilities, including essentials for their participation in contemporary life—fluency with language (written and spoken), a basic familiarity with mathematics, the learning of basic cultural values, and socialization.

Providing a basic level of basic skills to all young people.

INDICATORS

Index of mean performance in twelfth grade based on standard tests.

Percent of twelfth graders three or more years behind 1973 average.

An index of mean educational performance in verbal ability, reading comprehension and mathematics and the percent of students three or more years behind the 1973 average, both taken at the age of grade 12, are used as the principal indicators of basic education. The index is based on data for 1965 from the Equal Educational Opportunity Survey, published in 1966 and known as the "Coleman Report."[1]

Chart 7-1 shows mean raw scores for three grade levels for tests of mathematical achievement; similar data exist for verbal ability and reading comprehension.[2] The output indicators used here are an index number of

---

1   U.S. Department of Health, Education, and Welfare, Office of Education, National Center for Educational Statistics, *Equality of Educational Opportunity*, The Coleman Report (Washington, D.C.: U.S. Government Printing Office, 1966).

2   The scores are from tests administered to pupils in the sixth, ninth and twelfth grades. The tests were administered at a single period to students in different grades. In the chart, test scores are plotted on the vertical axis and grade levels on the horizontal axis. The mean for the population is shown by the heavy line. The heavy bars at grades 6, 9 and 12 show the dispersion of the scores by standard deviations, which increases with increasing school years.

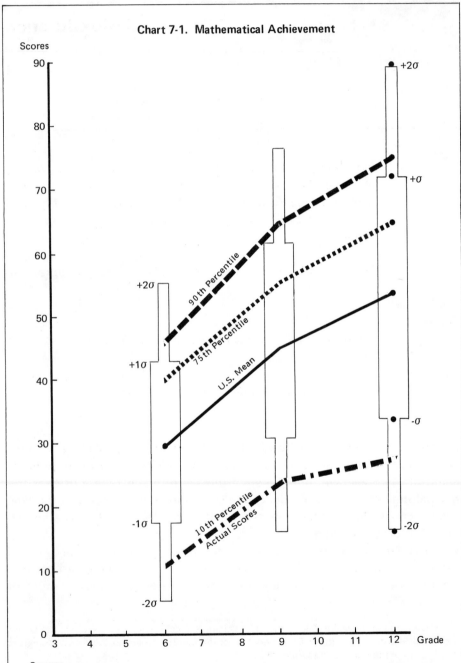

Chart 7-1. Mathematical Achievement

Source:
Tetsuo Okada and Davis S. Stoller, "Dynamics of Achievement: Differential Growth of Achievement for Negro and White Students by SMSA/Non-SMSA and Region," National Center for Educational Statistics, Technical Note No. 54, January 25, 1968, and HEW, unpublished materials.

average scores and the proportion of students three or more years below the index based upon this average of the three test scores for verbal ability, reading comprehension and mathematical achievement at the twelfth grade level. In calculating the index, the raw scores on the three tests were scaled so that the twelfth grade mean score equaled 100 in each case and then the three sets of points were averaged.[3] The resulting index is shown in Chart 7-2. Comparisons among the twelfth graders show that the top 10 percent of students had an achievement index of 135 or more and the top 25 percent, 119 or more, while the middle two-thirds (bracketed by a range of one standard deviation on each side of the mean) fell between 72 and 129. The scores for grade levels are translated into years of schooling behind the norm by looking at the change in average index scores as the grade level advances. Thus, 24 percent of twelfth grade students had an index score of 81 (the ninth grade mean), or less, and are therefore three or more years below the average for grade 12. The index reflecting the distribution structure of 1966 is set at the level of the 1973 average score equal to 100. It is assumed that the relative distribution remained unchanged.

BASE TRENDS

Indicators	1973	1983 Projection	Projected Change
Index of mean performance in twelfth grade based on standard tests	100	105	+5
Percent of students three or more years behind the 1973 average in twelfth grade	24%	19%	−6%

In estimating base trends, we have assumed that the percent of students three years behind the norm will drop to 19 percent because there will be a trend increase of 5 percent in the level of educational achievement by 1983. These

3   With the U.S. mean at grade 12 taken as 100, the ninth grade mean is 81.22 and the sixth grade mean, 53.28. The average difference per grade from the sixth to the twelfth grade is 7.8 points. The resulting distribution is a simple average of three separate distributions, not a one-dimensional scaling of a joint distribution of three variables.

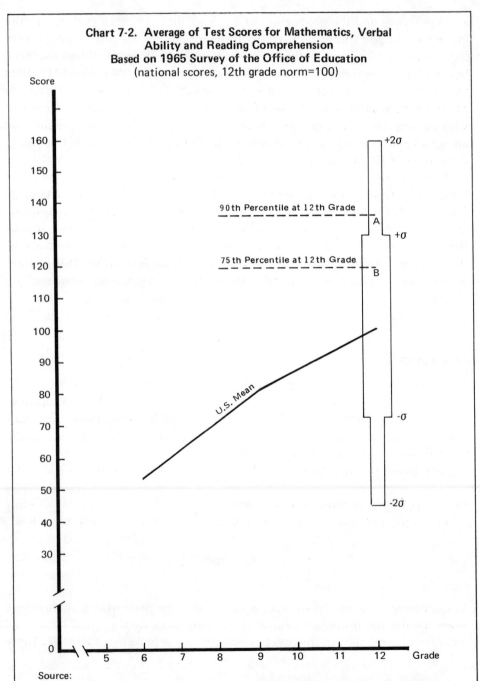

Chart 7-2. Average of Test Scores for Mathematics, Verbal
Ability and Reading Comprehension
Based on 1965 Survey of the Office of Education
(national scores, 12th grade norm=100)

Source:

Tetsuo Okada and Davis S. Stoller, "Dynamics of Achievement: Differential Growth of
Achievement for Negro and White Students by SMSA/Non-SMSA and Region," National
Center for Educational Statistics, Technical Note No. 54, January 25, 1968, p. 36, and
HEW, unpublished materials.

estimates are based on scattered evidence that such changes have taken place[4] and on the assumption of continuation of present educational methods, assuming that the achievement dispersion of the population will remain constant through 1983, and that, except for a 5 percent increase in the level, the proportionate relationship among the attainment levels in 1983 will be the same as shown in Chart 7-2.

ACTIVITIES TO INCREASE THE LEVEL OF BASIC SKILLS

There are no reasons to think that the current or projected levels of educational attainment are near any kind of a natural limit; indeed, existing evidence seems to suggest the opposite. The range of demonstrated attainment within the United States, such as 25 percent of the students performing at least 18 points above the national average, and international tests in mathematics administered to 13 year olds, showing a comparatively low performance of American students,[5] suggests that there may well exist room for substantial growth in the average attainment level in the United States. Presumably, this potential consists, to an important extent, of upgrading the performance of those students considerably below the mean, but it probably also includes possibilities for across-the-board growth, including growth by high achievers. There is no reason to assume that either biological or genetic limitations would pose any constraints in the range of the performance discussed. Several demonstrated instances of dramatic improvement which occurred on a small scale would tend to support the view that large improvements are at least theoretically possible.

Three activities to raise the level of basic skills beyond expected trend improvements are discussed below. Two are directly oriented toward basic education; the third is a multi-purpose activity concerned with providing teenagers with incentives to stay in school, opportunities for recreation and jobs.

In basic education, lead times are very long if achievement is measured at the twelfth grade. Consequently, the long-run impact of the activities dis-

---

4   After this chapter was completed, much of the analysis contained in it was refined and extended to embrace a 4-year and a 25-year time interval in addition to the 10-year period. See Edward L. Rhodes, *Performance Possibilities in Basic Education in the United States: 1974–1998,* A Technical Staff Paper (Washington, D.C.: National Planning Association, November 1974). Using time series information for certain test scores, that study arrived at a similar estimate of the trend rate of change of 8 percent in 14 years, equivalent to 6 percent in 10 years.

5   Torsten Husen, ed., "International Project for the Evaluation of Educational Achievement, Phase I," *International Study of Achievement in Mathematics: A Comparison of 12 Countries,* Vol. II (New York, 1967).

cussed below may be quite different from that shown by a measure of final output at grade twelve in 1983.

Remedial tutoring and augmenting educational inputs

Remedial tutoring and augmenting educational inputs include the subactivities of parent and student counseling and of providing books for students' homes. Their effects and costs are summarized below:

Activity	Index of Mean Performance in Twelfth Grade (points)	Students Three or More Years Behind the 1973 Average in Grade Twelve (percent)	Total 10-Year Cost (billions of 1973 dollars)
Remedial tutoring	+ 7	− 5%	$25
Parent counseling	+ 3	− 2	5
Student counseling	+ 4	− 3	33
Books for students' homes	+ 2	− 1	10
Total	+16	−11	$73

The effects of the subactivities on the index of mean performance are assumed to be additive, and the impact on students below the norm is estimated to be consistent with the shift in the index on the assumption that the relative distribution remains unchanged.

Remedial tutoring

In this subactivity, a massive remedial tutoring program would be established to train underachieving students in reading, mathematics and verbal skills. Such an approach to be successful should not involve payment by the hour for the tutor (which would probably provide counterproductive incentives) but rather offer a lump sum payment, in effect a bounty, to anyone raising a student's level of attainment as measured by achievement tests.[6] To

---

6 Sumner Myers, "A New Incentive Technique for All Our Children—'The Right to Read,' " *Looking Ahead* (Washington, D.C.: National Planning Association, June 1970).

prevent abuses, a careful administrative and testing system would be needed to accurately measure achievement before and after tutoring, and that system would entail considerable overhead cost.

Providing remedial tutoring for students near and below the national averages over an eight-year period is estimated, by 1983, to:

- bring about progress equivalent to three years for nearly one-third of the 19 percent of all twelfth graders three years or more behind, thereby raising them to the national average, and equivalent to two years for another two-thirds of these students plus 5 percent of all other students; bring about progress equal to one year for 30 percent of all students. This adds up to a gain of 0.82 years for all students. Converting years to index points by a ratio of 8 points per year yields a gain of 7 index points.

We assume for this subactivity a unit cost of $1,250 per student year.[7] Given the projection of 4.2 million twelfth graders for 1983, the 6 percent (252 thousand students) progressing three years would entail a unit cost of $3,750, the 17 percent (714 thousand) progressing two years would entail a unit cost of $2,500, and the 30 percent (1.3 million students) progressing one year would have a unit cost of $1,250. The total direct cost in 1983 would thus be $4.3 billion. We assume, however, phase-in increments of one-eighth a year with the build-up over seven years entailing an additional $16.8 billion in cost. Finally, an overhead cost of $4 billion for administration, research, etc., is assumed, yielding a total of $25.1 billion, or rounded, $25 billion.

Parent counseling

This subactivity would differ substantially from the guidance counseling and parent conferences currently provided by schools. Rather, this program would aid the parents of school children in understanding and encouraging those factors which facilitate learning. The subactivity is intended to provide a direct relationship between the student's home environment and the school elements of his education.

It is estimated here, roughly, that a total of 50 million students will be enrolled in primary and secondary education in 1983. It is further assumed that these 50 million students will come from 30 million homes, most of which will already be supportive of learning. For the parents in 20 percent (6 million) of the homes, the cost is calculated on the basis of an equivalent of providing eight-week classes on child development directly and other subjects that would directly aid them in understanding and encouraging those factors which

---

7   Since one student year under present definition consists of three subjects, in effect the unit cost is predicated on a cost on the average a little over $400 per subject per year. This is higher than the amounts established in performance contracts so far, but performance contracts are not good models for this subactivity since their results have been spotty and the scale of the present activity is much larger than any systematic contracting so far undertaken.

facilitate school learning, and providing, on the average, four one-hour conferences with a professional staff person a month. The subactivity is estimated to:

• improve the average performance of all twelfth graders by one-third of a grade level, or by 3 index points, and reduce the percent of students three years or more behind the norm in grade 12 by 2 percent.

Four one-hour conferences per month and eight weeks of classes for 6 million families translates into a need for 11,000 counselors spending 10 hours per week to conduct two classes in each of five eight-week periods, and spending 30 hours per week in counseling individual parents, plus an additional 4,000 counselors spending full time in counseling individual parents, or a total of 15,000 professional counselors. With an average estimated cost of $33,000 per professional, the annual cost comes to $495 million. Adding the cost of complementary inputs, mainly supporting staff, or $175 million yields $670 million a year. The activity is assumed to need eight years of full operation to yield the output by 1983, and would entail a total cost of $5 billion.

Intensive student counseling

This subactivity is designed to intensify and upgrade the school counseling services to include aid for personal problems, learning problems, school course selection, vocational or college choices, and even psychological and health problems.

Providing intensive student counseling to one-half the estimated 50 million primary and secondary students is assumed by 1983 to:

• increase the performance of those students receiving counseling by one year, yielding a total gain among all twelfth graders of one-half year, or 4 index points, and reduce by 3 percent the number of students three or more years behind the norm.

This subactivity assumes one-fourth of a day of professional counseling time per student per month for students requiring intensive counseling. At a rate of four students per working day and 22 school days per month, one counselor for each 88 students is needed. Rounding that ratio to 100 and assuming that one-half of the students either already have or do not need the intensified counseling gives a requirement of one counselor to every 200 students. With a projection of 50 million students, a quarter million counselors are therefore required. Assuming an annual cost per counselor of $33,000 gives a total annual cost of $8.25 billion. We postulate four years of full operation (or its equivalent) to achieve the 1983 effect, with the total cost therefore coming to $33 billion.

Books for students' homes

Providing a mechanism through which one-half of the estimated 30 million families with school-age children would obtain books and other durable learning tools is estimated to:

● improve the performance of one-half of the twelfth grade students in the program by one-half a year, yielding an improvement of 2 index points for all twelfth graders, and reducing the percent of students three or more years below the norm by 1 percentage point.

We assume an average cost of $110 per year per home, or a $1.65 billion annual cost, and six full years of operation, giving a total cost of $10 billion.

To sum up, all subactivities together are estimated to cost $73 billion, 17 percent of which would be required in the first period, and to be 90 percent financed by public funds.

Improved educational technology and approaches

This activity represents technological and conceptual developments in basic education aimed at raising educational attainment by means of changing important characteristics of the educational system. It consists of three subactivities: the introduction of new technologies (television, computers, etc.); the education of very young children, probably mostly by broadcasting and outreach involvement of parents; and the creation and nourishment of technical knowledge through the development of educational science and technology. A summary of the maximum effects and costs appears below:

Activity	Index of Mean Performance in Twelfth Grade (points)	Students Three or More Years Behind the 1973 Average in Grade Twelve (percent)	Total 10-Year Cost (billions of 1973 dollars)
New technologies	+13	− 9%	$161
Learning by the very young	—	—	17
R&D and the diffusion of innovations	+ 8	− 5	5
Total	+21	−14	$183

New technologies

This subactivity consists of the development and large-scale introduction into educational use of broadcasting, language and mathematical laboratories, and programmed instruction, and of the application of computers to instruction, information storage and processing, and administration. The introduction of such new technologies on a large scale is estimated to:

● improve average performance of twelfth graders by one and one-half years, or 13 points on the index of educational achievement, and reduce the percent below the norm by 9 percentage points.

We assume that the development and introduction into effective use of these new technologies would raise the annual cost per student by $650.[8] (Whether, when and what savings in other costs may be obtained from these technologies, and how, is not examined.) Given the projection of 50 million students for 1983, the estimated annual cost of this subactivity is $32.5 billion. It is further assumed that, to produce results by 1983 in any reasonable proportion to cost, three years of full operation are required, plus four years of phasing in by increments of one-fifth of the full level. The total cost is thus estimated to be $162 billion.

Learning by the very young

Since recent studies have indicated that very substantial learning occurs early in life, before school age,[9] this subactivity focuses on the introduction of opportunities for learning for children aged two to five. The activity would yield no output by 1983 as measured here because none of the children involved would reach twelfth grade by that date. Nevertheless, because the activity has a long-run productive potential, it is institutionally and politically improbable that the opportunity for the advancement of young children would be ignored should emphasis be placed on improving the technology of education. Therefore, this subactivity has been included as an integral part of the activity stressing new technology and new approaches in basic education.

Since the subactivity embodies substantial interest and work by parents, its financial cost is less than in formal schooling. We assume a cost per child of $225 a year. With an estimated 16 million children aged two to five in 1983, the annual cost at full operation would be $3.6 billion. We postulate, as in the preceding case, three years of full operation and four years for phase-in (in

---

8   This subactivity includes many components not yet well developed so that its cost and composition must be taken from existing experiments and applications. For example, the cost of purchasing a talking typewriter is estimated at $35,000. A computer system for drill and practice serving 100,000 students is estimated at $272 per student year. A general summary of such developments appeared in Carl Perkins, "To Improve Learning," *Report to the Committee on Instructional Technology* (Washington, D.C.: U.S. Government Printing Office, 1970). See also Lawrence Grayson, "Costs, Benefits, Effectiveness: Challenge to Educational Technology," *Science*, March 17, 1972; Maya Pines, *Revolution in Learning* (New York: Harper and Row, 1967); and C.N. Carter and M.J. Walker, *Costs of ITV & CAI*, Committee for Economic Development, Supplement 27, January 1967. See also discussion in Rhodes, *Performance Possibilities*.

9   J. McV. Hunt, *Intelligence and Experience* (New York: The Robald Press Company, 1961).

increments of one-fifth), beginning in 1977, and resulting in a total cost estimate of $18 billion.

*Strengthened educational research and development
and the diffusion of innovations*

This subactivity is aimed at building a science and technology base that
would support development, application and diffusion of educational innovations. We assume, perhaps conservatively, the output to be:

    • a gain in the performance of twelfth graders of one year, or 8 index
points, and a 5 percent reduction in students three or more years behind the
norm in grade 12.

The precedents for such rapid development of a large-scale base of
knowledge exist, for research, in the National Institutes of Health (NIH) and,
for development, in the space program. The NIH research program has grown
in terms of real input at a consistent rate of 15 percent per year, a figure used
here as a maximum sustainable real growth rate for educational R&D. We assume
a 1973 dollar base of $275 million. With the first increase in 1975, growth at 15
percent a year through 1983 would entail a total cost of $3 billion. Ninety percent
of that cost is assumed to require financing from public sources.

In summary, the total cost of all subactivities is estimated to be $183 bil-
lion, with 90 percent from public funds and with 4 percent of the total needed
in the first subperiod.

Employment and other opportunities for the young

This activity is designed to provide opportunities for young people, aged
14 to 18, in three areas—jobs, school and recreation. (See also Chapter 6.) A
summary of the effects and costs is given below:

Activity	Index of Mean Performance in Twelfth Grade (points)	Students Three or More Years Behind the 1973 Average in Grade Twelve (percent)	Total 10-Year Cost (billions of 1973 dollars)
Jobs	nes	nes	$26
School	nes	nes	17
Recreation	nes	nes	8
Total	+5	−4%	$51

nes = not estimated separately

This three-part activity is assumed to substantially raise high school reten-tion and completion rates. It is also expected to raise students' levels of attain-ment, including those of students who would be completing high school in any event. It is assumed that 30 percent of students would benefit from this activity and that their performance would improve by an average of two years by the twelfth grade. A two-year improvement for 30 percent of the students yields an average improvement of 0.6 of a year for all students and a gain in the index of 5 points. In addition, those students three or more years behind the norm in grade 12 are assumed to improve sufficiently to lower the indicator by 4 per-cent.

This activity is postulated to have a four-year phase-in period in the first subperiod and full operation in the second. The estimated costs are discussed below.

Jobs

Employment for the 1.2 million unemployed 16- to 19-year olds is assumed to cost $2,700 a year per person. At full-time equivalent of eight years of operation, the total cost of the subactivity is thus estimated at $26 billion.

School

The provision of part-time and summer jobs for 30 percent of the 8.5 million 14- to 15-year olds is estimated to cost $350 per person per year, and would cost $7.1 billion, while the part-time and summer jobs for 20 percent of the 8 million students 16 to 17 years old at $750 per person a year would total $9.6 billion. Total decade expenditure is therefore estimated at $17 billion.

Recreation

To provide well-staffed and well-kept facilities for year-round use by the 80 percent of the 25 million youths aged 14 to 19 is assumed to cost $50 per person per year. Total estimated cost for the decade is thus $8 billion.

For all three subactivities taken together, the total cost is estimated at $51 billion, $13 billion[10] of which would occur during the first subperiod and 80 percent of which is calculated as public funds.

INTERACTIONS AMONG ACTIVITIES

The summary of the activity effects and the interactions among these activities are shown in Table 7-1.[11] There is a comparatively large offset between reme-

---

10   In the tables and calculations discussed in Part I of this book, an earlier estimate of $9 billion was used erroneously instead of $13 billion.

11   Estimates of the activity effects obtained in the already mentioned follow-up study (Rhodes, *Performance Possibilities*) are somewhat lower than the present estimates for the 10-year period, but higher for the 25-year period.

Table 7-1. Effects of Activities on Performance in
Education Based on Standardized Tests

Activity*	Total Cost 1974-83 (billions of 1973 dollars)	Index of Performance in Education Based on Standard Tests	Percent of Students 3 or More Years Behind the 1973 Average in Grade Twelve
Base 1973	—	100	24%
Base 1983	—	105	19%
5. Employment and opportunities for the young	$ 51	5	- 4%
7. Remedial tutoring and augmenting educational inputs	73	16	-11
8. Improved educational technology and approaches	183	21	-14
Combinations of Activities			
5,8. Employment for the young; Improved technology	234	25	-15
7,8. Remedial educational inputs; Improved technology	256	26	-15
5,7. Employment for the young; Remedial educational inputs	124	17	-12
Total, all activities	**$307**	**27**	**-16%**

* The numbers preceding the activities refer to their order in the matrix, Table 2-4.

dial and augmenting activities (7) and employment opportunities for the young
(5), with (for the two goals) 25 percent and 27 percent, respectively, in terms of
the former activity estimated to be redundant, since both these activities represent, to some extent, different approaches to the same problem. In combining improved educational technology (8) and employment opportunities for
the young (5), a comparatively smaller redundancy is assumed.

Among the two solely educational activities (7 and 8), considerable offsets
are assumed to exist because the activities work with the same population.
Unadjusted, the effects of these two activities total 37 points and −25 points,
respectively; the adjusted combined effects, however, are 26 and −15 points.
The maximum effects of all three activities on the two goals are estimated at 27
and −16 points, respectively.

8

Higher education

OBJECTIVE

> *The attainment of a college education.*

Higher education is a widely held goal of individuals and families and it is also a publicly accepted goal as evidenced by public and governmental institutions to provide or support higher education. College education is viewed as an achievement in itself and as a requirement for earning capacity and achieving status in the present society.

INDICATOR

> *Number of persons completing college.*

It is the completion of college and attainment of a college degree that is most commonly seen as the object of higher education. While, as will be apparent from the discussion below, higher education and especially the processes and institutions providing higher education, in effect, provide multiple outputs, from the point of view of the individuals and families and probably as a primary public consideration, achievement of a baccalaureate-level degree or some equivalent of such a degree is probably the best criterion by which to measure output. In the available data, attainment of a degree shows up as producing nearly a 40 percent increment in income over completion of one to three years of college. How much of that is an artifact built in through the employment requirements process and how much of it reflects a functional increase in productivity is not clear, but regardless of the reasons, attainment of the degree at least has tangible manifest results from the point of view of individuals. This is illustrated by the data in Table 8-1 showing the greater lifetime earnings and job security of persons completing higher education compared with those who only finish high school. The impact on income of completing a two-year curriculum, of junior or technical college, or possibilities of providing the substance of education in less than traditional four-year spans should also be

Table 8-1. Indicators of the Value of Higher Education to Individuals
(dollar amounts in 1973 prices)

Income	High School	College	Advanced or Professional
Expected lifetime earnings			
1972:[1] (male)	$508,563	$754,624	$874,832
Median income age 40,			
1971:[2] (male)	10,693	16,026	17,860
Employment			
Unemployment rate (March 1972):[3]			
(male)	5.4	2.6	1.7
(female)	5.8	3.9	1.4
(total)	5.6	3.1	1.6

[1] U.S. Department of Health, Education, and Welfare, Office of Education, National Center for Education Statistics, *Digest of Educational Statistics, 1973* (Washington, D.C.: U.S. Government Printing Office, 1974), Table 22, p. 21, adjusted to 1973 price levels by the increase of 6.2 percent in the Consumer Price Index from 1972 to 1973.

[2] U.S. Department of Commerce, Bureau of the Census, "Money Income in 1971 of Families and Persons in the United States," *Current Population Reports,* Series P-60, No. 85 (Washington, D.C.: U.S. Government Printing Office, December 1972), Table 9; income is for persons aged 35 to 44 years.

[3] U.S. Department of Labor, Bureau of Labor Statistics, *Educational Attainment of Workers, March 1972,* Special Labor Force Report No. 148 (Washington, D.C.: U.S. Government Printing Office, November 1972), Table B, page A-8.

considered, but could not be measured. The estimates of possible changes provided here should be understood as implicitly including higher education obtained in these different modes, expressed for comparison in common units of conventional college degrees.

BASE TRENDS

Indicators	1973	1983 Projection	Projected Change
Number of persons completing college (thousands)	957	1,342	+385

The present levels of attainment in higher education in the United States are quite high. Of the traditional college-age group, 32 percent of men and 21 percent of women are enrolled in college.[1] Of those who enter college, the proportion completing is perhaps 53 percent.[2] That percentage has been increasing, as has the entrance rate.

The trend of college attainment is obviously up. In 1973, an estimated 957,000 bachelor and first professional degrees were awarded.[3] The basic outlook is given by a projection of trends of population growth, increase in attendance and decrease in the dropout rate. This projection gives 1,342,000

Table 8-2. Past and Projected Levels of Higher Educational Attainment
(number of persons in thousands)

	1940	1958	1973	1983
Population 21 years of age[1]	2,368	2,138	3,795	4,197
Number of bachelor degrees[2]	187	363	957	1,342
Bachelor's degrees as percent of population 21 years of age	7.9%	17.0%	25.2%	32.0%
Percent of labor force with college degree[3]	n.a.	10.2%	15.0%	18.0%

[1] U.S. Department of Commerce, Bureau of the Census: for 1940—"United States Summary, Detailed Characteristics," *1960 Census of Population,* PC(1)-1D (Washington, D.C.: U.S. Government Printing Office, 1960), p. 358, Table 157; for 1958—"Estimates of the Population of the United States, by Single Years of Age, Color, and Sex, 1900 to 1959," *Current Population Reports,* Series P-25, No. 311 (Washington, D.C.: U.S. Government Printing Office, July 2, 1965); for 1973 and 1983—interpolated from "Projections of the Population of the United States, by Age, Sex and Color to 1990, with Extensions of Population by Age and Sex to 2015," *Current Population Reports,* Series P-25, No. 381 (Washington, D.C.: U.S. Government Printing Office, December 18, 1967).

[2] Historical data: U.S. Department of Health, Education, and Welfare, Office of Education, National Center for Education Statistics, *Digest of Educational Statistics,* 1970 (Washington, D.C.: U.S. Government Printing Office, September 1970), p. 90, Table 120; 1973 and 1983 projections—OE/NCES, unpublished (data include first professional degrees).

[3] Denis F. Johnston, "Education of Adult Workers: Projections to 1985," *Monthly Labor Review,* August 1970, labor force 25 and over only; 1958 percentage is an average of 1957-59; 1973 percentage is interpolated from figures for 1967-69 and 1975; 1983 percentage is interpolated from figures for 1980 and 1985.

---

1   U.S. Department of Commerce, Bureau of the Census, "Social and Economic Characteristics of Students: October 1971," *Current Population Reports,* Series P-20, No. 241 (Washington, D.C.: U.S. Government Printing Office, October 1972). Data refer to the civilian noninstitutional population, ages 18-24, in college as of October 1971.

2   Office of Education, National Center for Educational Statistics. Estimate based on unpublished data, January 1973.

3   Based on unpublished data from the Office of Education, May 1973.

graduates with bachelor degrees for 1983.[4] The 1983 level includes an increase in the conventional college-age group plus perhaps 100,000 older persons receiving degrees for the first time. As a result of these trends, the proportion of the labor force 25 years and older holding college degrees is expected to rise from 15 percent in 1973 to 18 percent in 1983.[5] Past trends and projected increases in college completion (see Table 8-2), even in the absence of new programs, reflect the increasing interest and investment in higher education.

Further increases beyond the projected level can be viewed as desirable, since college attainment is considered desirable by most of the population. Increases are possible, both within the conventional age groups, where some competent prospective students might still be deterred by financial handicaps or cultural disadvantages in earlier preparation, and among persons not of conventional college age, who attend at various points in their lives for purposes of professional satisfaction and enhancement of earning capacity as well as for personal consumption or enjoyment. Thus, much larger numbers of college degrees are potentially possible. The size of this potential is discussed below.

DISCRETIONARY ACTIVITIES TO INCREASE COLLEGE COMPLETIONS

There are a number of ways in which an increase in the number of college degrees conferred (or their effective equivalent) could occur. The main lines of such developments divide them into three distinct but somewhat overlapping approaches. One is removal of financial obstacles along the lines suggested by the Carnegie Commission,[6] by various candidates for public office at national and local levels, or already embodied in many public policies of support, both of institutions and of students.

A related train of activities not entailing as large expenditures consists of modernization, improvement and upgrading of institutional productivity and of arrangements, modes and technologies for imparting higher education and interpreting its meaning. Public bodies, such as the Carnegie Commission and others, have recommended such activities. Under pressure of financial short-

---

4   Ibid. The data published by the U.S. Office of Education after the completion of the present calculations show a slightly higher level of 1973 completions and a substantially reduced 1982–83 projection of 1,064,000. However, enrollments rose again according to latest reports.

5   Denis F. Johnston, "Education of Adult Workers: Projections to 1985," *Monthly Labor Review,* August 1970, Table 2, p. 11, interpolated. Refers to civilian labor force 25 years old and older with four years or more of college.

6   Carnegie Commission, *Less Time, More Options: Education beyond the High School* (New York: McGraw Hill Book Company, 1971).

ages, some universities have attempted to experiment with less expensive but possibly no less efficacious modes of operation.

The third main line by which substantial enhancement in college attainment can be produced within the next 10 years would be for the public to stress heavily general maintenance and upgrading of skills on the part of individuals. This could entail completion of education perhaps interrupted long ago, acquisition of second careers and acquisition of job-relevant skills in a combination of job and academic environments.

In addition to these three main activity areas, some effects on higher education would result from increased high school attainment through improvement in elementary and secondary levels, since substantial populations now do not acquire the type of education which prepares them for study in college. Thus, an activity for massive remedial tutoring and one for improved educational technology at the high school level, and perhaps at lower educational levels, might each somewhat increase college completions during the 10-year period.

Universal access to higher education

Universal access to higher education would make college free to all persons otherwise qualifying but unable to pay the expenses. The total demand potential for higher education consists of persons traditionally of college age and older persons, usually already in the labor force (and in some cases possibly beyond), who would like to complete college or acquire an additional academic degree. A summary of the effect and cost appears below:

Activity	Number of Persons Completing College (thousands)	Total 10-Year Cost (billions of 1973 dollars)
Universal access to higher education	+1,050	$273

The number of potential enrollees of the traditional college age is comparatively simple to establish. It consists of those high school graduates who are not projected to attend college according to the base trend, but who, given their ability levels, would have attended if they were from high-income families.

This activity is estimated to:

• make it possible for all high school graduates to attend and graduate from college in the same proportions as are projected for those in the highest income quartiles.[7] Thus, 75 percent of those who graduate from high school are expected to enroll in college and 65 percent of that group are expected to complete college, thereby adding 450,000 graduates a year by 1983 (see Table 8-3);

• make it possible for 600,000 persons over 24 to receive or to complete college education a year.

The number of persons older than the traditional college age who have interrupted their education in the past runs in the millions. It is estimated that by 1983, 18 million people, or 13.3 percent of the population 25 years and over, will have begun but not completed a college education.[8] A rough estimate of potential candidates consists of that population plus a number about a fourth as large of those who never went to college or who would like to acquire another degree, whether they have changed their occupation or require a further degree in their own field. The total stock of such persons is thus gauged to be approximately 22 million. We assume that from this population, 50 percent would take advantage of the free higher education activity incentives and that about two-thirds of these persons would have enrolled within eight years after the program was offered. Their completion rates are projected as are those of the college entrants from the 1960s.[9] The number of additional graduations among persons 24 or older after an initial buildup period would probably amount to 600,000 annually. Allowing for the additional graduations of the usual college-age individuals who might complete college as a result of the activity, the limits of how many more persons could conceivably complete higher education in the United States are about 1,050,000 a year by 1983.

This improvement in access is priced out assuming four years of attendance plus living costs of the additional 1,050,000 people a year, and further assuming a buildup of one year at one-third operation, one year at two-thirds and two years at full operation to allow for full output by 1983. An average cost of $10,000 per person per year is assumed, including the opportunity cost. This amount is allocated proportionally to people at the traditional college age and

7 The proportions have been derived by projecting persistence rates in higher education for the top income quartile in the late 1960s, as given in Joseph Froomkin, "Aspirations, Enrollments and Resources," Planning Paper 69-1, HEW/OE, Office of Program Planning and Evaluation (Washington, D.C., may 1969).

8 Judgment estimate of persons 25 and over with one-three years of college in 1983 derived from U.S. Department of Commerce, Bureau of the Census, Current Population Reports, Series P-25, No. 476 (Washington, D.C.: U.S. Government Printing Office, February 1972), Table 5, pp. 21 and 23.

9 The proportions have been derived by projecting persistence rates in higher education for the top income quartile in the late 1960s, Froomkin, "Aspirations, Enrollments and Resources."

Table 8-3. Additional College Completions Resulting from the Activity Providing Universal Access to Higher Education
(bachelor and first professional degrees, thousands)

| Year | Without Activity[1] | | With Activity[2] | | | | | |
| | | | Additional among the "College Age" (18-24) | | Additional Older Persons (over 24) | | Total Additional "College Age" and Over | |
	Enrollment	Degrees	Enrollment	Degrees	Enrollment	Degrees	Enrollment	Degrees
1976	6,139							
1977	6,307		200		300		500	
1978	6,465		700		900		1,600	
1979	6,606		1,300		1,700		3,000	
1980	6,724	1,107	1,900	150	2,500	200	4,400	350
1981	6,829	1,159	2,200	300	2,900	400	5,100	700
1982	6,921	1,192	2,300	450	3,100	600	5,400	1,050
1983		1,221	2,300	450	3,100	600	5,400	1,050

Note: These figures assume full level of program operation can be reached by 1983 by starting with one-third full program completions in 1980, increasing to two-thirds in 1981 and full operation output level in 1982 and 1983.

[1] Source: Based on Office of Education, National Center for Education Statistics, unpublished projections, January 1973.

[2] Source: For "college age": unpublished, OE/NCES, and Joseph Froomkin, "Aspirations, Enrollments and Resources," Planning Paper 69-1, HEW/OE, Office of Program Planning and Evaluation (Washington, D.C., May 1969). Projection of entry and persistence ratios for highest income quartile. For older persons: for estimate of number entering, see text discussion; completions are estimated from the data in Froomkin for "college age."

those older, at $109 billion and $145 billion, respectively. In addition to these direct costs, overhead facility items of $15 billion and administrative costs of $4 billion are assumed.

The total cost is thus estimated at $273 billion, all of which would be public funds and would be concentrated in the second subperiod (1978-83); the output would materialize in 1980-83.

Structural improvements in higher education

This activity comprises the development of new institutional arrangements, improved design of educational processes and staff support, and the introduction and expansion of technological innovations. The production processes of the higher education institutions, viewed as an industry, have not been greatly affected by modern technology, and larger potential for improvement in productivity or expansion in output probably exists. The effect and cost of the activity are summarized below:

Activity	Number of Persons Completing College (thousands)	Total 10-Year Cost (billions of 1973 dollars)
Structural improvements in higher education	+350	$70

We estimate that the introduction of new institutional arrangements, technological changes and new teaching systems that would ease time and place requirements for taking courses would:

• lead to college graduation for 150,000 college-age persons not expected to complete college otherwise.

It has been estimated that three-fifths of prospective college students do not reside within a 45-minute commuting distance of a free-access college.[10] Of the 9.5 million prospective students of college age (18-24),[11] then 5.7 million, or 60 percent, would be potential users of access-improving techniques and devices, such as more flexible schedules, use of video tapes and TV broadcasting,

10   Warren W. Willingham, *Free-Access Higher Education* (New York: College Entrance Examination Board, 1970), and "Quality and Equality," Review of *Free-Access Higher Education* in *Science*, February 5, 1971.

11   U.S. Department of Commerce, Bureau of the Census, "Projections of the Population of the United States, by Age and Sex (Interim Revisions): 1970 to 2020," *Current Population Reports*, Series P-25, No. 448, Series C (Washington, D.C.: U.S. Government Printing Office, August 6, 1970), Table 2.

etc. This is not too different from the number estimated to enroll under the fellowship program.

Not all persons who would lack access to college during the time period studied, however, would be high school graduates or have the desire or ability to do college work even if it were cost free. Thus, of those in the traditional college-age group who would get degrees if offered fellowships, we estimate that only 60 percent would be potential degree recipients under this program. This could mean an additional 270,000 graduates (60 percent of the number graduating in 1983 due to fellowship aid) annually by 1983. If, however, it is estimated that half of these would need additional incentives, such as financial assistance, in order to complete college, then the number would be about 135,000. Of the remaining students of college age—those already having commuting access to college but not attending because of lack of time or financial resources—perhaps an additional 10 percent or about 14,000-15,000 would finish annually by 1983 as a result of the easing of time and place requirements for taking courses;

• lead to college graduations of 200,000 persons older than 24, primarily housewives and employed persons, who could thus attend college without major time and financial losses.

For persons over 24, the value of new institutional arrangements, technological changes and new systems would be especially significant, since these developments would reduce the time required to complete college as well as make it possible to meet many requirements without having to go to a college campus or even leave home. These features would mean housewives and employed persons would face much less of a burden in terms of time and financial loss in order to earn a degree. Because of these features, the impact by 1983 is estimated here to be about a third of that of providing universal fellowships, or an annual increase of 200,000 degrees. Thus, the total increase in the number of college completions in 1983 resulting from this activity would be about 350,000.

The total cost for the activity is estimated at $70 billion, calculated as $27 billion for new innovative institutions, $5 billion for the infrastructure to support new forms of service delivery, individual communication, testing and certification, and $38 billion for the basic technological programs, broadcasts and research and development. The activity probably would require about 90 percent financing by public funds; costs are divided here between the two subperiods by 18 and 82 percent, respectively. The cost also includes opportunity income foregone, but since this activity is predicated on reducing the time of attendance, this element is less per person and thus less in the total.

Maintenance, updating and improvement of job skills

A third type of activity with a major effect on higher education is maintenance, updating and improvement of job skills. This scenario includes acquisition of skills for secondary or second careers and maintenance of skills in any one particular career. The activity includes a number of ways in which human capital can be increased, including an important higher education component. But its main output is in growth of individuals' earnings, and its clientele includes persons who would not avail themselves of college fellowships.

A summary of the effect and cost is presented below:

Activity	Number of Persons Completing College (thousands)	Total 10-Year Cost (billions of 1973 dollars)
Improvement of job skills	+650	$342

Providing opportunities and incentives (including financial subsidies) to attend college to improve job skills is estimated to:

• lead to 600,000 college graduations annually by 1983 among those over 24 years of age. We have estimated a population of 11 million older persons who would take advantage of free higher education (see the discussion under universal access to higher education) and assume the same proportions of annual graduations among those older people as for the universal fellowship activity;

• lead to 45,000 college graduations among those 18-24. We assume here graduations equaling 10 percent of the annual number estimated for the program of universal fellowships.

In total, nearly 650,000 additional persons are thus estimated to complete college in 1983 due to these efforts. Most of the impact of this activity would occur in the group of persons beyond the usual college age who either never attended or never completed college. The activity, which would involve subsidization of part or all of the financial and time requirements, is seen as job skill oriented and likely to be utilized primarily by more experienced workers.

The total cost of the activity which includes a very substantial labor market component (see Chapter 9) is $342 billion, 67 percent of which is assumed to have to be publicly financed. The continued education option component which is a part of the activity, amounts to $232 billion, of which about 60 percent may be attributed to higher education.

Activities directed toward high schools

Two activities directed toward high schools are assumed to interest and prepare more students for college than expected by a continuation of current trends. A summary of the activity effects and costs is presented below:

Activity	Number of Persons Completing College (thousands)	Total 10-Year Cost (billions of 1973 dollars)
Remedial tutoring and augmenting educational inputs	+50	$ 73
Improved technology and approaches	+50	183

An activity to provide remedial tutoring, special counseling programs for parents and students, and vouchers to purchase books for students' homes is estimated to raise student interest and school performance and result in an additional 50,000 annual college completions by 1983. The 10-year cost of this activity which, in this period, would have its main impact on achievement in basic education (see Chapter 7), is estimated at $73 billion.

Improvements in educational technologies and approaches at the elementary and secondary levels are also estimated to lead to 50,000 additional college completions annually by 1983 at the total activity cost of $183 billion (see Chapter 7).

INTERACTIONS AMONG ACTIVITIES

There exist very definite demographic limits and less definite ability and preference limits on the total potential for maximum college attainment in the United States. The effect of the alternative activities used in combination obviously cannot exceed the total potential. In many ways, they are alternative routes toward the same thing. They would involve mostly the same people whether they would be taking advantage of institutional reforms making access easier and less expensive in terms of time or money, or whether they would be taking advantage of financial subsidies, direct or indirect. The estimated output of various activity combinations taking these interactions into account is illustrated in Table 8-4.

If the universal higher education activity (9) is combined with structural improvements (10), it is estimated that about 75 percent of the structural im-

Table 8-4. Effects of Activities on Number of Persons Completing College

Activity*	Total Cost 1974-83 (billions of 1973 dollars)	Number of Persons Completing College (thousands)
Base 1973	—	957
Base 1983	—	1,342
6. Remedial tutoring & augmenting of educational inputs	$ 73	50
7. Improved educational technology and approaches	183	50
9. Universal access to higher education	273	1,050
10. Structural improvements in higher education	70	350
11. Maintenance, updating and improvement of job skills	342	650
Combined Effects		
9,10. Universal access to higher education; Structural improvements	343	1,150
9,11. Universal access to higher education; Job skills	615	1,100
10,11. Structural improvements; Job skills	412	750
9,10,11. Universal access to higher education; Structural improvements; Job skills	685	1,200
Total, all activities	**$941**	**1,300**

* The numbers preceding the activities refer to their order in the matrix, Table 2-4.

provements activity would be redundant; the number of persons completing college would increase by 1.15 million. A large overlap—about 90 percent—is also assumed when universal higher education (9) operates simultaneously with the job skill activity (11) to produce a 1.1 million output. Structural improvements (10) interact with the job skill activity (11) producing a 75 percent output for each, resulting in an additional 750,000 graduates. When universal higher education is added to this combination, the output climbs to 1.2 million. This is based upon an assumed two-thirds offset effect of the structural improvement activity and 90 percent of the job skills activity when they are operated in conjunction with universal higher education. The relatively small individual outputs estimated for remedial tutoring (6) and improved technology (7) are assumed to be additive, producing 1.3 million as a total combined output for all activities.

The actual outputs of these activities may be less than estimated if the numbers of graduates are not absorbed into jobs commensurate with their education. The historical experience so far—both under the G.I. Bill, and with the absorption of very large increases in educational attainment, including college and professional level graduates, which have occurred in the past several decades by all indications without driving down the rate of return to education—contains no indications that a limit on the productive investment in higher education has already been approached (at least with regard to the returns to individuals).

9

General level of earnings

Increased real earnings of workers.

Earnings are the basis of living standards. In the aggregate, real earnings are defined by real productivity. The great importance of earnings to individuals and of earnings and productivity as an object of public concern are evident in much of the behavior of individuals, labor organizations and governments.

INDICATOR

Median real earnings of working individuals.

Median earnings have been selected because they reflect earnings (and productivity) of an "average" worker rather than the amount of money that workers earn on the average. We have used real earnings rather than current dollar earnings to exclude the inflationary element. The indicator represents earnings as usually defined—that is, wages or salaries and net income from self-employment before deductions for personal taxes, social security, etc., rounded to the nearest $100.

BASE TRENDS

Indicator	1973	1983 Projection	Projected Change
Median earnings of individuals (in 1973 dollars)	$5,900	$7,800	+$1,900

The 1973 level of median earnings of individuals of $5,900 has been derived from U.S. Census data.

In the 1950s and 1960s, the trend of labor productivity held rather constant at an average annual increase of about 2.3 percent, although it fluctuated about a percentage point above or below this trend, in, for example, the early and late 1960s, respectively. We have used the 2.7 percent NPA growth estimate made for the 1972-81 projection, raised to 2.8 percent to allow for the more rapid growth in the later years of the period.[1] The projected 1983 level of median earnings of individuals is therefore $7,800, in comparable 1973 dollars. It should be noted that the figures used refer to median total earnings for all persons who worked, whether for a few hours or full-time all year. They are therefore below the median for those who worked at year-round full-time jobs and also below the mean earnings of all workers which are weighted by the earnings at the higher levels.

DISCRETIONARY ACTIVITIES TO RAISE EARNINGS

The activities described below are estimated to have a maximum capacity to raise median earnings (in constant dollars) in the United States by $1,400 per year in 1983, or by 18 percent. Thus, the annual compound rate of growth in real median earnings would increase from the 2.8 percent per annum contained in the base projection to 4.5 percent. The activities discussed here include activities which have a potential to increase median earnings by means of increased human capital formation, local economic development or increased labor force participation. Not included are activities which would raise productivity and, hence, real earnings as part of general stimulation of economic growth by means of acceleration of technological change and innovations, increased formation of physical capital or improvements in industrial organization. The decision not to include economic stabilization and growth, discussed in Chapter 1, was made to limit the scope of the study, but it should be noted that, as a result of it, the set of activities with potential to raise median earnings discussed here is incomplete.

Maintenance, updating and improvement of job skills

The purpose of the activity is to improve the economic functioning of the labor market and make substantial investments in human capital, with the aim of

---

1 *U.S. Economic and Demographic Projections: 1972–81*, 1972 National Economic Projections Series, Report No. 72-N-2 (Washington, D.C.: National Planning Association, January 1973), p. 2. The projection published for the period 1974–84, after the present study was completed, contains a slightly lower productivity growth assumption. See Robert Dennis, *Clambering into the Eighties* (Washington, D.C.: National Planning Association, 1974). That change would affect the level of the base projection for 1983, but not the effects of discretionary activities discussed in this chapter.

raising productivity on the job and making possible increased mobility, and hence a better allocation of human capital, between jobs. The effect and cost are summarized below:

Activity	Median Earnings of Individuals (1973 dollars)	Total 10-Year Cost (billions of 1973 dollars)
Maintenance, updating and improvement of job skills	+$200	$342

This activity includes provision for job training and experience formation, career development opportunities, a job inquiry service, and transition subsidies to promote mobility to employed and unemployed persons as well as those outside the labor force, such as housewives and persons with various prior skill and income levels.[2] By 1983, this is assumed to:

● return in increased GNP 10 percent of the investment cost ($342 billion) or $34 billion.

Given 70 percent as the share of labor income and 100 million persons in the labor force, the result is a $200 increase in mean earnings, assumed to apply also to median earnings.

Assuming a depreciation of human capital on the job at 1 percent annually (even after allowing for learning occurring there) and a need for an additional 3 percent human capital investment to acquire transferable and generalized skills, then 4 percent of the national earnings share of total output would be required annually for this activity. Using NPA projections, the earnings share of the national product (70 percent) would average $1,160 billion (in 1973 dollars) per year over the decade. At 4 percent, the investment for updating and maintenance of job skills would be $46.4 billion a year. However, because many components of this activity require an initiation period, the total cost for the decade would be less than indicated by this average.

The component parts of this activity and their costs include:

● skills maintenance and updating, estimated to cost one-half of the total, or $23.2 billion annually (with 20 percent of the total allocated to increased job training and 80 percent to institutional training beyond high school);

● a career development program at an estimated cost of $100 billion for the decade (approximately $1,000 per member of the labor force) consisting of two

---

2 The importance of experience as a component of human capital is analyzed in Jacob Mincer, *Schooling, Experience and Earnings* (New York: National Bureau of Economic Research, Inc., 1974).

components, new careers for older workers and effective retraining of workers with skills which face declining demand;

• a job inquiry service and transition subsidies to promote job mobility at an estimated cost of $10 billion for the period.

The 10-year cost is thus $342 billion, about two-thirds of which would be public outlays. Funds for the major portion of the on-the-job training component are assumed to come from private sources. Of the total expenditure, 80 percent could be deferred to the last six years, and half to the last three years.

Aid to depressed communities

Income subsidies in the low range do not affect the median. But aid to depressed communities, unlike traditional welfare programs, would affect a broad range of income distribution. The effect and cost of such aid are given below:

Activity	Median Earnings of Individuals (1973 dollars)	Total 10-Year Cost (billions of 1973 dollars)
Aid to depressed communities	+$200	$171

Large-scale investment and development aid in economically depressed areas is estimated to:

• add $17 billion to the 1983 gross national product.

The labor share of the increment, 70 percent, would equal $12 billion. Part of this amount is assumed to leak out of the depressed areas and to be distributed among the general labor force of 100 million, yielding a $120 average increase in earnings. Since the increase is estimated to be concentrated in the lower two-thirds of the income distribution, however, median earnings are projected to go up by $200.

The aid program is calculated at a 10-year cost of $171 billion. It is described in more detail in Chapter 10.

Remedial and augmenting educational inputs and improved educational technology and approaches

The effects and costs of these two basic education activities are summarized below:

Activity	Median Earnings of Individuals (1973 dollars)	Total 10-Year Cost (billions of 1973 dollars)
Remedial and augmenting educational inputs	+$100	$ 73
Improved educational technology and approaches	+ 200	183

Offering remedial tutoring and improving educational inputs (assumed to enhance job skills through their impact on basic literacy and numerical skills and by inducing an increase in the level of educational attainment) are estimated by 1983 to:

• yield, respectively, an additional $44 billion and $60 billion of GNP in 1983.

By 1983, remedial activities are projected to have raised the level of basic educational attainment by 1.9 years for 11.2 million new workers. With an average gain of $1,500 in earnings for a year of schooling, each of these workers would receive an additional $2,800. Although average earnings for all workers would thus go up by about $300, median earnings are projected to rise by $100, since the addition would occur among new workers with incomes generally in the lower two-thirds of the income distribution.

Improving educational inputs is projected to add 2.52 years to attainment in basic education by 1983. At $1,500 additional income per year gained, the 11.2 million new workers benefiting would receive an average of $3,780 in increased earnings by the end of the decade. This represents an average earnings increase of about $400 for all workers. Median earnings are estimated to rise by about $200, since the workers benefiting are again new workers with generally lower than average incomes.

Tutoring and augmenting educational inputs are calculated to cost $73 billion over the decade. Improved technology is estimated to cost $183 billion over the period. Both activities are described in more detail in Chapter 7.

Universal access to and structural improvements in higher education

The effects and costs of these two higher education activities are given on the following page.

Universal access to higher education, by increasing productivity of the additional college graduates, is estimated by 1983 to:

Activity	Median Earnings of Individuals (1973 dollars)	Total 10-Year Cost (billions of 1973 dollars)
Universal access to higher education	+$200	$273
Structural improvements in higher education	+ 100	70

• raise the 1983 GNP by $29 billion. The 70 percent labor share spread among the 100 million people in the labor force yields a $200 increase in median earnings.

Structural improvements in higher education, assumed to yield similar gains in productivity, are estimated by 1983 to:

• add $10 billion to 1983 GNP. With the 100 million in the labor force receiving 70 percent of the increment, median earnings would increase by $100.

These activities and their costs are discussed in detail in Chapter 8.

Time-saving innovations

The effect and cost of introducing time-saving innovations, primarily in transportation and home operation, are summarized below:

Activity	Median Earnings of Individuals (1973 dollars)	Total 10-Year Cost (billions of 1973 dollars)
Time-saving innovations	+$400	$91

Saving, through time-saving innovations, an estimated 319 hours a year for the population 6 years and over, or an average of 425 hours per person 18 years and over per year, is estimated by 1983 to:

• add 6.7 billion hours to work time, assuming that 20 percent of the time gained is devoted to work.

The average GNP of an hour worked in 1983 is projected at $12.50, and the marginal product is assumed to be $7.50. These additional hours would then add $50 billion to GNP, of which 70 percent would go to labor. The addition to median earnings is thus $350 or, rounded, $400 for the projected labor force of 100 million persons in 1983.

This activity, estimated to cost $91 billion, is described in more detail in Chapter 20.

INTERACTIONS AMONG ACTIVITIES

The outputs of all these activities are assumed to be additive. While for some of the activities, especially those in higher education, considerable offsets exist in their other outputs, their effects on *median* earnings are relatively small and perhaps sufficiently independent to be treated as additive. The total output of all activities then gives an estimated $1,400 increase in median earnings of individuals in 1983 (see Table 9-1).

Table 9-1. Effect of Activities on Median Earnings

Activity*	Total 10-Year Cost (billions of 1973 dollars)	Median Earnings of Individuals (1973 dollars)
Base 1973	—	$5,900
Base 1983	—	$7,800
6. Remedial tutoring and augmenting of educational inputs	$ 73	$ 100
7. Improved educational technology and approaches	183	200
9. Universal access to higher education	273	200
10. Structural improvements in higher education	70	100
11. Maintenance, updating and improvement of job skills	342	200
16. Aid to depressed communities	171	200
28. Time-saving innovations	91	400
Total, all activities (output additive)	**$1,203**	**$1,400**

* The numbers preceding the activities refer to their order in the matrix, Table 2-4.

10

Ability to earn

OBJECTIVE

Employment with earnings above minimum living standards for all who want work.

INDICATOR

Number of persons not in the mainstream of the labor force.

The extent of the effective opportunity to participate fully in paid employment is determined by the number of persons who can obtain a regular job that supports them and their families at a level of minimum comfortable living.[1] The measure adopted as the indicator measures actually the opposite of the stated goal. The focus is on those who cannot participate fully—that is, on the number of persons working but not in the mainstream of the labor force. That includes persons employed but unable to earn enough to maintain themselves and their families above poverty levels,[2] the unemployed poor, and persons not in the labor force who would like to work.

BASE TRENDS

Indicator	1973	1983 Projection	Projected Change
Number of persons not in the mainstream of the labor force (millions)	11.1	8.8	−2.3

---

1   For a recent discussion of the measurement of employment and earnings conditions in the labor market, see Sar Levitan and Robert Taggart, "Employment and Earnings Inadequacy: A Measure of Worker Welfare," *Monthly Labor Review,* October 1973, p. 19.

2   Approximately 3,700,000 persons were earning less than the minimum wage per hour in January 1972, according to unpublished material from the Bureau of Labor Statistics, Wage and Hour Division.

**Table 10-1. Number and Characteristics of Persons not in the
Mainstream of the Labor Force, 1971, 1973 Estimate and 1983 Projection**
(millions)

	1971	1973 Estimate[1]	1983 Projection[1]
In labor force	7.2[2]	6.6[3]	4.3[3]
Working poor	4.5	4.2	3.0
Unemployed poor	2.7	2.4	1.3
Not in labor force but want to work	4.4[4]	4.5[5]	4.5[5]
In school	1.2	1.2	1.2
Ill health, disability	0.6	0.6	0.6
Home responsibilities	1.0	1.1	1.1
Think cannot get a job	0.8	0.8	0.8
All other reasons	0.8	0.8	0.8
Total	**11.6**	**11.1**	**8.8**

[1] Assumes constant real dollar poverty threshold at 1971 level.

[2] U.S. Department of Commerce, Bureau of the Census, "Characteristics of the Low-Income Population, 1970," *Current Population Reports,* Series P-60, No. 86 (Washington, D.C.: U.S. Government Printing Office, December 1972), Table 14, pp. 76-79.

[3] From projections based on unpublished OEO tabulation of the March supplement of the *Current Population Reports* prepared by the Bureau of the Census; interpolated for 1973 and extrapolated to 1983 from worksheets of the National Goals Project, directed by Leonard A. Lecht at the National Planning Association.

[4] Based on U.S. Department of Labor, *Manpower Report of the President* (Washington, D.C.: U.S. Government Printing Office, 1973), Table A-8, p. 137.

[5] Ibid. In the absence of any clear trend, the latest (1973) figures have been used.

In a recent study, Leonard A. Lecht estimated the components of this population, including persons who are in the labor force but are poor, who are long-term unemployed, and who would enter the labor force if an opportunity for a meaningful job arose.[3] Based on this study in the base year (1971), and its initial projection, interpolating the data for 1973 and including additional data on persons not in the labor force who want to work, it is estimated that 11.1 million persons did not participate in the labor force mainstream in 1973. Extending Lecht's projection (as modified) to 1983 yields an estimate of 8.8 million persons outside the labor force mainstream. Table 10-1 shows the breakdown of persons in this "universe of need" in 1971 with the 1973 estimate and projection to 1983.

3   Leonard A. Lecht, *Poor Persons in the Labor Force: A Universe of Need* (Washington, D.C.: National Planning Association, October 1970).

The 1983 projection allows for the effects of overall economic growth as well as currently operating manpower programs.

DISCRETIONARY ACTIVITIES TO BRING PERSONS INTO THE LABOR MARKET MAINSTREAM

It appears technically feasible that a combination of public, private and individual activities including improvement of skills, job creation and supportive services could reduce the number of workers without self-supporting jobs to near zero. Even if the experience of many past training programs would not warrant projecting high rates of success, it is hypothesized here that, within a 10-year time horizon, workable means for a general improvement in the ability to fully participate in the labor force could be developed if the objective of work participation actually became a widely shared high priority goal.[4] The individual activities, each being judged to have a potential capacity for measurable effect on the indicator over a 10-year period, are discussed below.

Specialized training, job creation and maintenance, and job placement

This activity is a combination of general manpower programs and services operated on a large and comprehensive scale. The effect and cost of the activity are summarized below:

Activity	Number Not in Mainstream (millions)	Total 10-Year Cost (billions of 1973 dollars)
Specialized training for those outside the mainstream of the labor force	−5.0	$94

Providing job training, job creation, job placement, and special workplaces for persons with difficulties (including assistance to older persons still vigorous

---

4   For a discussion of problems in evaluating past programs, see Joe N. Nay, John W. Scanlon and Joseph S. Wholey, "Benefits and Costs of Manpower Training Programs: A Synthesis of Previous Studies with Reservations and Recommendations," *Benefit-Cost Analyses of Federal Programs*, A Compendium of Papers submitted to the Subcommittee on Priorities and Economy in Government of the Joint Economic Committee, Congress of the United States, 92d Congress, 2d Session (Washington, D.C.: U.S. Government Printing Office, January 2, 1973), pp. 249-273.

but unable to find or retain jobs because of age-associated problems such as obsolescent skills, compulsory retirement, barriers to job entry, or inability to locate training and jobs drawing on the skills they have) would, we estimate:

• reduce the number of persons outside the mainstream of the labor force in 1983 by 5.0 million.

This activity consists of:

• job training programs, at an estimated cost of $32 billion;

• job placement and access, at an estimated cost of $8 billion, including transfer subsidies;

• special workshops for the physically or mentally handicapped, at a cost of $6 billion;

• child care to enable mothers, fathers of families without mothers, or underemployed or handicapped parents to maintain jobs, at an estimated cost of $18 billion;

• an investment in job creation of $30 billion—$15 billion in capital investment and $15 billion in operating subsidies.

The total amount, $94 billion,[5] is assumed to come entirely from public funds. We assume that an expenditure of 10 percent (or about $9 billion) would be needed within the first four years for designing and creating necessary organizational and research infrastructures, with 90 percent of the expenditures incurred in the second subperiod.

Aid to depressed communities

This activity would embrace a large developmental effort including aid, subsidies and special programs to stimulate economic and social investment and growth in depressed communities. Its effect and cost are given below:

Activity	Number Not in Mainstream (millions)	Total 10-Year Cost (billions of 1973 dollars)
Aid to depressed communities	−1.8	$171

Depressed communities are those identified by the Economic Development Administration of the Department of Commerce (under the *Public Works*

---

5   This cost would be balanced by an increase in GNP, realizing $21 billion annually by 1983 (see Chapter 23).

and Economic Development Act of 1965), and constitute areas designated for assistance because of low income or employment and include rural counties, Indian reservations and parts of cities. The criteria used are: chronic unemployment of 6 percent or more; average income of less than 40 percent of national median; or a combination of low income (40-50 percent of the national median) and 25 percent or more intercensal population loss. Based on estimated median income (although statistics are not directly available), we estimate that the resident population of those areas thus qualifying for development aid will be 10 percent of the U.S. population, or 24 million people in 1983.[6] Total labor force plus persons wanting to work but not in the labor force of these communities is estimated as one-third of the population, or 8 million, of whom 40 percent (3.2 million) are assumed not to be in the mainstream of the labor force in 1983.

We estimate, arbitrarily, that an aid and investment effort with components (see below) totaling $21,400 per member of the labor force (or about a third of this amount per resident) would:

● develop in the depressed communities structurally self-maintaining employment, raise median income on a self-sustaining basis above 40 percent of the national median, and bring 1.8 million persons into the labor force mainstream. This figure is calculated by assuming the same overall rate of effectiveness (57 percent) relative to the number of persons not in the labor force mainstream as for activity number 12, specialized training for persons outside the mainstream of the labor force.

We approximate that such a development effort would require:

● infrastructure and physical capital investment of $84 billion ($10,500 per member of the labor force or about one-third of this amount per resident);

● human capital investment averaging $3,500 per person for one-half of the total population, or $42 billion;

● operating subsidies of $45 billion, of which $17 billion (or 10 percent of the total outlay) could be expected to be returned from normal market activity brought about by these investments.

Of the $171 billion total, we estimate that 90 percent would come from public funds and 10 percent from private funds and that 12 percent of the total would be expended in the first subperiod.

The benefit-cost ratio (the unit cost of output increment compared to that of other activities) of this activity does not appear very impressive within the 10-year period, but there is no reason to assume a short payout period from such a monumental investment effort. If such domestic development became a

---

6   Figures on resident population of qualifying areas jumped from about 25 million in June 1970 to about 46 million in July 1971, and thus appear to reflect cyclical as well as structural conditions. Figures on median income in qualifying areas are unavailable.

priority, this activity would be likely to be accepted on the basis of its inherent economic viability in the longer run, and its components presumably would be designed accordingly.

Other activities

Three other discretionary activities discussed in more detail in other chapters are assumed to decrease the number outside the mainstream of the labor force—the improvement of job skills, creation of employment opportunities for the young, and provision of day-care facilities. Their effects and costs are summarized below:

Activity	Number Not in Mainstream (millions)	Total 10-Year Cost (billions of 1973 dollars)
Maintenance, updating and improvement of job skills	−3.4	$342
Employment and other opportunities for the young	−1.5	51
General day care for children	−1.8	126

Maintenance, updating and improvement of job skills
Offering to employed and unemployed persons job training and job placement services designed to raise productivity on the job and increase mobility is assumed by 1983 to:
● move one-half, or 1.5 million, of the working poor, into the labor force mainstream;
● reduce the number of unemployed and those not currently in the labor force but wanting to work on the order of one-third, or a total of 1.9 million.
We thus estimate that 3.4 million people would enter the labor market mainstream as a result of this activity, which is calculated at a cost of $342 billion for the 10-year period. The activity is described in detail in Chapter 9.

Employment and opportunities for the young
Providing employment, special education and recreational opportunities for 16- to 19-year olds is estimated by 1983 to:
● bring 1.5 million unemployed 16- to 19-year olds into the mainstream of the labor force (the 1.2 million from those unemployed or in low-paying or

intermittent work and 0.3 million, or one-fourth the number, gaining employment through the job component of the activity, as a result of special education and recreational opportunities).

This activity, estimated to cost $51 billion over the decade, is described in more detail in Chapter 7.

General day care for children

Providing day care for about 10.8 million children is assumed to:

● permit 1.8 million persons to enter the mainstream of the labor force, primarily women who are mothers of young children and who are sufficiently skilled to get jobs, or more regular or better paying jobs, or who could acquire training to qualify for such jobs if provided with child-care facilities.

The total cost is calculated at $126 billion. The activity is described in Chapter 15.

Table 10-2. The Effect of Activities on Participation in the Labor Force Mainstream

Activity*	Total Cost 1974-83 (billions of 1973 dollars)	Number Not in Mainstream (millions)
Base 1973	—	11.1
Base 1983	—	8.8
5. Employment and other opportunities for the young	$ 51	-1.5
8. General day care for children	126	-1.8
11. Maintenance, updating and improvement of job skills	342	-3.4
12. Specialized training for those outside the mainstream of the labor force	94	-5.0
16. Aid to depressed communities	171	-1.8
Combined Effects		
11,12. Job skills; Specialized training	436	-6.1
8,11. Day care; Job skills	468	-4.6
8,12. Day care; Specialized training	220	-5.2
5,8. Employment for the young; Day care	177	-3.3
5,8,11. Employment for the young, Day care; Job skills	519	-5.4
8,16. Day care; Aid to depressed communities	297	-3.0
8,5,16. Aid to depressed communities; Employment for the young; Day care	348	-3.8
5,8,11,16. Employment for the young; Day care; Job skills; Aid to depressed communities	690	-5.7
11,16. Job skills; Aid to depressed communities	513	-4.0
Total, all activities	**$784**	**-7.2**

*The numbers preceding the activities refer to their order in the matrix, Table 2-4.

INTERACTIONS AMONG ACTIVITIES

The specialized training activity (12) is specifically aimed at assisting persons to gain full participation in the labor force and yields by far the greatest proportion of output of any single activity, diminishing by 57 percent the number, 8.8 million, of workers outside the mainstream. In combination with the job skill activity (11), the assistance provided would mean nonpoverty jobs for 6.1 million persons. The total of all the activities other than that concerned with specialized training (12) would reduce the number not in the mainstream by 5.7 million. These combinations and others, given in Table 10-2, all yield output totals less than the sum of their individual outputs, since different activities to some extent serve the same populations. An example is day care (8) and maintenance of job skills (11). The employment opportunities gained, whether through day care or improved job skills, would serve an estimated 0.6 million people. Since there are redundancies between the two activities, the sum of their individual outputs has therefore been reduced from 5.2 million persons to 4.6 million. In considering the interactions between day care (8) and specialized training (12), even larger interactions occur. Indeed, a substantial part of the specialized training activity includes provisions for child-care services. Together, the two activities result in an output of 5.2 million persons who could enter the mainstream.

Other activity combinations which exclude specialized training (12) produce smaller outputs. For example, employment for the young (5) and day care (8) combine to produce a reduction of those not in the mainstream of the labor force by 3.3 million. If the job skills activity is subsequently added, the effect would be an increase of 5.4 million.

11

Adequacy of Income

OBJECTIVE

An adequate income to meet a minimum standard of living.

INDICATORS

Percent of population below the poverty standard.

Percent of population in conditions of near-poverty.

Since the objective is adequate income, the concern is with those whose incomes are inadequate—the poor and near-poor.

Poverty is defined here by a minimum living standard, with income needed to support that living standard as a criterion of measurement. The assumption is made that a particular level of income, given corrections for cost of living and family size, will in all cases sustain this minimum living standard.

In the present study, the Office of Economic Opportunity-Social Security Administration indices of poverty and near-poverty are used as the criteria for minimum adequate income. The poverty and near-poverty levels for 1973 in 1973 prices were $4,540 and $5,675 for a nonrural family of four.[1] The poverty index, originally developed by Dr. Mollie Orshansky of the Social Security Administration, is calculated in the following way:[2] U.S. Department of Agriculture estimates are used to establish the cost of a minimum adequate diet to comprise one-fourth of the family's income. The percentage of family income spent on food is then assumed to be constant for families throughout the low- and moderate-income ranges. Since the diet estimates vary with the size of family and place of residence, income cutoffs vary as well.

---

1   U.S. Department of Commerce, Bureau of the Census, *Current Population Reports*, Series P-60, No. 88 (Washington, D.C.: U.S. Government Printing Office, June 1973). This report defines the 1972 levels, which were then converted to 1973 prices.

2   Mollie Orshansky, "Counting the Poor: Another Look at the Poverty Profile," *Social Security Bulletin*, January 1965, and Orshansky, "Who's Who among the Poor: A Demographic View of Poverty," *Social Security Bulletin*, July 1965.

In part to reduce the arbitrariness of a poverty line cutoff, the Office of Economic Opportunity instituted the concept of near-poverty, defined as 125 percent of the poverty line income for each category. By extending the poverty line 25 percent, the concept of minimum necessities is relaxed somewhat to include low-income persons whose situations merit social concern although their safety and their ability to function socially and economically may not be endangered by severe deprivation.

The indicators are, therefore, the percent of population poor and near-poor identified in federal statistics.

A comparison of the poverty index with various other income benchmarks is shown in Table 11-1.

The poverty standard we are using is set at a fixed real income level. An alternative would be based on a concept of relative poverty, the rationale for which is that poverty is best defined by a person's income position relative to the rest of society rather than along a scale of physical needs. One implication of this approach is that the poverty line changes in response to real income growth. (A possible cutoff appears in Table 11-1 as 40 percent of median income.)[3] Or one might specify a minimum-income level and apply a growth factor to this level.[4]

The indicator based on a fixed minimum-consumption standard is chosen here in preference over a relative poverty indicator for two reasons: first, it is based on analysis of consumption needs, and, second, relative income is more a distributional issue than a question of consumption standards and involves concepts of economic equality (see Chapter 13), rather than income adequacy.

BASE TRENDS

Indicator	1973	1983 Projection	Projected Change
Percent of population below the poverty standard	11.4%	8.7%	−2.7%
Percent of population in conditions of near-poverty	4.8	3.5	−1.3

3   U.S. Department of Commerce, Economic Development Administration, "Qualified Areas . . . Criteria and Data" (Washington, D.C., December 1970). If median income grows at the same rate as NPA projections for average income over the decade, the near-poverty line would increase from $5,552 to $9,305 by 1983.

4   Robert Levine, The Poor Ye Need Not Have with You (Cambridge: The MIT Press, 1970), pp. 15-18, and Chong Kee Park, "Human Resource Development—Skill Training for the Poor" (Washington, D.C.: National Planning Association, June 1971).

Table 11-1. Income Maintenance Indicators in Force in the United States
and Related Data, 1972 and 1973

Indicators	Income Standard (or cut-off)	Number at or below Standard (millions)
Minimum wage/hour[1]	$1.60	3.9 workers
Poverty (1973):[2] Nonfarm family of four	4,540	19.6 persons
Nonfarm unrelated individual	2,240	4.9 "
Near- poverty (1973):[2] Nonfarm family of four	5,675	28.2 "
Nonfarm unrelated individual	2,799	6.4 "
Social security average benefit:[3] Retiree	1,997	15.4 recipients
Disabled	2,196	2.0 "
Survivors	1,624	7.1 "
Maximum veteran pension:[4] Individual	2,600 ⎱	2.3 veterans (cases)
Married	3,800 ⎰	
Qualification for medical assistance (1972):[5]		
Individual	1,400-3,000 ⎱	18.3 persons
Family of four	2,800-5,000 ⎰	
B.L.S. low-income budget (1973):[6]		
Urban (family of four)	8,181	
State public assistance plans: AFDC average of three to four recipients:[7]		10.9 recipients
High (state)	3,240	
U.S. (average)	2,244	
Low (state)	624	
40% of U.S. median (1972):[8] Family of four	5,123	1.1 (10%) families of four
U.S. median family income (1972):[8] Family of four	12,808	5.3 (50%) "
U.S. mean family income (1972):[8] Family of four	14,387	6.2 (58%) "

[1] U.S. Department of Labor, Employment Standards Administration, March 1974.

[2] U.S. Department of Commerce, Bureau of the Census, "Characteristics of the Low-Income Population, 1972," *Current Population Reports,* Series P-60, No. 91 (Washington, D.C.: U.S. Government Printing Office, December 1973), Tables 1 and 2. Levels for 1972 were converted to 1973 prices by the Consumer Price Index.

[3] U.S. Department of Health, Education, and Welfare, Social Security Administration, Spring 1974.

[4] Veterans Administration, April 1974.

[5] U.S. Department of Health, Education, and Welfare, Social and Rehabilitation Service, April 1974.

[6] U.S. Department of Labor, Bureau of Labor Statistics, USDL 74-304, June 1974.

[7] U.S. Department of Health, Education, and Welfare, Social and Rehabilitation Service, National Center for Social Statistics, April 1974.

[8] U.S. Department of Commerce, Bureau of the Census, "Money Income in 1972 of Families and Persons in the United States," *Current Population Reports*, Series P-60, No. 90 (Washington, D.C.: U.S. Government Printing Office, December 1973), Table 20.

The 1973 base numbers and the 1983 projections have been derived from trends in income distribution for selected years,[5] and numbers of persons in poverty as reported by the U.S. Census Bureau together with the poverty and near-poverty income cutoffs.[6] Chart 11-1 shows the trends in the income distribution of families. (In 1972, the income cutoff for a nonfarm family of four was $4,540 and $2,240, in 1973 prices, for an unrelated individual; the near-poverty cutoffs were at the 125 percent of these levels.[7]) The projection to 1983 reflects assumptions of continued trends and continued expansion of present welfare programs.[8] Proposed new income maintenance activities such as the family assistance program, however, are not reflected in the base projection. Assuming three persons per family, the percent of the population in poverty is expected to drop from 11.4 percent in 1973 to 8.7 percent in 1983, and the percent of population near-poor is expected to decline from 4.8 percent in 1973 to 3.5 percent in 1983.

ACTIVITIES TO REDUCE POVERTY AND NEAR-POVERTY

Poverty involves not only an immediate absence of money but often a lack of the resources that enable people to earn money. Consequently, the activities to reduce poverty include human development and improvement of employment opportunities as well as income-maintenance programs.

Extended welfare

Unless serious handicaps exist that prevent effective use of the money, poverty and near-poverty, as defined by the currently accepted minimum-consumption standards, can be eliminated by a transfer of funds.[9] The effect and cost of such a transfer aiming at the full effect by 1983 are summarized below:

---

5   The source of the data for 1950, 1960 and 1970 was *Current Population Reports*, Series P-60, published by the Census Bureau. The income categories were adjusted on the basis of 1973 prices. The 1980 projection was based on the National Planning Association's projection of the distribution of consumer unit income for 1980 (Washington, D.C.: NPA, National Economic Projections Series Report No. 70-N-1, March 1970), broken down into income of families and unrelated individuals on the basis of the 1950 to 1970 trend by income class in the relative income of these two categories. The 1973 estimate was interpolated and the 1983 extrapolated from the data shown in Chart 11-1.

6   *Current Population Reports*, Series P-60, No. 88, June 1973.

7   Ibid.

8   See footnote 5 above.

9   Such handicaps as physical disabilities, mental health problems, discriminatory barriers against buyers, and severe supply imperfections in economic markets undoubtedly exist, but their overall quantitative significance beyond the point at which they correlate with poverty as defined is probably small and they are not included explicitly in this aggregate calculation.

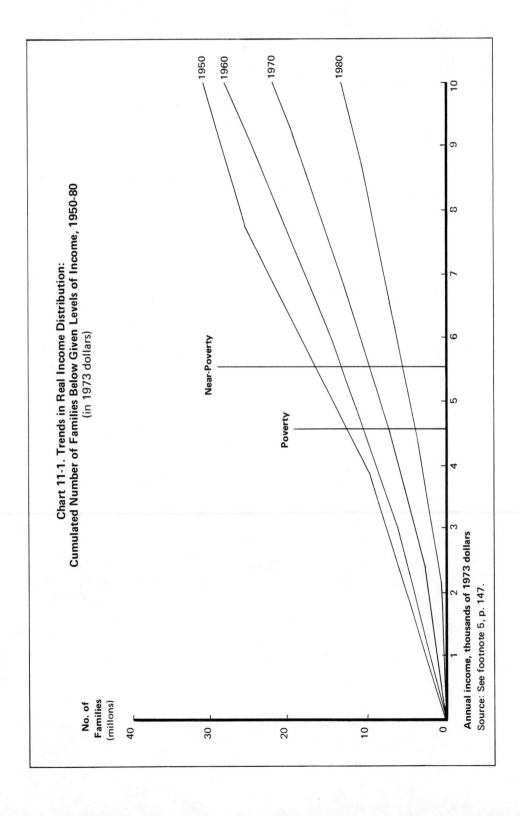

Chart 11-1. Trends in Real Income Distribution:
Cumulated Number of Families Below Given Levels of Income, 1950-80
(in 1973 dollars)

Annual income, thousands of 1973 dollars
Source: See footnote 5, p. 147.

Activity	Percent of Population below Poverty Standard	Percent of Population in Near-Poverty Conditions	Total 10-Year Cost (billions of 1973 dollars)
Extended welfare	−8.7%	−3.5%	$76

The transfer activity defined here is a "negative income tax" system that would provide a minimum-income level for all at the near-poverty cutoff level ($5,552 for a nonfarm family of four, in 1973 dollars), with a marginal tax rate of 50 percent on earned income.[10] The minimum-income level payment assures that no one remains below the near-poverty level even if they have no other source of income. The 50 percent marginal tax rate allows those in poverty and near-poverty to supplement the transfer with half of their earned income, minimizing the incentive to leave the labor force.[11]

The cost estimate for this program is derived as follows. Using cost figures tabulated by Edward Moscovitch and based on the Urban Institute model developed by Nelson McClung,[12] the net additional federal cost in 1973 of a payment system with a minimum-income level of $5,552 and a marginal tax rate of 0.5 is $63 billion. This figure is then multiplied by 0.6 to account for the reduced target population projected for 1983. The estimated annual cost is thus $37.8 billion. The three-year phase-in schedule—33 percent the first year, 67 percent the second year, and 100 percent the target year—would give a total cost of $76 billion, all of which would come from public sources and occur in the second subperiod.

Since the output for this income program is calculated for 1983, most of the spending could be deferred until late in the period. This does not mean that it is in any sense desirable to postpone the reduction of poverty until some distant point in the future, but it simply follows from the specification of 1983 as the base

---

10 This type of tax-transfer scheme is described in Levine, *The Poor Ye Need Not Have*, pp. 200-210; President's Commission on Income Maintenance Programs, *Technical Studies* (Washington, D.C.: U.S. Government Printing Office, 1970); and *New England Economic Review*, Federal Reserve Bank of Boston, January/February 1971.

11 With a minimum above the near-poverty level and a low marginal tax rate, payments become very large and in part go to persons with income substantially above the minimum level.

12 Edward Moscovitch, "Income Supplement—How High Should They Be?," *New England Economic Review*, Federal Reserve Bank of Boston, January/February 1971, pp. 22-23; and Nelson McClung, "Estimates of Income Transfer Effects," *Technical Studies*, President's Commission on Income Maintenance Programs (Washington, D.C.: U.S. Government Printing Office, 1970), pp. 135-142.

year for achievement of outputs and the calculation of only the cost required to achieve 1983 outputs, as part of the methodology of this study. In the future, the methodology may be generalized to deal with flows of outputs and costs over periods of time.

Education, training and employment activities

Five activities aimed primarily at education, job training and employment opportunities may also have some effects on the prevalence of poverty and near-poverty. The estimated effects and costs of these activities are summarized below:

Activity	Percent of Population below Poverty Standard	Percent of Population in Near-Poverty Conditions	Total 10-Year Cost (billions of 1973 dollars)
Employment and other opportunities for the young	−0.9%	−0.4%	$ 51
Day care for children	−1.7	−1.3	126
Universal access to higher education	0	−0.4	273
Improvement of job skills	−0.9	−0.9	342
Specialized training	−1.3	−0.4	94

Employment and other opportunities for the young
The present poverty population contains approximately 4.0-4.5 million young people 13-18 years old who will be affected by this activity. There are approximately 6.5-7.0 million aged 3 to 15, some of whom will be 13-18 years old and poor by 1983.

Providing educational and job training opportunities to the 3 million young poor (aged 13-18) assumed to be unemployed or not in school in 1983 (based on the size of the 1983 poverty population and the age profile of the 1973 poverty population) is estimated to:

• reduce the population in poverty by 2 million, or 0.9 percentage points, and the population in near-poverty by 1 million, or 0.4 percentage points, assuming that 80 percent of these young people would make effective use of the opportunities.

The activity is estimated to cost $51 billion over the decade. A more detailed description appears in Chapter 6.

General day care for children

Providing general day-care services for children is assumed to:

● make earnings from work possible for the estimated 1.5 million poor and 1.1 million near-poor women who could not otherwise work because of small children. Assuming that 1 million of the poor and 3/4 million of the near-poor women go to work, 4 million persons (assuming on the average three additional family members)[13] would be raised above the poverty level and 3 million above the near-poverty level. This amounts to a reduction of 1.7 and 1.3 percent, respectively, in the poor and near-poor populations.

The total cost is calculated at $126 billion. A more detailed description of the activity appears in Chapter 15.

Universal access to higher education

Offering universal access to higher education is estimated to:

● raise 1 million persons, or 0.4 percent of the population, above the near-poverty level. The activity is assumed not to benefit the poverty population within the 10-year time span.[14]

The cost of the activity is calculated at $273 billion. It is discussed in more detail in Chapter 8.

Maintenance, updating and improvement of job skills

This activity is assumed to affect primarily those already in the labor force, and therefore a smaller percentage of those in poverty (10 percent) compared to those in the near-poverty population (26 percent).

Offering skill improvement, career development and job inquiry programs is estimated by 1983 to:

● reduce the poverty and near-poverty portions of the population by 0.9 percent each by opening up higher-paying employment opportunities to 2 million poor and 2 million near-poor (assuming 2.3 million poor and 1.5 million near-poor and working full time in 1983, and assuming that a significant number, at least 0.5 million, of the near-poor would enter the labor force if training and jobs were available).

This activity, estimated to cost $342 billion, is described more fully in Chapters 9 and 10.

Specialized training for those outside mainstream of the labor force

This activity is expected to have its output among the poor and nonpoor

---

13   Three children per family is assumed for women who cannot work because of children, even though the *overall* average in our base projection is three persons per family.

14   We have assumed only 1 million persons benefit because the age and educational composition of the poverty population is such that only a very small reduction in the numbers of poor would be likely to result from improved access to higher education within a 10-year period.

who have not been working full time or have not been working at all. Allowing a margin for those unable or unwilling to work, offering specialized training to the 3.5 million poor and 2 million near-poor[15] estimated to be outside the mainstream of the labor force in 1983, is assumed to:

• raise 3 million poor and 1 million near-poor above the poverty and near-poverty lines, respectively. It would thus reduce the portion of population poor and near-poor by 1.3 and 0.4 percent, respectively.

The activity is estimated to cost $94 billion. It is discussed in greater detail in Chapter 10.

Specialized income maintenance activites

Two specialized income maintenance activities are also judged to affect the number of persons in poverty and near-poverty. Their output and costs are summarized below:

Activity	Percent of Population below Poverty Standard	Percent of Population in Near-Poverty Conditions	Total 10-Year Cost (billions of 1973 dollars)
Private savings, insurance and pension plans	−0.9%	−0.6%	$200
Old age pensions at 40% of current median earnings	−1.7	−0.6	30

Private savings, insurance and pension plans
The extension of private savings, insurance and pension plans by providing a larger retirement reserve income by 1983 is estimated to:

• lift 2 million aged poor (from an estimated 5 million aged poor, approximately the same number as in 1973) out of poverty;

• lift 1.5 million aged near-poor (from an estimated 2 million aged near-poor, approximately the same as in 1973) above near-poverty, assuming that the aged near-poor are more likely to be able to utilize these savings improvements.

The expansion of savings, insurance and pension plans would thus reduce the poverty and near-poverty portions of the population by 0.9 and 0.6 percent-

---

15 National Planning Association estimates. See Park, "Human Resource Development," extrapolated.

age points, respectively, and is estimated to cost $200 billion. The activity is described in more detail in Chapter 12.

Old age pensions at 40 percent of current median earnings

This activity is aimed at the same population as the previous activity, but, based on a social insurance approach, it is expected to have a broader impact on the poor. The poor will not have been able to work at jobs allowing them to participate in improved savings plans to as great an extent as will the near-poor; on the other hand, more poor will have worked enough to   qualify for social security-type benefits. Making available old age pensions averaging 40 percent of current earnings is estimated to:

• reduce the number of aged poor by 4 million (out of an estimated 5 million);

• reduce the number of aged near-poor by 1.5 million (out of an estimated 2 million).

This activity, which is described in more detail in Chapter 12, is estimated to cost $30 billion and reduce the poor and near-poor percentages of the population by 1.7 and 0.6, respectively.

Other activities

Two other activities are assumed to have a secondary effect on the number of poor and near-poor. Their effects and costs are summarized below:

Activity	Percent of Population below Poverty Standard	Percent of Population in Near-Poverty Conditions	Total 10-Year Cost (billions of 1973 dollars)
Aid to depressed communities	−0.9%	−0.9%	$171
Construction and mainte-nance of housing	−0.4	−0.4	108

Aid to depressed communities

This activity consists of a large developmental effort aimed at stimulating economic and social investment in depressed communities. The output in reducing numbers of poor and near-poor will result primarily from moving persons in depressed communities who had been suffering from employment difficulties into the mainstream of the labor force. This will be achieved directly through the development of human capital (training and education) and indirectly through the development of physical capital. Aid to the communities identified as depressed, thus providing job opportunities and job training, is estimated to:

• move 1.8 million people into the mainstream of the labor force. Assuming that 2.2 million family members also benefit, the result is a decrease in the number of poor by 2 million and in the number of near-poor also by 2 million, or a 0.9 percent drop each in the portions of population poor and near-poor.

The estimated cost of this activity is $171 billion. Its components are described in Chapter 10.

Construction and maintenance of housing

Census and other government survey figures clearly indicate that the correlation between poverty and substandard housing is extremely high. Many social scientists have hypothesized about the deleterious effects of living in slum housing, effects that appear to influence the economic success of the inhabitants. We assume that improved housing will have some effect on the health, self-esteem and educational attainment, and hence on the economic productivity, of those living in it. In addition, the subsidy element inherent in the activity would have some effects equivalent to increases in real incomes. Unfortunately, there is no empirical basis for estimating the magnitude of these effects. They are probably not very large, but perhaps not negligible. We therefore arbitrarily estimate, pending further analysis, that improved housing for all the 28 million poor and near-poor would, on a net basis:

• move 1 million persons, or 0.4 percent of the population, above the poverty level;

• move 1 million persons, or 0.4 percent of the population, above the near-poverty level.

The estimated cost for the activity, detailed in Chapter 16, is $108 billion.

INTERACTIONS AMONG ACTIVITIES

By definition, there is a limit set by the size of the poverty and near-poverty population on the total output of all the activities in combination. Since the extended welfare program (15) is designed to completely eliminate poverty and near-poverty, the effects of other activities are redundant, and the offsets among activity combinations that include the income transfer program are complete. Offsets among other activities are less complete, since the populations affected by each of them are to a large degree separable. A summary of the interactions appears in Table 11-2.

Several combinations of activities are assumed to produce additive or near-additive outputs. Employment for the young (5) aids a completely different population than old age pensions (14) and so the effects of the two activities should be additive. Maintenance of job skills (11) affects those working or having worked, while specialized training for those outside the labor force mainstream (12) primarily affects people who have not been working. There is also some overlap in these populations among those who have worked but are not now working because of job obsolescence or other reasons. However, the two populations are mostly separate and therefore the combined output offsets amount to only a small portion of their added total. The aged poor are also largely separate from the populations affected by skills improvement and job training activities (11 and 12), which are oriented toward earning capacity. Therefore, the output of these three activities is additive.

In contrast, employment for the young (5) and skill improvement and job training (11 and 12) would have offsets. The major offset would be with activity 12 since most young people have not yet acquired many skills to be improved but are in need of specialized training in order to participate fully in the labor market.

In addition, it is assumed that there will be some offset between aid to depressed communities (16) and the construction of housing (17) because part of the aid to depressed communities would most likely consist of improved physical living conditions.

Table 11-2. Effects of Activities on Poverty and Near-Poverty

Activity*	Total Cost 1974-83 (billions of 1973 dollars)	Percent of Population below Poverty Standard	Percent of Population in Near-Poverty Conditions
Base 1973	—	11.4%	4.8%
Base 1983	—	8.7%	3.5%
5. Employment for the young	$ 51	-0.9	-0.4
8. General day care for children	126	-1.7	-1.3
9. Universal access to higher education	273	0	-0.4
11. Maintenance, updating and improvement of job skills	342	-0.9	-0.9
12. Specialized training	94	-1.3	-0.4
13. Private savings, insurance, pension plans	200	-0.9	-0.6
14. Old age pensions up to 40%	30	-1.7	-0.6
15. Extended welfare program	76	-8.7	-3.5
16. Aid to depressed communities	171	-0.9	-0.9
17. Construction and maintenance of houses	108	-0.4	-0.4

Table 11-2. Effects of Activities on Poverty and Near-Poverty (continued)

Selected Combined Effects**	Total Cost 1974-83 (billions of 1973 dollars)	Percent of Population below Poverty Standard	Percent of Population in Near-Poverty Conditions
13,14. Private savings; Old age pensions	$ 230	-2.2%	-0.9%
5,14. Employment for the young; Old age pensions	81	-2.6	-1.0
8,12. Day care; Specialized training	220	-2.2	-1.5
11,12. Job skills; Specialized training	436	-1.7	-1.1
11,12,14. Job skills; Specialized training; Old age pensions	466	-3.4	-1.7
5,11,12. Employment for the young; Job skills; Specialized training	487	-2.2	-1.3
16,17. Aid to depressed communities; Construction of houses	279	-1.1	-1.1
5,9,11,12. Employment for the young; Universal access to higher education; Job skills; Specialized training	760	-2.2	-1.7
5,11,12,16,17. Employment for the young; Job skills; Specialized training; Aid to depressed communities; Construction of houses	766	-3.0	-2.2
5,8,11,12,16,17. Employment for the young; Day care; Job skills; Specialized training; Aid to depressed communities; Construction of houses	892	-3.5	-2.4
5,8,9,11,12,16,17. Employment for the young; Day care; Universal access to higher education; Job skills; Specialized training; Aid to depressed communities; Construction of houses	1,165	-3.5	-2.6
All activities (excluding extended welfare)	1,395	-5.6	-3.5
Total, all activities	$1,471	-8.7%	-3.5%

* The numbers preceding the activities refer to their order in the matrix, Table 2-4.

**Since activity #15 alone is designed to reduce the projected incidence of poverty and near-poverty to zero, any combination including this activity also has maximum output; therefore, such combinations are not included in this table.

12

Continuity of income

OBJECTIVE

Income security.

INDICATOR

Percent of population with a living standard loss of over 30 percent.

The concept dealt with in this chapter is impoverishment rather than poverty. Impoverishment can be defined as a significant and permanent loss of a permanently attained living standard. Such losses occur through losses of real income, and can result from death, disability, loss of a job, or retirement.[1] That income security is a major concern can be gauged from the amount of private and public resources allocated to it; see Table 12-1.

The most prevalent cause of impoverishment is retirement, as can be inferred from empirical studies that relate to the economic status of the aged.[2] These studies permit two important observations. The first is that there does occur a very large drop of income, and presumably a drop of living standard, as a result of retirement. Consequently, a large number of Americans live in

---

1 Equivalent losses of value of assets (e.g., through damage) or of real consumption streams (e.g., through estrangement within families) are subsumed under the income losses.

2 See, for example, Milton Moss, "Consumption: A Report on Contemporary Issues," *Indicators of Social Change,* Eleanor B. Sheldon and Wilbert E. Moore, eds. (New York: Russell Sage Foundation, 1968); Michael Brannon, Philip Taft and Mark Schupack, *The Economics of Age* (New York: Norton, 1967); Otto Eckstein, ed., *Studies in Income Maintenance* (Washington, D.C.: The Brookings Institution, 1967); Lenore A. Epstein and Janet H. Murray, *The Aged Population of the United States: The 1963 Social Security Survey of the Aged,* SSA Research Paper No. 19 (Washington, D.C.: U.S. Government Printing Office, 1967); James Schultz, *The Economic Status of the Retired Aged in 1980,* SSA Research Report No. 24 (Washington, D.C.: U.S. Government Printing Office, 1968); Arnold Strasser, "Pension Formula Summarization," *Monthly Labor Review* (Washington, D.C.: U.S. Government Printing Office, April 1971); John Reinecke, "Expenditures of Two-Person Units and Individuals after Age 65," SSA Staff Paper No. 9 (Washington, D.C.: U.S. Government Printing Office, May 1971).

**Table 12-1. Selected Flows of Outlays Identifiable with the
Objective of Income Continuity in the United States, 1972-74**
(in billions)

Outlays	Amount
Social security contributions	$65.3[1]
Unemployment insurance taxes	6.7[2]
Personal consumption expenditures for insurance	19.2[3]
Pension fund receipts	35.4[4]
Personal savings	74.4[5]

[1] Figure for 1974 (preliminary): U.S. Department of Health, Education, and Welfare, Social Security Administration, *Social Security Bulletin* (Washington, D.C.: U.S. Government Printing Office, November 1974), Tables M-5, M-6 and M-7.

[2] Figure for 1973: U.S. Department of Commerce, Bureau of Economic Analysis, *Survey of Current Business* (Washington, D.C.: U.S. Government Printing Office, July 1974), Table 3.8, p. 28.

[3] Ibid., Table 25, p. 24; premium receipts of U.S. insurance companies on health, life and automobile insurance.

[4] Figure for 1972: *Life Insurance Fact Book 1974* (New York: Institute of Life Insurance), pp. 39-41; includes private insured and non-insured pension plans plus government-administered pension plans.

[5] Figure for 1973: *Survey of Current Business,* July 1974, Table 2, p. 2.

circumstances much reduced from their previous levels. (It should be emphasized that the concern dealt with here relates to permanent levels and to changes in permanent levels of living, not to temporary fluctuations.)

The second observation is that in spite of the growth of coverage and benefits of private pension plans and of the social security payment system, as well as probable trends in savings, by 1983 the picture will not be too different.[3] Large numbers of persons will still be living at a standard of living greatly reduced from their prior levels.

In addition to the change in income flow due to retirement, there are age-related changes in income needs and expenditure requirements. Some living expenses diminish among older people, work-related expenditures are discontinued, and family obligations are smaller. Therefore, a less than full replacement of income may be sufficient to maintain a given standard of living. A counter trend usually sets in at later ages as increasing incidence of infirmities and illness require added outlays for medical, and eventually personal care. Because the consumption patterns, by necessity, change with age, a

---

3 See especially Schultz, *Economic Status of Retired Aged*, and Strasser, "Pension Formula."

Table 12-2. Estimated Budget Required to Maintain a Moderate Low-Income
Standard of Living, by Age and Family Size, 1973

Age of Head of Family	One Person		Two Persons		Family of Four	
	Budget	Equivalence Scale	Budget	Equivalence Scale	Budget	Equivalence Scale
Under 35	$2,863	35	$3,845	47	$6,054	74
35-54	2,945	36	4,827	59	8,181	100
55-64	2,618	32	4,827	59	8,917	109
65 or over	2,291	28	4,254	52	7,445	91

Source: U.S. Department of Labor, Bureau of Labor Statistics, "Revised Equivalence Scale," *Bulletin No. 1570-2* (Washington, D.C.: U.S. Government Printing Office, November 1968); and "Autumn 1973 Urban Family Budgets and Comparative Indexes for Selected Urban Areas," U.S. Department of Labor Press Release No. 74-304, June 16, 1974, Table A.

The family unit of four persons with head aged 35 to 54 is used as the index. The 1973 BLS low-income budget for this family unit is $8,181. The equivalence scale was estimated by BLS to compare budget requirements since family size and age vary. The equivalence scale number is the ratio of the given family unit's budget requirement to the index unit's budget requirement multiplied by 100 percent.

direct quantitative comparison of living standards, using income changes, cannot be made.

An attempt to provide an estimate of the cost of maintaining a fixed moderate standard of living for persons and families in four age categories is shown in Table 12-2. This age comparison is based on the Bureau of Labor Statistics Revised Equivalence Scale derived from the 1960-61 consumer expenditure surveys. A family of four members with the head aged 35 to 54 is used as the index base, and the fixed standard of living corresponds to the BLS Low-Income Budget. In each family-size category, one person, two persons or four persons, the budget requirement decreases after age 65. From this information, one can estimate that the family income required to maintain living standards after age 65 is reduced by approximately 17 percent. The 17 percent factor is the percentage drop for a family of four from the level shown in the equivalence table (12-2) for the age of head 55-64 to age 65 or over.

A criterion of what constitutes a serious income loss is not readily apparent. A 30 percent drop in living standard is taken as the basis for measuring the target population. The choice is arbitrary. (A 10 percent loss would be too small to be viewed as an object of important existing concern, and a 50 percent loss might be too catastrophic and would exclude a large number of hardship cases that are actually part of the effective public concern with income security.)

For purposes of measurement here intended, the loss of living standard must be translated into an income loss. The BLS equivalence scale indicates that a 17 percent drop in income after retirement might be sufficient to maintain a former living standard. A 42 percent loss of income, incorporating the 17 percent factor, would mean a 30 percent loss in living standard. The criterion for measuring the extent of impoverishment is therefore chosen to be an income loss of 42 percent.[4] This criterion does not account for the asset holdings that a retired person may use to maintain his standard of living. It is unlikely, however, that asset holdings, which for the retired person consist mostly of home ownership,[5] would much distort the present criterion, and the resulting estimates and discussion. This criterion of loss of 30 percent of the standard of living is applied uniformly to all groups in the impoverished population.

BASE TRENDS

Indicator	1973	1983 Projection	Projected Change
Percent of population with living standard loss of over 30 percent	8.6%	8.7%	+0.1%

To determine base trends, we begin with a base target population made up of four components: the retired with income loss, the disabled with income loss, survivors of a deceased income earner, and those with permanent job losses due to economic conditions.

Using Social Security Administration estimates of the number of retired workers eligible for benefits[6] and a cohort grouping of men and women,[7] we estimate that 8.5 million men and 1.2 million women suffered an income loss greater than 42 percent and therefore a drop in living standard greater than 30 percent. These figures assume that nearly all retired men suffer this magnitude of income loss, while a smaller percentage of women do because women have a lower average income before retirement and, hence, not as

---

4   The 42 percent was calculated in the following manner:
$(1.00 - .30) = .70; (1.00 - .17) = .83; (.70)(.83) = .58; (1.00 - .58) = .42.$

5   Schultz, *Economic Status of Retired Age*.

6   Office of the Actuary, Social Security Administration, June 1973.

7   Mary F. Henson, "Trends in the Income of Families and Persons in the United States 1947–1964," Bureau of the Census Technical Paper 17 (Washington, D.C.: U.S. Government Printing Office, August 1967).

Table 12-3. Number of Persons Suffering Permanent Income Loss
(in millions)

Cause of Income Loss	1973	1983 Projection
Retirement	9.7[1]	10.2[3]
Disabilities	2.6[2]	3.3[4]
Death of income earner	5.2[2]	5.4[4]
Permanent loss of job	1.0	1.0
Estimated total base population	18.5	19.9

[1] Office of the Actuary, Social Security Administration (June 1973).

[2] Ibid., 75 percent of the 3.5 million disabled and 7 million survivors in 1973.

[3] Social Security Administration projections; projected beneficiaries of OASDHI.

[4] Ibid., 75 percent of the 4.4 million disabled and 7.2 million survivors projected for 1983.

large a percentage drop. The numbers of persons suffering an income loss due to disability or death of an income earner in the family are estimated from social security figures for beneficiaries of OASDHI payments. In 1973, 3.5 million persons are estimated to have received benefits for disability reasons, and 7 million as survivors of beneficiaries.[8] It is assumed that in these two groups, 75 percent of the persons, 2.6 million and 5.2 million persons respectively, will have suffered at least a 42 percent drop in income. We have placed the number of persons having suffered a permanent economic job loss at 1.0 million. The total 1973 base population of income loss sufferers is thus estimated at 18.5 million, or about 8.6 percent of the population (see Table 12-3).

The 1983 projection is based on population projections and the Social Security Administration's projections of beneficiaries. Social Security projects that there will be 4.4 million beneficiaries due to disabilities and 7.2 million survivors in 1983, and it is again assumed that 75 percent of the disabled and survivors will have suffered a living standard loss of at least 30 percent.[9] The 1983 base population is estimated to include 9.1 million retired men, 1.1 million retired women, 3.3 million disabled workers, 5.4 million survivors of deceased workers, and 1 million permanently jobless due to changes in economic condi-

---

8   Ibid.

9   It should be noted that the estimate of disabled persons here is much smaller than the estimate of disabled persons given in Chapter 5. This is because the population qualifying for social security is much smaller, but here it is used as better representing the population who had been previously maintaining comfortable living standards. Dependents are included in all these estimates as provided by social security data.

tion, totaling 19.9 million persons, or about 8.7 percent of the population (see Table 12-3).

DISCRETIONARY ACTIVITIES TO EXTEND INCOME SECURITY

Private savings, insurance and pension plans

The design of this activity, which draws on no previous work, must be considered very tentative in magnitude. A summary of the effect and cost is given below:

Activity	Percent of Population with Living Standard Loss over 30%	Total 10-Year Cost (billions of 1973 dollars)
Private savings, insurance, pension plans	−4.3%	$200

We assume that a variety of specific activities, including financial, institutional and regulatory innovations, perhaps such as constant dollar savings instruments and improvements in the private pension systems, all aimed at improving the capacity of private savings to serve the objectives of individuals, with funds accumulated basically from employee and employer contributions, could, if generally adopted by 1983:

● be utilized by about 10 million persons in the target population (slightly more than one-half), thus providing income security for 10 million persons who otherwise would have suffered a severe decrease in their living standard.

This activity can be described as a 10-year annuity with average payment of $2,000 per person per year to 10 million persons mainly to supplement other income sources. The resulting payment stream of $22 billion annually by 1983 requires a capitalization of $200 billion by that date, assuming a 10 percent yield. The total cost of the activity is, therefore, $200 billion, 40 percent of which would be required in the first period since building up capital of this magnitude has to be stretched out in time,[10] and 20 percent of which is as-

---

10   For the past growth in private pension funds, see Walter W. Kolodrubetz, "Employee-Benefit Plans, 1972," *Social Security Bulletin* (Washington, D.C.: U.S. Government Printing Office, May 1974), pp. 20-21.

sumed to be from public sources, representing the proportion of public employment.

Old age pensions at 40 percent of current median earnings

As for the previous activity, the assumptions and estimates for this activity are not based on previous studies, since none exist, but are "best guesses" of the effect and cost of such an effort. A summary appears below:

Activity	Percent of Population with Living Standard Loss over 30%	Total 10-Year Cost (billons of 1973 dollars)
Old age pensions	−2.6%	$30

The replacement ratio of social security payments to current income is about 25 percent. We assume that an increase in benefits, which is set at 40 percent of current median earnings, would allow many beneficiaries to maintain living standards at 70 percent of their previous permanent level. By tying benefits to current median earnings, an adjustment factor is introduced which allows the retired to benefit from future increases in the productivity of the economy as a whole. There are problems with this assumption, namely, that the benefit increase relates to median earnings for the nation, and the indicator refers to particular individuals' permanent incomes. Without knowing the distributions of benefits and permanent income levels, no concrete estimates can be made. We postulate, however, that the distributions would be such that raising social security benefits to 40 percent of current median earnings in 1983 would:

• permit maintenance of former living standards within the 30 percent margin for 60 percent of retirees, or an estimated 6 million persons (2.6 percent of the population), who otherwise would not be able to maintain them.

Using NPA projections for GNP growth over the next decade, median earnings (of all working individuals) for 1983 are projected to be $7,800. Forty percent of this is $3,120 per year, or $260 per month. If we assume that the social security system replacement ratio will be around 30 percent of income (30 percent is the informal estimate made by Social Security for the equilibrium replacement ratio), then the median benefit will be $2,340 per year, or $195 per month. To reach the target benefit outlay, an additional annual benefit of $780 per retiree will be required, or about a 33 percent increase.

If the social security outlays for OASDI (i.e., excluding medicare) increase at the rate displayed from 1960 to 1971, then its total outlay will be $68.4 billion (in 1973 dollars). Charles Schultze projects the social security outlay at $78 billion.[11] Using the past growth projection, the increased payment of 40 percent would cost $27.4 billion as a yearly increment. Using Schultze's projection, the incremental cost would be a higher $31.6 billion. Thus, roughly, a $30 billion yearly increment to the 1983 social security outlay would allow the system to increase the average benefit by nearly 40 percent (enough to cover the 33 percent requirement mentioned earlier), bringing it to 40 percent of 1983 median earnings.[12]

Although conceivably some amount of increased private philanthropic contributions might be included in the $30 billion estimated total 1983 outlay for this activity, it is assumed here to be entirely publicly financed. It is also assumed that the program can be initiated in 1983 without any lead time for phasing in, since the necessary administrative apparatus already exists, and the political and legislative preparations would not generate any perceptible activity costs in the earlier years.

OTHER ACTIVITIES

Four other discretionary activities are assumed to improve the standard of living of those otherwise expected to have a serious drop in living standard. The effects and costs of the activities are summarized below:

---

11 Charles L. Schultze et al., *Setting National Priorities: The 1974 Budget* (Washington, D.C.: The Brookings Institution, 1973), p. 57.

12 Questions may be raised about the fiscal feasibility of future large increases in the social security benefit rates which even with conventional demographic projections have been causing some concern recently. See, for example, a recently released consultant study for the Secretary of the Treasury (Robert S. Kaplan and Roman L. Weil, "An Actuarial Audit of the Social Security System," September 1974) and the recent report by the board of trustees of the social security trust funds (1974 Annual Report, House Document No. 93-313). With increases in longevity of the magnitudes considered feasible in Chapter 5, should such increases result in raising the proportion of total population over 65 (which need not be the case but which requires further analysis), these increases may be incompatible with the ongoing economic, labor market, fiscal, and administrative systems. The present study can only address some basic technical and economic feasibilities as currently apparent. The activity discussed is not incompatible with the basic economic trends. Specifics of implementation cannot be seriously explored in a study such as this. However, it may well be the case that implementation of this activity may require discovery of means to provide wider range of equitable work and retirement options for older persons other than the present system of largely compulsory retirement. Or implementation may require discovery of means of financing, in effect, a continuously improving living standard for a continuously increasing fraction of dependent population without cutting off growth of the living standards of the working population. This would probably require a quantum jump in the productivity growth rate of the American economy to the level of rates comparable to those which have prevailed in Europe and Japan in the recent decades.

Activity	Percent of Population with Living Standard Loss over 30%	Total 10-Year Cost (billions of 1973 dollars)
Changes in health-related habits	−0.9%	$64
Health services related to specific conditions	−0.4	66
Specialized job training	−0.4	94
Extended welfare	−1.3	76

Changes in health-related habits and patterns

Eliminating smoking, improving nutrition and fitness, preventing accidents, and reducing alcohol and drug abuse are estimated to:

• reduce the number of persons suffering from major disabilities by about 20 percent and extend the average life expectancy by over five years. Applying the 20 percent figure to those suffering an income loss due to disability or the death of a wage-earner, with a small increased margin to account for increased life expectancy, gives an estimate of 2 million persons, or 0.9 percent of the population, prevented from suffering substantial income loss.

This activity, described in Chapter 5, is calculated to cost $64 billion.

Health services related to specific conditions

Expanding health services for diagnosis and treatment of cancer, mental illness and arthritis should decrease disabilities and mortality from these conditions. In the face of uncertainty regarding the likely maximum size of this effect, the activity is here arbitrarily assumed to:

• reduce the number of persons suffering an income loss due to disability or death of a wage-earner by 1 million, or 0.4 percent of the population. (Since this activity does not have as broad an effect as the preceding health activity, we assume a considerably smaller output.)

The cost of this activity is estimated to be $66 billion. The activity is described in more detail in Chapter 5.

Specialized training for those outside the mainstream of the labor force

Providing specialized training for those outside the mainstream of the labor force, with the assumed consequence that 5 million persons would enter the labor force mainstream, is estimated by 1983 to:

● provide jobs, and therefore improve the standard of living, for those 1 million impoverished (0.4 percent of the population) who lost their jobs due to structural economic changes.

This activity, estimated to cost $94 billion, is described in Chapter 10.

Extended welfare—taxes and transfers
to abolish poverty and near-poverty

We project the population of the aged poor and near-poor (65 and over) to decline from 5.2 million in 1973 to 3.8 million in 1983. Extending welfare to raise all persons above near-poverty by 1983 is assumed to:

● assure a standard of living at least 70 percent of their previous permanent levels to the 75 percent of the aged poor who had not been poor previously (about 3 million people, or 1.3 percent of the population). (The income gain of those persons who had been in poverty or close to poverty before retirement cannot be counted against the base population of those experiencing sizable income losses.)

This transfer and tax program, discussed fully in Chapter 11, is estimated to cost $76 billion.

INTERACTIONS AMONG ACTIVITIES

A summary of the activity interactions is presented in Table 12-4. Both the health-related habits activity (1) and the health services activity (2) will affect the number of persons suffering an income loss due to disability or death. Here we assume that the offset will be 500,000, or 0.2 percent, resulting in a combined reduction of 2.5 million persons (1.1 percent of the population) who suffer a living standard loss of over 30 percent. If the extended welfare activity (15) is added to this combination, output would increase to 4.5 million, or 1.9 percent of the population. The overlap between the populations affected by private savings (13) and old age pensions (14) is considerable. Many persons would benefit from either private or public pension improvements, and to this extent the two activities offset each other. However, it is assumed that some persons not able to participate in the private savings improvements would be helped by public pension improvements. Thus, the combined effect is estimated at 12 million persons, or 5.2 percent of the population. If an extended welfare program (15) is added to the above combination, output is expected to be 13.5 million persons (6.1 percent of population). The additional 1.5 million persons above the combination of activities (13) and (14) is composed of some aged poor who will not have been covered by private plans and are not participating in the social security system and pensions. In addition, some disability or death-related cases may exist in which the transfer amount is sufficient, with what pension provisions exist, for the individual to bring living standards up to 70 percent of the previous permanent levels.

Combining old age pensions (14) with the extended welfare activity (15) results in an offset of 1 million persons (about 0.4 percent of population); output is estimated at a reduction in the number of persons with more than 30 percent living standard loss of 8 million (3.5 percent of population). Similarly, there is an offset of 1 million between private savings plans (13) and the extended welfare program (15), with the combined output reducing the number

Table 12-4. Effects of Activities on the Continuity of Income

Activity*	Total Cost 1974-83 (billions of 1973 dollars)	Reduction in Percent of Population with Living Standard Loss over 30%
Base 1973	—	8.6%
Base 1983	—	8.7%
1. Change in health related habits and patterns	$64	-.9%
2. Health services related to specific conditions	66	-0.4
12. Specialized training for those outside the mainstream	94	-0.4
13. Private insurance, savings, pension plans	200	-4.3
14. Old age pensions at 40% of current median earnings	30	-2.6
15. Extended welfare—taxes and transfers to abolish poverty and near-poverty	76	-1.3
Combined Effects		
1,2. Health related habits; Health services	130	-1.1
1,2,15. Health related habits; Health services; Extended welfare	206	-1.9
13,14. Private savings; Old age pensions	230	-5.2
13,14,15. Private savings; Old age pensions; Extended welfare	306	-6.1
14,15. Old age pensions; Extended welfare	106	-3.5
13,15. Private savings; Extended welfare	276	-5.2
12,13,15. Private savings; Extended welfare; Specialized training	370	-5.4
Total, all activities	**$530**	**-6.9%**

* The numbers preceding the activities refer to their order in the matrix, Table 2-4.

of persons suffering a substantial living standard loss by 12 million (5.2 percent of population). The activity of specialized training (12) will add 0.5 million (0.2 percent of population) to the output of activities (13) and (15) in combination because some of those outside the labor force mainstream will qualify for the extended welfare program.

The total effect of all activities in combination is a reduction in the number of persons experiencing a living standard loss of 30 percent or more of 16 million, or 6.9 percent of the population.

13

General economic equality

OBJECTIVE

    Equality of opportunity.

Concern with equality is one of the oldest expressed American goals. Many statements of public policy and popular expressions throughout American history are explicitly concerned with promoting equality, especially equality of opportunity. More recently, distinctions have been made between equality of opportunity and equality of results, *ex ante* and *ex post* equality, equality in law and equality in fact.

One important aspect of equality is economic equality. While economic equality is not a complete reflection of all the basic concerns with equality, it is an important dimension of equality by itself as well as a prerequisite for many others.

Economic equality is measured here by the equality of income. Using an income indicator does not imply primacy of monetary values. But income is a very basic operational indicator of what individuals and families can actually do, what opportunities their children can have, how they may be accorded status and respect by their fellowmen, and, indeed, the extent to which they are free to pursue their own better judgments.

This chapter is included on a trial basis. The criteria for economic equality in general (as distinct from specific issues discussed in other chapters) are not readily apparent. There is also a host of conceptual and statistical questions in actually defining an indicator of economic equality. The answers to all these questions are not clear.[1] And yet, the measurement of economic equality in the population at large appears to be sufficiently important to warrant inclusion of this chapter which is built around an indicator perhaps much more experimental than most of the others included in this study.

---

1 A rigorous analysis of properties of a number of different indicators of inequality and of differences in the results they may produce is contained in D.G. Champernowne, "A Comparison of Measures of Inequality of Income Distribution," *The Economic Journal,* December 1974, pp. 787-816.

One conceptual issue involves the correspondence between income and opportunity or income and social mobility. Any income distribution is theoretically consistent with both large and no social mobility. In fact, any distribution short of identical incomes, i.e., zero inequality, is consistent with either complete mobility where status of a person is uncorrelated with status of his parents (or even of himself at an earlier time) or zero mobility where it is completely determined by and identical to it. (Logically, it is also consistent with inverse correlations of status between generations, but this has no practical significance.) Another question is whether it is possible to specify desirable direction of change in any measure not involving either of the extremes of the distribution of an actual distribution of the annual ·money income of families and individuals for which a normative consensus could be claimed (as distinct in the abstract long run in which all other things are assumed to hold equal). Is it important?

It would be desirable to include an indicator of distribution of wealth along with the one for income or to have data for lifetime incomes rather than annual incomes. However, both the data on the distribution of wealth and the conceptual formulation of wealth distribution are not sufficiently developed and the experimental state of this chapter does not warrant use of two indicators.[2]

INDICATOR

Family income ratio: 20th percentile to 90th.

Equality is approached here by means of this particular indicator of the range of incomes in the population at large.[3] It measures concerns distinct from those already identified as goals and measured by their indicators elsewhere in this work, such as a minimum adequacy of income, income equality by race and by sex, continuity of income, and ability to earn income.

In order to reflect income differences for a large proportion of the population, but to exclude the special problems of the extremes of income, a wide range is needed. For that purpose, the median income of the top 20 percent and the median income of the bottom 40 percent, i.e., the 90th and the 20th percentiles of the income distribution, are adopted. The reason for the asym-

---

2   For measurement and theoretical discussions of the distribution of wealth see Lee Soltow, "The Wealth, Income and Social Class of Men in Large Northern Cities of the United States in 1860," *The Personal Distribution of Income and Wealth*, James D. Smith, ed., Vol. 39 of Studies in Income and Wealth (New York: National Bureau of Economic Research, 1975).

3   For other indicators and for detailed tabulation of the family income time series and indicators, see Murray S. Weitzman, "Family (Money) Income 1947–1971: Summarizing Twenty-five Years of a Summary Statistic," U.S. Bureau of the Census Technical Paper 35 (Washington, D.C.: U.S. Government Printing Office, July 1974).

metrical cut-off points is that the wealthy population is often defined as the top 5 percent (sometimes top 1 percent) of income recipients (or wealth holders), while the poor constitute nearly 10 percent of the total population at the opposite end. The cut-off points are twice the percentages indicated. The resulting indicator reflects the dispersion or the range of incomes for the 70 percent of the population located well within the extremes of wealth and poverty. This range is estimated for 1973 to extend from $6,200 to $25,000 annual income. The lower limit is 25 percent of the upper limit, or, stated another way, the income at the upper end of the range is 4 times that at the lower end.

Incomes of all families during one year are included in the distribution from which the indicator is derived. (However, incomes of unrelated individuals not in a family are not included.) No measures of distribution of permanent income or of lifetime income are available. For comparison, it may be noted that among the husband and wife families, with employed male head aged 35-44, income of the 90th percentile is 2.5 times greater than the income at the 20th percentile. However, the ratio for all families is more inclusive and is used in this chapter.

The range between the 90th and 20th percentiles used as the indicator for economic equality, abstract and inelegant as it may be, seems preferable to the alternatives available for this goal and sufficiently related to the specific concern with economic equality within the bulk of the population to be included on an experimental basis.

BASE TRENDS

Indicator	1973	1983 Projection	Projected Change
Family income ratio: 20th to 90th percentile	25%	25%	0
Family income, 20th percentile	$ 6,200	$ 9,050	+46%
Family income, 90th percentile	24,860	36,300	+46

In the absence of a clear long-run trend, continuation of the estimated 1973 ratio of 25 percent is projected to 1983 even though the ratio declined somewhat between 1961 and 1971.

DISCRETIONARY ACTIVITIES

A number of activities have a large effect on the equality of income. However, in some cases, the effect is not realized or is realized only in a small part by 1983, and the 1983 estimates shown here do not represent the long-run effects. Also, since the indicator chosen is that for families at the 20th and 90th income percentile levels, activities dealing with other, lower-income population groups simply would not have any appreciable impact on this indicator. Thus, no effect is assumed to accrue from income transfers aimed at abolishing poverty and near-poverty. Such effects would probably become apparent in a longer-term, 25-year analysis.

Remedial and augmenting educational inputs

Improving students' performance in the basic skills of mathematics, reading comprehension and verbal ability will also augment their earnings potential. The effect and cost of this activity are estimated to be as follows:

Activity	Family Income Ratio: 20th to 90th Percentile	Income at Percentile: 20th 90th	Total 10-Year Cost (billions of 1973 dollars)
Remedial and augmenting educational inputs	+2%	$740 0	$73

Of the $44 billion output increment estimated to result from these improvements in basic skills, about $31 billion would represent additional income. Assuming the proportion of this income gain received by families is the same as the family proportion of total income, then $23.6 billion (or 76 percent of the $31 billion) would be added to family income. On the assumption that all of the gain would go to families in the lower half of the income distribution, since the students benefiting would tend to be those initially with lower potential incomes, then these 32 million families would each gain $740 annually by 1983. This would raise the ratio of family income at the 20th percentile level by two percentage points in relation to the base income of families at the 90th percentile, which would remain unchanged.

The cost of this activity is estimated at $73 billion. It is discussed in more detail in Chapter 7.

Improved educational technology and approaches

Modernizing the technology and approaches in basic education will improve the general equality of earnings by 1 percentage point:

Activity	Family Income Ratio: 20th to 90th Percentile	Income at Percentile: 20th 90th	Total 10-Year Cost (billions of 1973 dollars)
Improved educational technology and approaches	+1%	$500 $500	$183

The introduction of new educational technologies could have a very significant impact in raising basic educational skills of all students and also in reducing the percent lagging seriously behind the average performance. Students entering the labor force by 1983 would produce an additional $60 billion of output. The full impact of the activity, however, would not be felt until some years later, when those benefiting from the activity's provision for educating the very young also reached working age. Of the $42 billion additional income produced by 1983, $32 billion would go to families. It is estimated that all families would share approximately equally in the gain, thus yielding an average increase of $500 for each. Income at the 20th percentile would go up to $9,550 and at the 90th to $36,800, which raises the income ratio of the lower-income families by 1 percentage point.

The cost of this activity is estimated at $183 billion. Both the cost and the composition of the activity are discussed in more detail in Chapter 7.

General day care for children

Providing general day care is expected to increase opportunity to participate in the labor force. Its effect and cost are summarized below:

Activity	Family Income Ratio: 20th to 90th Percentile	Income at Percentile: 20th 90th	Total 10-Year Cost (billions of 1973 dollars)
General day care for children	2%	$700 0	$126

General availability of day care for smaller children and for school-age children at hours other than school hours will have a large effect on earnings of women because of greater flexibility of time of work, ability to have jobs at all, and ability to increase their educational levels. Similarly, it would have some effect on the flexibility of men with respect to job and time opportunities. Participation of women in the labor force is estimated to be about 46 percent in 1983 (compared to about 79 percent for men) and is estimated to increase to 51 percent as a result of this activity. Based on the 1983 average earnings for year-round full-time workers of $7,500 for women and $12,500 for men, this will bring an income increment of $7,500 per family for 4 million families (estimating a full-time equivalent increase of 4 million women workers). Assuming all of this increase applies only to families in the lower two-thirds of the income distribution, then the $43 billion of additional output produced, of which $30 billion represents additional earnings, yields an average income gain of $700 for these 43 million families. At the 20th percentile, income would thus rise to $9,750 per family, while at the 90th percentile, it would remain at $36,300. Relative income equality would increase by two percentage points.

The cost of this activity is estimated at $126 billion, and is discussed in detail in Chapter 15.

Universal access to higher education

Offering universal access to higher education is estimated to increase the number of persons who have completed college by 1983. The projected impact on their earnings would affect the equality indicator as follows:

Activity	Family Income Ratio: 20th to 90th Percentile	Income at Percentile: 20th 90th	Total 10-Year Cost (billions of 1973 dollars)
Universal higher education	1%	$480 0	$273

Income increases consistently with education. A number of persons in the labor force having incomplete higher education would be likely to complete it if they had an opportunity. The difference in expected male lifetime earnings between high school and college graduates amounted to about $6,000 a year in 1968.[4] Allowing for economic growth, it can be expected to rise to $10,600 in

---

4   U.S. Department of Health, Education, and Welfare, Office of Education, National Center for Education Statistics, *Digest of Educational Statistics, 1971* (Washington, D.C.: U.S. Government Printing Office, 1972), Figure 4, p. 16.

1983, in 1973 dollars. If 20 percent is deducted from this amount to allow for partial completions and simple transfer effects (nonfunctional increases in pay based on college degrees without any real productivity difference), then the 1983 differential comes to $8,500.

As a result of the activity, 3,150,000 additional persons would earn college degrees by 1983. Estimating that 75 percent, or 2.4 million, of these are employed at the $8,500 rate by this date yields an additional $20 billion in earnings. Of this, an estimated $15 billion would be additional family income. On the assumption that families in the lower half of the income distribution are the ones benefiting from the activity, the average gain is thus $480 per family. This is equivalent to 1 point increase in the income ratio at the 20th percentile. (It is assumed that no effect accrues to income at the upper end of the distribution since these persons are already fully using their education potential or capabilities.)

This activity and its cost are discussed in greater detail in Chapter 8.

Maintenance, updating and improvement of job skills

Job training and placement assistance under this activity would increase productivity and mobility of workers. The cost and impact on equality are given below:

Activity	Age Adjusted Family Income Ratio: 20th to 90th Percentile	Income at Percentile: 20th 90th	Total 10- Year Cost (billions of 1973 dollars)
Maintenance and improvement of job skills	2%	$560 0	$342

Both employed and unemployed persons, as well as those outside the labor force and, generally, persons with varied prior skill and income levels would participate in this activity.

The resulting increased productivity would, in 1983, add $24 billion to income, of which the family share would be $18 billion. Assuming those in the upper half of the income distribution already have access to training, mobility and placement services, the average gain for the other families would be $560. Added to income at the 20th percentile, this represents a gain of 2 percentage points in relation to income at the 90th percentile.

The cost of this activity is $342 billion; it is discussed in detail in Chapter 9.

Private savings, insurance and pension plans

Public measures to improve private savings arrangements would have the effect and cost given below:

Activity	Family Income Ratio: 20th to 90th Percentile	Income at Percentile: 20th 90th	Total 10- Year Cost (billions of 1973 dollars)
Private savings, insurance, pension plans	1%	$350 0	$200

This activity would yield an additional $2,000 per year for 10 million people, mainly retired persons, surviving dependents of deceased income earners, and persons becoming disabled or permanently unemployed. An annual total of $20 billion would thus become available to these persons. Assuming all those benefiting are among the lower two-thirds of income recipients, the average family share would be $350. Assuming also that families at the 20th percentile are, on the average, net recipients of this amount, the ratio of their income to that at the 90th percentile would increase by 1 percentage point.

A more extensive discussion of this activity and its cost appears in Chapter 12.

Old age pensions up to 40 percent of current median earnings

If pensions are increased from the present 30 percent replacement ratio of Social Security payments to income to a level of 40 percent of current median earnings, the cost and impact will be as follows:

Activity	Family Income Ratio: 20th to 90th Percentile	Income at Percentile: 20th 90th	Total 10- Year Cost (billions of 1973 dollars)
Old age pensions up to 40% of current earnings	1%	$200 0	$30

This measure would permit 60 percent of retirees—an estimated 6 million persons—to maintain living standards at 70 percent of their former permanent level. Assuming that those eligible have incomes in the lower 30 percent of the distribution, that 20 percent of them are unrelated individuals and that retiree families average 1.6 retirees each, then three million families would receive these benefits. Thus, 16 percent of the 19 million families with incomes in the lower 30 percent would gain income amounting to $1,248 (or 1.6 times the difference between 30 and 40 percent of 1983 median earnings), and the average gain for this income group is $200. At the 20th percentile, this increase raises the income ratio by 1 percentage point as compared with the 90th percentile.

The activity and its $30 billion cost are explained in more detail in Chapter 12.

Aid to depressed communities

This activity would enlarge opportunities for those living in depressed communities who would benefit from jobs, education and other opportunities offered. Its effect and cost are given below:

Activity	Age Adjusted Family Income Ratio: 20th to 90th Percentile	Income at Percentile: 20th 90th	Total 10-Year Cost (billions of 1973 dollars)
Aid to depressed communities	1%	$260 0	$171

The infrastructure, physical and human capital investments, and operating subsidies comprising this activity are estimated to increase the average income of consumer units in depressed communities by an amount equal to 10 to 15 percent of the 1983 average consumer unit income projected for the United States. This would add $1,375 on the average to the 1983 annual incomes of the eight million persons in the labor force in the depressed areas. For families in these areas, the average addition would be $2,100. If the incomes of the estimated four million families involved are assumed to be in the lower half of the distribution, then the average gain for the 32 million families in this income group is $260. At the 20th income percentile, this would add 1 percentage point in relation to income at the 90th percentile, which remains unchanged.

A detailed cost analysis for this activity can be found in Chapter 10.

Time-saving innovations

Implementing measures to reduce time spent on "consumer production" activities, especially those relating to household chores, would affect the income equality indicator as follows:

Activity	Family Income Ratio: 20th to 90th Percentile	Income at Percentile: 20th 90th	Total 10-Year Cost (billions of 1973 dollars)
Time-saving innovations	1%	$420 $420	$91

Increasing the mechanization of home activities and improving shopping, delivery, maintenance and repair, and other services is estimated to save an average of 319 hours per year for every person six years old and over. Twenty percent of this gain, or 6.7 billion hours, is assumed to be used for gainful employment at a level of productivity 60 percent that of the average base hour, or $7.50 per additional hour worked. Total output would thus rise by $50 billion, of which $35 billion represents the labor income share. Dividing the estimated $26.6 billion family portion of this among all families yields an additional $420 income for each. Although families at both the 20th and the 90th income percentiles are thus assumed to receive equal increments, the ratio of income of the former to that of the latter would rise by 1 percentage point.

This activity and its cost are discussed in Chapter 20.

COMBINED EFFECTS

The separate effects of the nine activities add up to a 12 percent increase in income at the 20th percentile relative to income at the 90th percentile. However, except for that of the private savings (13) and old age pension (14) activities, the output of activities is not generally additive. The maximum attainable net effect of all the activities would raise the ratio by 9 points from 25 percent to 34 percent.

The outputs and cost estimates are shown in Table 13-1. The remedial (6) and educational technology (7) activities overlap to produce a combined output of 2.4 points. The time-saving activity (28) would overlap only moderately with these four. This combination would produce an increase of 5.2 points in the family income ratio. A moderate offset also results when it is paired with day care (8): the income ratio is raised by 2.8 points. The job skills activity (11) overlaps in combination with these two, producing a total of 4.0 points. In combination with the remedial and educational technology activities, it yields a 3.6 percentage point increase at the 20th family income percentile. Adding day care (8), universal access to higher education (9) and aid to depressed communities (16) to these three yields an increase of 6.6 points. Another 0.4 of a point is gained by including the time-saving innovations with these six, bringing the total to 7.0 percentage points. A grand total yield of 9 percentage points results from full capacity use of all nine activities.

Table 13-1. Effects of Activities on Equality of Income

Activity*	Total Cost 1974-83 (billions of 1973 dollars)	Annual Income of Family Income at Percentile		Family Income Ratio: 20th to 90th Percentile
		20th	90th	
Base 1973	—	$6,250	$24,950	25 %
Base 1983	—	9,050	36,300	25 %
6. Remedial tutoring and augmenting educational inputs	$ 73	$ 550	$ 0	2
7. Improved educational technology and approaches	183	500	500	1
8. General day care for children	126	700	0	2
9. Universal access to higher education	273	480	0	1
11. Maintenance, updating and improvement of job skills	342	560	0	2
13. Private savings, insurance, pension plans	200	350	0	1
14. Old age pensions up to 40% of current earnings	30	200	0	1
16. Aid to depressed communities	171	260	0	1
28. Time-saving innovations	91	420	420	1
Combined Effects				
6,7. Remedial educational inputs; Improved educational technology	256	1,050	500	2.4
13,14. Private savings; Old age pensions	230	550	0	2.0
6,7,13,14. Remedial educational inputs; Improved educational technology; Private savings; Old age pensions	486	1,600	500	4.4
6,7,13,14,28. Remedial educational inputs; Improved educational technology; Private savings; Old age pensions; Time-saving innovations	577	2,020	920	5.2
8,28. Day care; Time-saving innovations	217	1,120	420	2.8
8,11,28. Day care; Job skills; Time-saving innovations	559	1,680	420	4.0
6,7,11. Remedial educational inputs; Improved educational technology; Job skills	598	1,610	500	3.6

Table 13-1. Effects of Activities on Equality of Income (continued)

Activity*	Total Cost 1974-83 (billions of 1973 dollars)	Annual Income of Family Income at Percentile		Family Income Ratio: 20th to 90th Percentile
		20th	90th	
Combined Effects				
6,7,8,9,11,16. Remedial educational inputs; Improved educational technology; Day care; Universal access to higher education; Job skills; Aid to depressed communities	$1,168	$3,050	$500	6.6
6,7,8,9,11,16,28. Remedial educational inputs; Improved educational technology; Day care; Universal access to higher education; Job skills; Aid to depressed communities; Time-saving innovations	1,259	3,470	920	7.0
Total, all activities	**$1,489**	**$4,020**	**$920**	**9.0**

*The numbers preceding the activities refer to their order in the matrix, Table 2-4.

14

Economic equality of races

OBJECTIVE

    Economic equality regardless of race.

INDICATOR

    Mean family income of blacks as a percentage of mean family income of whites.

Economic equality, as discussed in the preceding chapter, is viewed as a good, though not complete, representation of the broader objective of social equality. The basic concern with equality, of course, embraces all racial, ethnic, religious, occupational, geographic, and cultural groups. However, at present in the United States, the economic equality between blacks and whites is quantitatively perhaps the largest element of the concern with the equality of groups and is the only aspect of the equality of particular groups treated here, other than the economic equality of the sexes discussed in the next chapter. The black-white income equality may represent the broader concern rather well in the context of this chapter because the discretionary activities discussed are not race specific. But it would be desirable to develop a fuller set of indicators of group equality in the future.

    Although economic equality can be measured by a number of indicators, mean family income has been selected as the principal indicator. The mean income lends itself more readily to calculation and analysis than do the alternative measures, notably, median family income, per capita income, or median income or earnings of persons. (Median family income of blacks was 60 percent that of whites in 1968, while mean income was 64 percent. Another measure, an index of overlap of income distribution, was 0.71.[1])

---

1   The definition of income is that used by the Census Bureau; thus, it consists of money wages and salaries, earnings from self-employment, dividends, interest, social security benefits, public assistance, unemployment compensation, pensions, alimony, and other periodic income. These amounts represent income before deductions for taxes, social security contributions, etc. See Murray S. Weitzman, "Measures of Overlap of Income Distributions of White and Negro Families in the United States," U.S. Department of Commerce, Bureau of the Census, Technical Paper 22 (Washington, D.C.: U.S. Government Printing Office, 1970), p. 13, for a discussion of the different indicators.

BASE TRENDS

Indicator	1973	1983 Projection	Projected Change
Mean family income ratio, blacks to whites (trend values)	65%	70%	+5%

The projection of a base trend in the black to white mean family income ratio is based on the 1947-72 trend in a related series. See Chart 14-1. The black/white mean family income ratio is available only for the years after 1967. Since this is a short period when compared with the length of the projection period, the 1983 projection was made on the basis of trends in the nonwhite/white median family income ratio, which, for the period in which the two series overlap, shows parallel movement. The average annual increment of change in the trend for the period 1947-72, calculated from the two three-year averages at the beginning and the end of the period, respectively, when applied to the ratio of black to white mean family income averaged for 1970-72, gives a projection in that ratio of 70 in 1983. The 1973 estimate of 65 is an extrapolated trend value.[2]

Such a simple extrapolation of the past rates of change from a related time series was the only practical way to project the income ratio by race. After the present estimates were complete, however, two studies appeared which suggest possibilities of much improved analysis and projections of income trends

---

2   The actual value for the ratio in 1973 according to the data reported while this study was in press was 62. See U.S. Department of Commerce, Bureau of the Census, "Money Income in 1973 of Families and Persons," *Current Population Reports*, Series P-60, No. 97 (Washington, D.C.: U.S. Government Printing Office, 1975), p. 17. This amounts to a considerable departure from the projected trend value of 65 for 1973. However, the difference is wholly explainable by the level of the unemployment rate in 1973. Historically, the family income ratio has been quite sensitive to the current economic conditions, as can be seen from its fluctuations in Chart 14-1. The equation for the ratio of median family income nonwhite to white, calculated using data for 1948-73:

$$R = 58.0 \quad + \quad .457T \quad - \quad 1.64U \; : \quad R_c^2 = .72$$

$$(27.80) \quad\quad (7.70) \quad\quad (3.89)$$

with the income ratio, R, and the national unemployment rate, U, measured in percent and the time, T, measured in years, with 1948 = 1, gives a projected value of 68 percent for 1983 assuming a 4 percent unemployment rate. The t-ratios for the coefficients in the equation are shown in parentheses. This projection is equivalent to 69 percent for the ratio of mean incomes of black and white families.

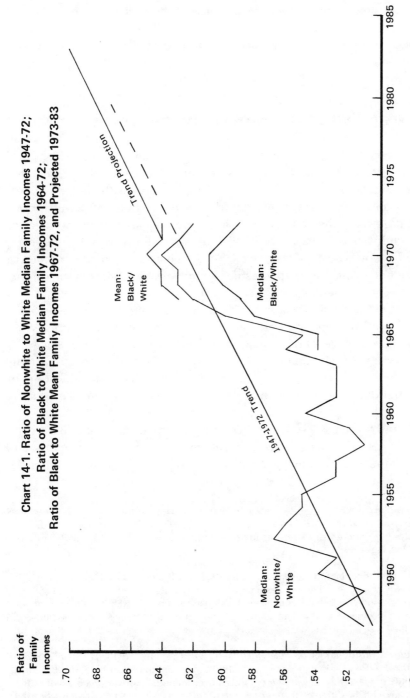

Chart 14-1. Ratio of Nonwhite to White Median Family Incomes 1947-72;
Ratio of Black to White Median Family Incomes 1964-72;
Ratio of Black to White Mean Family Incomes 1967-72, and Projected 1973-83

Sources:
U.S. Department of Commerce, Bureau of the Census. "Social and Economic Status of Negroes in the United States in 1970," 1971; Murray S.
Weitzman (U.S. Department of Commerce, Bureau of the Census), "Measures of Overlap of Income Distributions of White and Negro Families
in the United States," April 1970; U.S. Department of Commerce, Current Population Reports, P-60, Numbers 66, 75, 80, 85, and 87, December
1969, December 1970, October 1971, December 1972 and June 1973, respectively.

by race by focusing on the income experience of the individual age cohorts.[3] Implications of such an analysis for projections is explored briefly at the end of the following discussion of the characteristics associated with the income differences by race.

CHARACTERISTICS ASSOCIATED WITH INCOME DIFFERENTIALS BY RACE

Some factors relating to the differences in average incomes between black and white families are presented in Table 14-1. Unfortunately (and surprisingly), information about individual characteristics associated with income differences is available only singly.[4] We could find no analysis of simultaneous effects for more than one characteristic at a time. We also found no data for some characteristics that may have very large correlations with income level, notably occupation. Nevertheless, the table suggests some major sources of income differences and may help to estimate the possible effects of the various activities on economic equality of races.

As shown in the table, the largest single factor accounting for the disparity between mean family income of blacks and whites is education.[5] When income is adjusted for level of education, the income disparity is reduced by nearly 14 points, from 63.9 percent to 77.8 percent. (This adjustment is strictly for the number of years of schooling, not for the subject of education or institution attended, which, when included, might have still greater explanatory power.)

The second largest single factor, accounting for a difference of 8 percent, is type of income, i.e., the relative prevalence of income from property and self-employment. The third major factor is type of family, that is, whether the

---

3   Richard B. Freeman, "Changes in the Labor Market for Black Americans, 1948–72," *Brookings Papers on Economic Activity, 1: 1973* (Washington, D.C.: The Brookings Institution, 1973); Finis Welch, "Black-White Differences in Returns to Schooling," *The American Economic Review*, Vol. LXIII, No. 5, December 1973.

4   *Current Population Reports*, Series P-60, No. 66, 1969. A simultaneous analysis might make it possible, in theory at least, in addition to estimating more accurately the effects of the individually measured factors, also to explore the unexplained residuals for possible effects of the current racial discrimination on incomes. Past discrimination, on the other hand, is likely to be embodied in the difference in the levels of the explanatory factors themselves.

5   A recent study, Christopher Jencks et al., *Inequality: A Reassessment of the Effect of Family and Schooling in America* (New York: Basic Books, Inc., 1972), questions the importance of education for income equality by race. It has not yet been thoroughly examined. However, the present analysis dealing essentially with the differential rates of economic growth may reflect different relationships than those examined by Jencks et al., consisting largely of cross-section comparisons. The two more recent studies, by Freeman and by Welch (see note 3 above), which study time trends directly, suggest large effects of education on the differences in incomes by race.

Table 14-1. Ratios of Mean Incomes of Families and Persons,
Black as Percent of White, 1968

	Ratio of Mean Incomes	Difference from Mean	Percent of Gap*
Actual Mean Incomes Standardized for:	.639	.000	100.0
Education	.778	.139	38.5
Type of income	.719	.080	22.2
Family type	.709	.070	19.4
Regional location	.694	.055	15.2
Sex of earners	.684	.045	12.5
Age of head	.634	-.005	-1.4
Number of earners	.628	-.011	-3.3

*Effects are not additive.

Source: U.S. Department of Commerce, Bureau of the Census, "Income in 1968 of Families and Persons in the United States," *Current Population Reports,* Series P-60, No. 66 (Washington, D.C.: U.S. Government Printing Office, December 23, 1969).

family heads were male or female. Statistical adjustments for regional location and sex of earners reduce the gap by about 5 points each. On the other hand, adjusting for the differences in the number of family earners or for the age of family head actually increases the gap slightly.

These are, it should be repeated, comparisons based on single characteristics, standardized for one factor at a time. Until a more thorough analysis is available, it is possible only to speculate about the compound effects of these factors.

Perhaps most important are the differentials suggesting increasing equality with level of education past high school and a diminishing equality with age. If relative educational attainment is correlated with age, as the evidence suggests it is, then the projection of relative incomes to 1983, reflecting increasingly greater equality in educational attainment, would suggest a higher growth in the income ratio than a projection based on the widening relative income gap observed from cross sections of the two populations by age alone. The corresponding income trend rate may be assessed roughly in the following simplified manner. Given the 1973 income ratio of 65 percent on the trend basis, the income gap is 35 points. Of this, about 10 points represent income from business and property and the remaining 25 points represent mostly earnings. Assuming that property and business income is being equalized at 0.20 points a year (i.e., assuming an equalization period of 50 years) and that the remaining income is being equalized at a rate of 0.56 assuming a 45-year (average working life) equalization period, the annual increase in the ratio would be 0.76 points. Rounding the numbers, the increase over 10 years would be 8 points and the 1983 projection for the income ratio would be 73 percent. However, in the absence of a more detailed analysis which would permit construction of an income growth model, the extrapolation of trends in Chart 14-1 which yields a ratio of 70 percent is used for the projection for 1983.

DISCRETIONARY ACTIVITIES TO REDUCE INCOME DIFFERENTIALS BY RACE

A large number of activities identified in this study are likely to have an effect on the black/white family income ratio. They include activities in education, skill improvement, income maintenance, and community development.

Remedial tutoring and augmenting of educational inputs

The activity providing extensive remedial tutoring in high school would narrow the income differences between blacks and whites. The estimated effects and costs are summarized below:

Activity	Mean Family Income Black as Percent of White	Total 10-Year Cost (billions of 1973 dollars)
Remedial tutoring and augmenting of educational inputs	+1%	$73

Given that mean scores for black children in school are appreciably lower on the average than the mean scores for white children,[6] we estimate that remedial tutoring would:

---

6   U.S. Department of Health, Education, and Welfare, Office of Education, National Center for Educational Statistics, *Equality of Educational Opportunity*, The Coleman Report (Washington, D.C.: U.S. Government Printing Office, 1966).

• be translated by 1983 into higher average incomes for young blacks and equalization or at least substantial convergence of unemployment rates for all young workers. We assume that 10 percentage points (representing roughly the proportion of youth to all black workers) of the gap between black and white mean family income would be eliminated for 10 percent of the labor force, resulting in a 1 point decrease for the total population.

The component parts of this activity, estimated to cost $73 billion, are described in Chapter 7.

Employment and skill improvement activities

Three activities directed toward employment opportunities and job training are judged to affect the income differential between blacks and whites. The estimated effects and costs which are discussed below are summarized as follows:

Activity	Mean Family Income Black as Percent of White	Total 10-Year Cost (billions of 1973 dollars)
Employment and other opportunities for the young	+2%	$ 51
Maintenance, updating and improvement of job skills	+4	342
Specialized training for those outside mainstream of the labor force	+3	94

Employment and other opportunities for the young

The unemployment rate for black teenagers has commonly been 2 to 2½ times that for whites.[7] As shown in Table 14-2, labor force participation rates for black teenagers are also much lower relative to those of white teenagers. The participation rate, averaged for both sexes, was 40 percent among the nonwhite teenagers compared to 55 percent among the white age group.

---

7 During 1970, the teenage unemployment rate averaged 29.1 percent for nonwhites, more than double the rate for the white teenage group. This group typically has the highest unemployment rate in the labor force. See U.S. Department of Commerce, Bureau of the Census, "Social and Economic Status of Negroes in the United States in 1970" (Washington, D.C.: U.S. Government Printing Office, 1971), p. 49.

Table 14-2. Percent of Population Participating in the
Labor Force by Age, Sex and Race, 1972

Age Group	MALES		FEMALES	
	White	All Other	White	All Other
Teenagers	62%	48%	48%	32%
20-24	86	84	60	57
25-54	96	91	50	60

Source: U.S. Department of Labor, Bureau of Labor Statistics, *Employment and Earnings* (Washington, D.C.: U.S. Government Printing Office, January 1973), Table A-1, pp. 122-123.

Providing employment opportunities for teenagers not in school is thus estimated to:

● reduce unemployment rates among teenagers by 6-8 percent, raising participation rates to about 70 percent for males and 50 percent for females. (This estimate is based on the experience of the 20-24 age group, keeping in mind that more teenagers will be in school and not in the labor force.) We assume also that with the added job training that is a part of this activity, the wage gap between blacks and whites would be narrowed as well, so that the income ratio would be increased by 2 percent for the entire population.

The cost of this activity is calculated at $51 billion. Its components are described in more detail in Chapter 7.

Maintenance, updating and improvement of job skills

Out of the total differential in the family incomes of blacks and whites projected to be 30 percentage points in 1983, about 8 percent can be attributed to the relative prevalence of income from property and self-employment. Of the remainder, perhaps 10 points can be associated with the differences in the average earnings of workers in the mainstream of the labor force, and the rest with all other causes. A job skill improvement activity because of its comprehensiveness would have its largest effects on incomes of workers within the mainstream of the labor force. But it would also have important effects on the incomes of workers not in the mainstream who constitute a larger proportion of the black workforce. Such a massive activity would by 1983 in all likelihood:

● decrease that part of the family income gap which arises from differences in the mean earnings of workers to a significant extent. At this point, it is assumed that 20 percent of the gap associated with mainstream workers would be eliminated by such an activity, resulting in a 2-point increase of the income ratio for the whole population. Another 2-point increase would result from its effects on workers not in the mainstream of the labor force.

The cost of this activity is $342 billion and is described in Chapter 10.

*Specialized training for those outside
the mainstream of the labor force*

Providing specialized training for the 8.8 million projected to be outside the mainstream of the labor force in 1983 but desirous of employment (of whom 37 percent are estimated to be blacks and 63 percent whites), with a 57 percent success rate in securing employment among both blacks and whites, is estimated to:

● result in an average increase in income for this population of $2,940, yielding an increase of $515 in average family income of blacks and of $127 in that of whites (assuming 7.7 million black families and 56.3 million white families). The mean family income ratio of blacks to whites would rise by 2 percentage points.[8]

This activity, calculated to cost $94 billion, is discussed in Chapter 10.

Income maintenance activities

Three income maintenance activities are assumed to affect the disparity between black and white family income. Their effects and costs are summarized as follows:

Activity	Mean Family Income Black as Percent of White	Total 10-Year Cost (billions of 1973 dollars)
Private savings, insurance and pension plans	+1%	$200
Old age pensions at 40% of current median earnings	+1	30
Extended welfare program—tax and transfers to abolish poverty and near-poverty	+3	76

Private savings, insurance and pension plans

Analyses of relative savings by black and white families in comparable income situations suggest the existence of comparable savings rates.[9] The holdings of pensions and annuities, however, is assumed to be relatively less

---

8   An output of 3 appears erroneously in the matrix, Table 2-4.

9   Marjorie Galenson, "Do Blacks Save More?," *The American Economic Review*, Vol. LXII, No. 1, March 1972, p. 211.

prevalent among the black population than among the white population and, in view of higher average unemployment rates, the average pension entitlement is likely to be lower among the blacks. No figures were found on the subject, however, so the numbers are assumed. An activity designed to support greater rates of return and continuity of participation in private pension funds and greater rates of return and safety from inflation in individual savings behavior is thus likely to:

• have a differential effect on the black families, and is hence assumed to increase the mean family income ratio of blacks to whites by 1 percentage point.

This activity, calculated to cost $200 billion, is described in Chapter 12.

Old age pensions at 40 percent of current median earnings

The availability of old age pensions at 40 percent of current median earnings is assumed to:

• have a differential effect on the income of black families, and to increase the mean family income ratio by 1 percentage point.

This activity, estimated to cost $30 billion, is described in Chapter 12.

Extended welfare—taxes and transfers
to abolish poverty and near-poverty

Establishing a tax and transfer program to raise the incomes of the estimated 28 million poor and near poor in 1983 (of which, based on present proportions, 9 million are estimated to be black and 19 million white), with an assumed average benefit payment of $2,000 per family or $500 per person, is estimated to:

• provide an average benefit (assuming 56.3 million white families and 7.7 million black families with 3.3 members per family) of $234 per white family and $768 per black family. Average taxes levied to pay for the program are estimated (dividing the total among nonpoor families) at $286 per white family and $230 per black family, leading to a reduction of white family income, on the average, by $52 and an increase in black family income, on the average, by $538. Given 1983 projected mean family incomes of about $22,100 for whites and $15,500 for blacks, the net effect is to decrease the mean family income disparity by 3 percentage points.

The estimated cost of the activity is $76 billion. A more detailed description appears in Chapter 11.

Other activities

Two other discretionary activities are judged to have an effect on the disparity between the incomes of blacks and whites. They are summarized below:

Activity	Mean Family Income Black as Percent of White	Total 10-Year Cost (billions of 1973 dollars)
Aid to depressed communities	+2%	$171
Construction and maintenance of housing	+1	108

Aid to depressed communities

The total population of economically depressed communities in 1983 is estimated at 24 million, one-third of whom are assumed (on the basis of proportions of the total number of persons with incomes below the poverty minimum) to be black families and two-thirds, white families. Supplying aid to these communities is estimated to:

• provide a net income gain of $151 per family ($439 per black family and $114 per white family, based on an estimate of additional GNP generated), equivalent to an increase in the ratio of mean family incomes of 2 percentage points.

The cost of this activity is calculated at $171 billion. A more detailed description appears in Chapter 10.

Construction and maintenance of housing

The construction and maintenance of houses is assumed to increase the demand for workers, upgrade jobs in the construction industry, and increase the real income value of the resulting housing.

Assuming that 20 percent of blacks and 6 percent of whites live in deficient housing in 1983, this activity is assumed to:

• advance the mean family income ratio by 1 percentage point.

This activity costs $108 billion and is discussed in Chapter 16.

INTERACTIONS AMONG ACTIVITIES

The many combinations of activities that would serve to raise the black/white family income ratio are shown in Table 14-3. When the extended welfare activity (15) is combined with employment of the young (5), construction of houses (17), or aid to depressed communities (16), a 4 percentage point increase is assumed to occur in each case given the overlaps.

Maintenance of job skills (11) and specialized training (12) have substantial overlaps and thus together result in an output of 5 percentage points. When the extended welfare program (15) and aid to depressed communities (16) are combined with the above two activities, the output increases to 8 points. If the activities designed for the elderly (13, 14) are also included, the net effect is an increase in the income ratio of 10 points.

Job skills (11) and specialized training (12) combined with activities for the elderly (13, 14) produce a joint output of 7 points. If employment for the young (5) is included, one-half of that activity is considered redundant and the resulting increase is 8 points.

The total effect of all activities in combination is 12 points, which would raise the mean income ratio of black families to that of white families from the projected 70 percent to 82 percent.

Table 14-3. Activity Effects on Mean Family Income, Black as Percent of White

Activity*	Total Cost 1974-83 (billions of 1973 dollars)	Mean Family Income Black as Percent of White
Base 1973	—	65%
Base 1983	—	70%
5. Employment and other opportunities for the young	$ 51	+2
6. Remedial tutoring and augmenting educational inputs	73	+1
11. Maintenance, updating and improvement of job skills	342	+4
12. Specialized training for those outside mainstream of labor force	94	+3
13. Private savings and pension funds	200	+1
14. Old age pensions at 40% of current median earnings	30	+1
15. Extended welfare program—tax and transfer to abolish poverty and near-poverty	76	+3
16. Aid to depressed communities	171	+2
17. Construction and maintenance of housing	108	+1
Combined Effects		
5,15. Employment for the young; Extended welfare	127	+4
15,17. Extended welfare; Construction of houses	184	+4
15,16. Extended Welfare; Aid to depressed communities	247	+4
11,12. Maintenance of job skills; Specialized training	436	+5

*The numbers preceding the activities refer to their order in the matrix, Table 2-4.

Table 14-3. Activity Effects on Mean Family Income, Black as Percent of White (continued)

Combined Effects	Total Cost 1974-83 (billions of 1973 dollars)	Mean Family Income Black as Percent of White
11,12,15,16. Job skills; Specialized training; Extended welfare; Aid to depressed communities	$ 683	+ 8%
11,12,13,14,15,16. Job skills; Specialized training; Private savings and pensions; Old age pensions; Extended welfare; Aid to depressed communities	913	+10
11,12,13,14. Job skills; Specialized training; Private savings and pensions; Old age pensions	666	+ 7
5,11,12,13,14. Employment for the young; Job skills; Specialized training; Private savings and pensions; Old age pensions	717	+ 8
13,14,15,16. Private savings; Old age pensions; Extended welfare; Aid to depressed communities	477	+ 6
5,15,16. Employment for the young; Extended welfare; Aid to depressed communities	298	+ 5
11,12,13,15,16. Job skills; Specialized training; Private savings and pensions; Extended welfare; Aid to depressed communities	883	+ 9
13,14. Private savings and pensions; Old age pensions	230	+ 2
5,6. Employment for the young; Remedial educational inputs	124	+ 2
Total, all activities	$1,145	+12

15

Economic equality of sexes

OBJECTIVE

Economic equality of sexes.

INDICATOR

Hourly earnings of women as percentage of earnings of men.

BASE TRENDS

Indicator	1973	1983 Projection	Projected Change
Hourly earnings, women as percent of men	60%	60%	0%

Based on 1959 information from the Bureau of the Census, the mean hourly earnings ratio of women to men observed by Fuchs was 60 percent.[1] With statistical adjustments for differentials related to race, schooling, age, and city size, the ratio was 61 percent; with further adjustments for martial status, class of workers (self-employed, private wage and salary, government), and the length of trip to work, the ratio was 66 percent.[2]

Since the ratio of female to male earnings for full-time, year-round workers has remained around 60 percent in recent years, [3] we have used that ratio for the

---

1 Victor R. Fuchs, "Differences in Hourly Earnings between Men and Women," *Monthly Labor Review*, May 1971, p. 9.

2 Women, because of their greater responsibilities at home, often seek employment nearer home, where they will earn 26 percent less, other things being equal, than those who travel to their jobs. Ibid., p. 10.

3 U.S. Department of Commerce, Bureau of the Census, "Consumer Income," *Current Population Reports*, Series P-60, 1970–73. This has been true even though income differentials both by sex among blacks and by color between blacks and whites have narrowed appreciably over the 1959–69 decade. See Victor R. Fuchs, "Recent Trends and Long-run Prospects for Female Earnings," Working Paper No. 20 (New York: National Bureau of Economic Research, December, 1973).

1973 base and, projecting no change over the decade, for the 1983 base as well.[4]

DISCRETIONARY ACTIVITIES TO EQUALIZE EARNINGS BY SEX

The activities described below were identified as those which, over a 10-year period, are judged to have potential for a measurable effect on equality of earnings. Other discretionary activities that may have an effect on the relative income of women as compared with men do not affect the indicator used here. Pension and saving activities, for example, have no effect on hourly earnings. Activities to promote higher education increase productivity and earnings capacity of men and women but probably would have no special differential effect on the earning capacity of women.

General day care for children

Child-care facilities are assumed to make possible career continuity of women and opportunities in jobs that require nearly full-time work. This regularity of working hours and continuity of employment are assumed to increase the productivity of female relative to male workers and thus raise the relative earnings of women. The effect and cost are summarized below:

Activity	Earnings of Women as Percent of Earnings of Men	Total 10-Year Cost (billions of 1973 dollars)
General day care for children	+3%	$126

Providing day-care facilities in 1983 for all of the estimated 18 million children six years old or younger of 10 million women (assuming the birth of 3 million children per year for the preceding six years), is estimated to:

• give 10 million women the opportunity to participate in the labor market, of whom 60 percent would enter the labor force. We assume that, on the average, these 6 million women newly entering or increasing their labor force participation would increase the hourly earnings ratio by 20 percentage points. Projecting the labor force at 104 million with one-third women, this influx amounts to 17 percent of all women in the labor force. The increase of 20 percent

---

4 For all men and women, the comparative earnings used for the base are without adjustment.

for 17 percent of working women averages to 3 percentage points in unadjusted average hourly earnings of all women relative to men.

The activity consists of operating child-care systems (possibly eventually reaching the level of universality of present elementary school systems) for 10.8 million children in 1983 (60 percent of all children six years and younger). We assume a cost of a little over $2,000 per child per year, higher than elementary education but not as high as infant care in hospital-type nursing. The facilities and personnel would need to be built up over the 10-year period. The total cost for the period would thus be $126 billion, with 17 percent needed in the first subperiod. Such an activity would entail heavy public financing but private participation would be somewhat higher than in elementary schools. Therefore, while elementary schools are projected to be 90 percent publicly financed by 1983, the child-care activity is assumed to be 80 percent publicly financed.

Maintenance, updating and improvement of job skills

This activity aims at improving the functioning of the labor market by increasing opportunities for individuals to acquire skills and to find jobs or move into better ones. To the extent that either underdevelopment or undermaintenance of human capital exists more commonly among women than among men, there would be a differentially greater effect of this activity on the earnings of women. The effect and cost are summarized below:

Activity	Earnings of Women as Percent of Earnings of Men	Total 10-Year Cost (billions of 1973 dollars)
Maintenance, updating and improvement of job skills	+6	$342

A skill-improvement program is arbitrarily assumed to:

● increase the earnings of women relative to the earnings of men by 6 percentage points. No clearly defined basis exists for calculating the reduction of the earnings gap, so an assumed procedure has been adopted here, based on the existing differentials as reported by Fuchs.[5] The unadjusted ratios of female to male average hourly earnings for married women with spouse present,

---

5 Fuchs, "Differences in Hourly Earnings."

women who never married, and other women are assumed to remain the same in 1983 as they were in Fuchs' data for 1959. Relative to the earnings of men in comparable categories, projected ratios of mean hourly earnings for the three groups are thus 58 percent, 88 percent and 69 percent, respectively. We assume arbitrarily that the activity will reduce 20 percent of the earnings differential for the three groups. Weighting all these differentials in proportion to women in the labor force as of 1959 (the latest date for which data are available as of this writing) gives an overall increase in the earnings of women relative to the earnings of men of 6 percentage points.

This activity, estimated to cost $342 billion, is described further in Chapter 9.

Time-saving innovations

Although time-saving innovations are likely to expand discretionary time for both men and women, many are directed toward home operations and can therefore be expected to have some differential impact on the relative earnings of women. This would follow from the impact in increasing the relative productivity of women workers by making it more often possible for more of them to avoid job or career interruptions due to household responsibilities. A summary of the effect and cost is given below:

Activity	Earnings of Women as Percent of Earnings of Men	Total 10-Year Cost (billions of 1973 dollars)
Time-saving innovations	+2%	$91

The introduction of time-saving innovations in household management and service industries and the estimated resulting time savings of 319 hours per person (over six) per year are estimated to lead to:

- 62 percent of that free time being used for gainful employment, primarily by women, with a resulting increase in the hourly earnings of women relative to men of 2 percentage points.

The cost of this activity is calculated at $91 billion. It is described in detail in Chapter 20.

INTERACTIONS AMONG ACTIVITIES

The three activities, in combination, are estimated to raise the earnings of women relative to those of men by 11 percentage points (see Table 15-1). The overlap between activities is so small that the outputs are treated as additive. Child care (8) and skill improvement (11) could overlap in that some women might approach parity of incomes either through improved child-care opportunities or through improved functioning of the labor market, but the group that could take advantage of both activities is small. The possible offsets between child-care (8) and time-saving innovations (28) are also small because the populations affected overlap very little. It is possible that in combinations the three activities might even reinforce each other by, for example, supporting women's roles in the labor market or facilitating the transition from fragmented to more integral career patterns for women. For these reasons, and in the absence of concrete evidence to the contrary, we have treated the combined effects as additive.

Table 15-1. Effects of Activities on Equality of Income by Sex

Activity*	Total Cost 1974-83 (billions of 1973 dollars)	Earnings of Women as Percent of Earnings of Men
Base 1973	—	60%
Base 1983	—	60
8. General day care for children	$126	+ 3
11. Maintenance, updating and improvement of job skills	342	+ 6
28. Time-saving innovations	91	+ 2
Combined Effects		
Total, all activities (output additive)	$559	+11

*The numbers preceding the activities refer to their order in the matrix, Table 2-4.

16

Housing and neighborhoods

OBJECTIVES

    Adequate housing.

    Adequate neighborhood environments.

INDICATORS

    Percent of persons living in adequate housing.

    Percent of persons living in adequate neighborhoods.

The indicator for adequate housing is based primarily on the existing statistics for substandard housing while the indicator for adequate neighborhoods represents an attempt to assess judgmentally the proportion of the population residing in neighborhoods with one or more specific undesirable characteristic. It should be possible in the future to develop indicators of the quality of neighborhoods and perhaps also of housing based on actual measurements of the characteristics of neighborhoods and of housing, possibly combined by weights implicit in the actual behavior of individuals in choosing their residences. Such weights can be derived by means of the available research techniques.[1]

    Two measures of housing inadequacy, the lack of hot water and full plumbing within the unit and occupancy of the unit by more than one family, are the chief determinants of a substandard unit. Other factors can also make a unit inadequate, such as the existence of rats in the building, the lack of an elevator in working condition in a tall building, paints with lead content, etc., but

---

1 For an analysis of characteristics of housing and neighborhoods and the relative valuation of these characteristics estimated for a local area, see A. Thomas King, "The Demand for Housing: A Lancastrian Approach," *Household Production and Consumption,* Studies in Income and Wealth Vol. 40 (New York: National Bureau of Economic Research, 1975).

because statistics are not available for these, only a judgmental adjustment of data for substandard housing can be made.

Neighborhood adequacy is based here upon a judgmental evaluation of four physical characteristics—the condition of housing, the presence of basic facilities and amenities (such as lighting, garbage and litter pick-ups, street repair, etc.), the availability of recreational opportunities, and the presence of pollution, omitting at this time such social aspects as crime.

BASE TRENDS

Indicators	1973	1983 Projection	Projected Change
Percent of persons living in adequate housing	88%	92%	+ 4
Percent of persons living in adequate neighborhoods	77	87	+10

The 1973 estimate of persons living in inadequate housing is based upon data from the 1970 Census of Housing. Table 16-1 shows the percent of units lacking some or all plumbing (i.e., the unit does not have all three specified plumbing facilities—hot and cold piped water, flush toilet and bathtub or shower inside the structure—or the toilet or bathing facilities are for the use of occupants of

Table 16-1. Indicators of Substandard Housing in the United States, 1970

	Percent of Total Occupied Units
Year-round units lacking some or all plumbing[a]	6.9%
Occupied units lacking some or all plumbing[a]	6.0
Units with 1.01-1.50 persons per room[b]	6.0
Units with 1.51+ persons per room[b]	2.2

Source: U.S. Department of Commerce, Bureau of the Census, *1970 Census of Housing:* [a]"Plumbing Facilities and Estimates of Dilapidated Housing," Vol. 6, November 1973; [b]"Detailed Housing Characteristics," Vols. 1 and 2, 1971 (Washington, D.C.: U.S. Government Printing Office).

other housing units) and the percent of occupied units with more than one person per room. As shown in Table 16-1 for the country as a whole in 1970, 6 percent of all occupied units lacked complete plumbing while 6 percent (not necessarily the same 6 percent) were moderately crowded and 2 percent more heavily crowded. Allowing for other factors of inadequacy mentioned above but not measured by the available statistics, we assume that approximately 9.5 percent of all units, or 6.4 million units, were inadequate in 1970. As an additional allowance, we apply the same percentage to 1973. (For comparison, it may be noted that the 1968 estimate of substandard units in the *Second Annual Report on National Housing Goals* was 6,149,000 units. This estimate includes both the units lacking plumbing facilities and those that were classified as dilapidated.[2]) We further assume that 4 persons lived in each inadequate unit as contrasted to 3.1 persons per adequate unit (the national average), thus giving a total of 25.6 million persons or 12 percent of the population housed in inadequate units.

The 1983 projection of persons in inadequate housing is calculated by comparing the projected "need" for housing with the projected building rate. (This approach follows that of the federal government in estimating housing needs for the country.) Table 16-2 shows the projected need for housing by 1983, which we estimate to be 27.4 million units over the decade. The building rate used in the table is a projection made by Charles Schultze and others, based on economic and demographic factors such as the relationship between housing starts and the level of household formation, the price of housing relative to the general price level, changes in after-tax personal income, and monetary conditions.[3] The projection assumes favorable economic factors. The present calculation further assumes that 23 million housing units will be constructed by 1983, as projected by the Department of Housing and Urban Development.[4] (It should be noted that the present calculations have not been updated to reflect the most recent trends in household formation and housing construction.) We define the difference between the projected need and the building rate, 4.4 million, as the number of units inadequate in 1983. Again assuming 4 persons per inadequate unit, the number of persons in inadequate housing is thus estimated to be 17.6 million, or 7.6 percent of the population, in 1983.

---

2   U.S. Department of Housing and Urban Development, *Second Annual Report on National Housing Goals* (Washington, D.C.: U.S. Government Printing Office, 1970), p. 22.

3   Charles L. Schultze et al., *Setting National Priorities: The 1972 Budget* (Washington, D.C.: The Brookings Institution, 1971), pp. 285–286. The specific projection made in this chapter is obsolete as of early 1975 when this book is being printed. But the method and the general order of magnitude are probably still applicable.

4   *Housing Goals.*

Table 16-2. Projected Housing "Need," 1983

Category	Million Units
Increase in household formation	13.5
Inadequate in 1973	6.4
Becoming inadequate by 1983	3.5
Loss of stock	2.0
Increase in vacancies	2.0
Total	**27.4**

Sources: Charles L. Schultze et al., *Setting National Priorities: The 1972 Budget* (Washington, D.C.: The Brookings Institution, 1971), p. 283; U.S. Congress, *Second Annual Report on National Housing Goals*, 91st Congress, 2d Session, House Document No. 91-202 (Washington, D.C.: U.S. Government Printing Office, 1970), p. 67. The estimates made for 1970-80 are used here for 1973-83.

The 1973 estimate of persons living in inadequate neighborhoods is based on rough (since no hard data on this topic exist) quantitative estimates of four physical conditions in neighborhoods. First, we judge that 12 percent of the population live in neighborhoods made unsatisfactory by inadequate housing. This proportion is based on the assumption that the number of persons living in good neighborhoods but inadequately housed is offset by the existence of adequate housing in unsatisfactory neighborhoods. In addition, we judge that pollution, especially air and noise pollution, is sufficiently bad for 9 percent of the population to make their neighborhoods unsatisfactory. Lack of amenities, such as parks and recreation facilities, and the presence of visible disamenities, such as streets in disrepair, vandalized buildings and litter, are judged to make the neighborhoods of 5 percent of the population unsatisfactory. Altogether, allowing for the presence of several of these conditions in some neighborhoods, we estimate that 23 percent of the population lived in inadequate or unsatisfactory neighborhoods in 1973 and, conversely, that 77 percent did not.[5]

The 1983 projection is based on projections for housing, pollution and recreation trends, all of which we estimate to improve moderately over the decade. We therefore project the number of people living in satisfactory neighborhoods to increase by 10 percentage points, reaching 87 percent by 1983. The

---

5   Eighty percent of respondents in a 1971 survey of opinion on the quality of life carried out by the Institute for Social Research at the University of Michigan reported they were "satisfied" with their neighborhood. See Executive Office of the President, Office of Management and Budget, *Social Indicators, 1973* (Washington, D.C.: U.S. Government Printing Office, 1974), p. 200.

effects of the activities on housing are discussed next, followed by a discussion of the effects of activities on the quality of neighborhoods.

ACTIVITIES TO IMPROVE HOUSING

We have identified three discretionary activities to upgrade housing—the construction and maintenance of housing, the design and testing of new environments, and, with an indirect effect, aid to depressed communities.

Construction and maintenance of housing

This activity, consisting of single-unit starts, multi-unit starts, new mobile homes, and rehabilitations, summarizes the construction, rehabilitation and maintenance activities which would reduce the number of persons living in inadequate housing to zero. Its effect and cost are summarized below:

Activity	Percent of Persons Living in Adequate Housing	Total 10-Year Cost (billions of 1973 dollars)
Construction and maintenance of housing	+8%	$108

Constructing 1.9 million single housing units, 1.5 million multiple housing units and 0.8 million mobile homes and rehabilitating 0.5 million existing units by 1983 is estimated to:
 • increase the percentage of persons living in adequate housing by 8 percentage points to 100 percent.
The components and costs of this activity are summarized in Table 16-3. The components include:
 • the construction and rehabilitation of 4.7 million units, at an estimated total cost of $98 billion.
In 1970, the median price for a conventionally built new home was $27,000, which, according to the Department of Housing and Urban Development, was the price that more than four-fifths of all American families could reasonably afford to pay given prevailing interest rates.[6] We therefore assume a percentage

---

6 *Housing Goals*, p. 32.

**Table 16-3. Discretionary Activity Components:
Construction and Maintenance of Housing, 1974-83**

	Number of Units Involved (millions)[1]	Percent of Total No. of Units Involved	Unit Cost[2] 1973	Total Cost (billions of 1973 dollars)
Rehabilitations	0.5	9.7%	$ 8,800	$ 4.5
New single-unit dwellings	1.9	40.6	28,600	58.9
New multi-unit dwellings	1.5	31.7	18,200	28.5
New mobile homes	0.8	18.0	6,500	5.6
Research and development	—	—	—	5.0
Maintenance and repairs	—	—	—	5.0
Total	4.7	100.0	21,500	107.5

[1] Based on past experience, the national housing goals projection and Schultze's economic projection.

[2] Estimates from the *Second Annual Report on National Housing Goals,* Table C-3, p. 67.

Sources: Charles L. Schultze et al., *Setting National Priorities: The 1972 Budget* (Washington, D.C.: The Brookings Institution, 1971); U.S. Congress, *Second Annual Report on National Housing Goals,* 91st Congress, 2d Session, House Document No. 91-202 (Washington, D.C.: U.S. Government Printing Office, 1970), Table C-3, p. 67.

of subsidized new units and rehabilitations, with the subsidies amounting to $42 billion. The success of this activity depends on maintaining a substantial volume of new construction so that the subsidies would not simply be absorbed by the increased cost of existing housing, but would result in physical improvements;

- research and development, including construction and maintenance technology; housing unit design; materials; housing market operation; and management, legal and financial practices;
- repair and maintenance.

Of the $108 billion total cost, 46 percent is assumed to come from public funds and, because of fixed capacity in many elements of the construction industry, 29 percent is assumed to be needed in the first subperiod.

The design and testing of new environments and aid to depressed communities

Two additional activities would also have some effects on housing. These effects and costs are summarized below:

Activity	Percent of Persons Living in Adequate Housing	Total 10-Year Cost (billions of 1973 dollars)
Design and testing of new neighborhood, city and regional environments	+2%	$202
Aid to depressed communities	+;4	171

The design and testing of large-scale habitats in cities and neighborhoods, including new housing patterns, new zoning patterns, landscape development, and alleviation of major eyesores and pollution is estimated to:

• increase by 2 percentage points the number of persons living in adequate housing in 1983. (Only a small increase is assumed since the full effects of the activity would not be realized in 10 years.)

This activity, estimated to cost $202 billion over the decade, is described in more detail later in this chapter.

Providing aid to economically depressed communities, a long-term development program, is assumed to:

• increase by 4 percentage points the number of persons living in adequate housing.

This activity, calculated at $171 billion, is described in Chapter 10.

INTERACTIONS AMONG ACTIVITIES

The construction and maintenance of housing (activity 17) is specifically designed to increase the percentage of persons living in adequate housing to 100 percent in 1983. Therefore, any combination of activities that includes this activity would also produce the maximum output but at a greater cost. Aid to depressed communities (16) and the design and testing of new environments (18), in combination, are judged to have an overlap of 1 percentage point and therefore increase the percentage of persons in adequate housing by 5 percentage points. The output, cost and interactions of these activities are shown in Table 16-4.

ACTIVITIES TO IMPROVE NEIGHBORHOODS

Activities to substantially improve the quality of neighborhoods include the

Table 16-4. Effects of Activities on Percent of Persons Living in Adequate Housing

Activity*	Total Cost 1974-83 (billions of 1973 dollars)	Percent of Persons Living in Adequate Housing
Base 1973	—	88%
Base 1983	—	92
16. Aid to depressed communities	$171	+4
17. Construction and maintenance of houses	108	+8
18. Design and testing of new neighborhood, city and regional environment	202	+2
Combined Effects **		
16,18. Aid to depressed communities; Design and testing of new environments	373	+5
Total, all activities	**$481**	**+8 %**

*The numbers preceding the activities refer to their order in the matrix, Table 2-4.

**Since the activity designed for construction and maintenance of houses serves to increase the percent of persons living in adequate housing to 100 percent, any combination including this activity would also provide maximum output.

construction of new and maintenance of existing housing; the design and testing of new neighborhood and city environments; the provision of recreational facilities; the implementation of programs to improve the quality of air, water and land; and aid to depressed communities.

Design and testing of new neighborhood, city and regional environments

The full effect of this long-term activity to revitalize neighborhoods and cities and develop new metropolitan patterns would not be realized in the 10-year period. The effect and cost anticipated by 1983 are summarized on the following page.

The design and construction of whole, large-scale habitats that would include testing concepts of environmental design, evaluation of assumptions about economic development, industrial development, and migration prac-

Activity	Percent of Persons Living in Adequate Neighborhoods	Total 10-Year Cost (billions of 1973 dollars)
Design and testing of new neighborhood, city and regional environments	+10%	$202

tices, the design of component functional areas, enhancement of natural environment, the development of new patterns of transportation, recreation and education, is assumed by 1983 to:

• increase the percentage of persons living in adequate neighborhoods by 10 percentage points.

The components of the activity include:

• the design and construction of new towns and city areas, at an estimated cost of $38 billion;

• the design and testing of new apartment arrangements, at an estimated cost of $38 billion;

• the design and testing of new neighborhood arrangements, at an estimated cost of $90 billion;

• the design and testing of overall development schemes, at an estimated cost of $32 billion;

• research, development and component testing, at an estimated cost of $4 billion.

Of the total cost of $202 billion, 16 percent is assumed to be needed in the first subperiod and 50 percent is assumed to be public funds. (We assume that in general land preparation and other infrastructure costs would be covered by private investment.)

The reason for the relatively high cost of this "design and testing" activity is that in dealing with the entire residential area, much actual new construction appears necessary. Failure of many new residential approaches in recent years suggests that there exist great difficulties in developing such large-scale projects successfully.

Construction and maintenance of housing

We assume in this activity the elimination of substandard housing throughout the country, with a consequent improvement in neighborhood quality. The effect and cost of the activity are summarized below:

Activity	Percent of Persons Living in Adequate Neighborhoods	Total 10-Year Cost (billions of 1973 dollars)
Construction and mainte-nance of housing	+5%	$108

Upgrading the 2.9 million substandard housing units we estimate to be in low-quality neighborhoods (we assume that one-third of inadequate housing units are in good neighborhoods and two-thirds are in low-quality neighborhoods) is assumed to:

• increase the number of persons living in adequate neighborhoods by 5 percentage points.

This activity, estimated to cost $108 billion, is described in more detail earlier in this chapter.

Other activities

Three other activities are assumed to have an effect on neighborhood quality. The effects and costs are summarized below:

Activity	Percent of Persons Living in Adequate Neighborhoods	Total 10-Year Cost (billions of 1973 dollars)
Pollution control	+5%	$171
Recreation facilities in neighborhoods	+5	127
Aid to depressed communities	+5	171

Pollution control

Reducing the levels of air, water and noise pollution (the latter mainly in and around heavily populated residential areas) and cutting down on land pollution from solid waste disposal is assumed by 1983 to:

• increase the number of persons living in adequate neighborhoods by 5 percentage points.

The activity, estimated to cost $171 billion, is discussed fully in Chapter 17.

Recreation facilities in neighborhoods

Providing local parks, playgrounds and sports facilities within easy reach of residents is assumed to:

● increase the number of persons living in adequate neighborhoods by 5 percentage points.

This activity is estimated to cost $127 billion and is described in detail in Chapter 18.

Aid to depressed communities

Economic aid to depressed communities, designed in part to improve housing and neighborhoods, is assumed to:

**Table 16-5. Effects of Activities on Percent
of Persons Living in Adequate Neighborhoods**

Activity*	Total Cost 1974-83 (billions of 1973 dollars)	Percent of Persons Living in Adequate Neighborhoods
Base 1973	—	77%
Base 1983	—	87
16. Aid to depressed communities	$171	5
17. Construction and maintenance of houses	108	5
18. Design and testing of new neighborhood, city and regional environments	202	10
20. Pollution control	171	5
22. Recreation facilities in neighborhoods	127	5
Combined Effects		
16,18. Aid to depressed communities; Design and testing	373	11
17,18. Construction of houses; Design and testing	310	11
18,22. Design and testing; Recreation facilities	329	12
16,17. Aid to depressed communities; Construction of houses	279	6
16, 17, 20. Aid to depressed communities; Construction of houses; Pollution control	450	9
17,18,20. Construction of houses; Design and testing; Pollution control	481	12
16,17,18,20. Aid to depressed communities; Construction of houses; Design and testing; Pollution control	652	13
17,18,20,22. Construction of houses; Design and testing; Pollution control; Recreation facilities	608	13
Total, all activities	**$779**	**13%**

*The numbers preceding the activities refer to their order in the matrix, Table 2-4.

• increase the number of persons in adequate neighborhoods by 5 percentage points.

This activity, at a cost of $171 billion, is detailed in Chapter 10.

INTERACTIONS AMONG ACTIVITIES

All combinations of the discretionary activities discussed here affect to some extent the same populations and therefore yield less than the sum of their individual outputs. The interactions are summarized in Table 16-5.

Design and testing of the new environments activity (18) has the greatest output individually (a 10 percent increase) and, when combined with other activities, substantially offsets their effects. For example, when this activity is combined with aid to depressed communities (16), 80 percent of that activity appears to be redundant. When combined with the construction and maintenance of the housing activity (17), the overlap is again 80 percent. When combined with improved recreational facilities (22), the output is reduced by 60 percent. Similar overlaps exist among the other combinations of activities. The total output of all five activities is an increase in the number of persons living in adequate neighborhoods of 13 percent, the maximum possible since we postulated that 87 percent of the population would be living in adequate neighborhoods by 1983.

17

Pollution control

OBJECTIVE

   To reduce pollution.

INDICATOR

   Percent of population affected by bothersome pollution.

The choice of the indicator is based on the premise that in order to measure environmental quality (or pollution control) as a dimension of the quality of life, it is necessary to proceed from the physical measurements of environmental quality to a social measurement. Such a step is taken here even if only a very rough estimate can be made of the indicator. But no indicator exists as yet showing directly or indirectly the prevalence or the severity of the effects of pollution on people, although specific indicators for measuring particular types of pollution and standards for aggregating them into environmental quality indexes are being developed and continuously improved at a fairly rapid pace.[1]

   Quite substantial extrapolation from the available information is required to assess the number of persons affected by pollution, both with regard to the facts of incidence of the different types of pollution and with regard to the criteria adopted to consider the effects large enough to be counted. We have defined "affected" to include one or more of the following: repeated irritation; respiratory and other diseases related to pollution; perceptible decrease in the use of the outdoors or in its quality; and financial losses through increased cleaning costs, corrosion, decrease in real estate values, etc. This approach means, however, that both the indicator and the estimates of the effects of discretionary activities on it must be judgmentally postulated rather than directly derived from quantitative data.

---

1 Successive annual reports of the Council on Environmental Quality reflect these improvements. The materials in this chapter reflect the information in the third report: Executive Office of the President, Council on Environmental Quality, *Environmental Quality,* Third Annual Report of the Council on Environmental Quality (Washington, D.C.: U.S. Government Printing Office, August 1972).

SOURCES AND EFFECTS OF POLLUTION

The major sources, types and amounts of pollution in the United States have been broken down into four categories: air, water, solid waste, and noise. Table 17-1 shows our estimates of the population affected by the different kinds of pollution.[2] Since there is substantial overlap among individuals affected by the different types of pollution, and any one effect is sufficient for our population count, the figures have been adjusted for overlap within each category and among categories. Most of the estimates are based on data from the Council on Environmental Quality and on the population of various areas of the country.

The estimates for air pollution include persons who are frequently and for long periods of time exposed to smog or noxious substances in the air and who suffer damage to their persons or property. The water pollution estimates encompass those who experience deterioration in their drinking water, limitation of recreational opportunities, and the presence of bacterial or chemical hazards in water resources. Land pollution affects those with proximity to eye-sores—junk yards, dumps, strip mines—and those who are near contaminated soil. Infestation by vermin and exposure to obnoxious odors also are included in the definition of being affected by land pollution. Persons affected by noise pollution include those who have developed symptoms of discomfort such as difficulty in sleeping and the resulting tension and anxiety or physical impairment, which in some cases may even lead to loss of hearing.

We have based our estimates on the population of regions where substantial pollution exists. (The notes to Table 17-1 give the specific assumptions used.) Although the definitions and estimates are quite loose, we propose them as a basis for discussion. We believe that sufficient data exist or are being prepared on which to base future estimates of a social index of environmental quality. We also believe that not linking the pollution problem to people would be a more serious error in this type of analysis than inaccurate initial estimates of the populations involved.

BASE TRENDS

Indicator	1973	1983 Projection	Projection Change
Percent of population affected by pollution	62%	46%	−16

2   Information which became available after these calculations were made should permit a number of improvements in the derivations of such estimates in the future.

Table 17-1. Effects of Pollutants on Population, 1973

Primary Sources	Effects on Health	Type of Persons Affected	Number of Persons Affected (millions)		
			Unadjusted	Adjusted for Overlap within Environment (cumulative)	Adjusted for Overlap, All Environments (cumulative)
Air					
Internal combustion powered transportation	Contributes to incidence of emphysema, bronchitis & other respiratory ailments; linked to higher mortality rates from cancer & heart disease; eye irritation; "killer smogs"	Primarily urban dwellers and transportation workers[1]	75	75	
Stationary fuel combustion sources	See above	Urban dwellers[2]	20	80	
Industrial processes	See above	Urban dwellers[3]	20	90	90
Water					
Municipal sewage systems	Sources of typhoid, dysentery & salmonellosis; toxic substances	Persons affected by inadequate sewage treatment[4]	25	25	
Industrial wastes	Toxic substances	Persons located near primary industrial sources[5]	50	50	
Steam-electric power plants	See above	Assume 2.5% of population	5	52	115
Solid					
Agriculture	Breeding of flies & other disease-carrying insects; animal wastes can contaminate water supplies	Persons exposed to contaminated water and smells[6]	10	10	
Metropolitan solid wastes	Breeding of rats and flies which carry disease	Urban dwellers[7]	25	35	
Soil pollution:	Pesticides: Acute poisoning from highly toxic pesticides; accumulation in the body through the food chain	Rural dwellers and certain consumers	5	37	130

Table 17-1. Effects of Pollutants on Population, 1973 (continued)

| | | | Number of Persons Affected (millions) | | |
Primary Sources	Effects on Health	Type of Persons Affected	Unadjusted	Adjusted for Overlap within Environment (cumulative)	Adjusted for Overlap, All Environments (cumulative)
Soil pollution: (continued)	Radiation: High levels associated with cancer & leukemia; low levels—possible genetic damage	Mostly through contaminated water supply[8]			
Noise					
Motor vehicles, airplanes, drills and construction equipment; industry	Steady exposure to about 90 decibels can cause permanent hearing loss; temporary changes in man's physiological state constriction of smaller arteries, speeded-up pulse; might be a cause of hypertension or ulcers; emotional effects	Those with proximity to principal sources of noise[9] (number is assumed)	80	80	
Total					135

Source: *Environmental Quality,* First Annual Report of the Council on Environmental Quality, August 1970.

[1] From 1970 Census figures, 71,033,000 people live in 25 largest SMSAs. Estimate on the average that 75 percent either live or work in the city proper or in other parts of the SMSAs which are congested = 53.2 million affected by car exhaust. Seventy-five percent used since, although one might expect the proportion to be much smaller in some areas, it probably exceeds 90 percent in others. Assume rural population to be constant at 54 million and that only 10 percent of rural inhabitants suffer air pollution from highway traffic, etc. = 5.4 million. Population not of 25 largest SMSAs or of rural areas estimated to be about 79.9 million. Of these perhaps 20 percent experience smog = 16 million. Total = approximately 75 million people.

[2] The number of stationary fuel combustion sources nationally and in 298 metropolitan areas in 1967 is given in *Economics of Clean Air* (1971):

Source	Total No.	No. in 298 Areas	Percent of Total
Commercial-institutional heating plants (thousands)	999	952	95%
Industrial boilers (thousands)	307	256	83
Residential heating plants (millions)	58	47	81
Steam-electric power plants	516	387	75

Most of the pollution from these sources would affect the population in the 298 areas which was 166,882,000 in 1967. Allowing for overlaps among the different sources, we assume that 10 percent of this population is affected by pollution from stationary fuel combustion sources. With rounding, this would come to a total of approximately 20 million people.

Table 17-1. Effects of Pollutants on Population, 1973 (continued)

[3] The following information for 1967 about the number of sources of industrial air pollution is presented in *Economics of Clean Air Act:*

Source	Total No.	No. in 298 Areas	Percent of Total
Brick and tile	469	301	64%
Grain handling	11,124	4,098	37
Iron and steel	142	134	94
Petroleum refineries	256	199	78
Copper	19	10	53
Sulfuric acid	213	180	85

[4] Based on data from *Clean Water for the 1970's,* FWQA (June 1970). Sixty-eight percent of population have sewer systems = 138 million people. Forty-six percent of these have overloaded or inadequate treatment facilities = 63 million. Estimate the number of people affected often enough from the storm overloading or odors from excess runoffs and other inconveniences to be about 10 percent = 6.3 million. Seven percent of population with sewer systems have no treatment = 9.7 million. Of these, we assume 20 percent experience some inconvenience = 1.9 million. Thirty-two percent of population have septic tanks, leaching systems, etc. Of these, we estimate 25 percent are affected by pollution = 16 million. Total equals approximately 25 million people.

[5] The First Annual Report of the Council on Environmental Quality states that the greatest volume of industrial wastes is discharged in the Northeast, Ohio River Basin, Great Lakes states, and Gulf Coast states. Significant volumes are discharged in some areas of the Southeast and Pacific Coast states. Population estimates made from this information.

[6] The First Annual Report of the Council on Environmental Quality gives the following distribution of agricultural wastes: cattle in Midwest, West, Southeast; poultry in South and Mid-Atlantic states; hogs in Midwest and South.

[7] This estimate is slightly larger than previous estimates of urban dwellers since the Council on Environmental Quality reports that inadequate sanitation and garbage removal are listed as significant grievances by residents in 9 out of 20 cities surveyed by the National Advisory Commission on Civil Disorders.

[8] Based on a reasonable approximation. Assumed to be small since this type of pollution will occur largely in rural areas.

[9] It is estimated that approximately 40 million people are directly exposed to potentially hazardous noise while a total of 80 million people are in some way directly affected by noise sources. *Report to the President and Congress on Noise,* Environmental Protection Agency (March 1971).

The estimated reduction in the number of persons affected by pollution from 62 percent of the population in 1973 to 46 percent of the population in 1983 is based upon the assumption that present interest in environment problems and the demands for action will be sustained sufficiently throughout the decade to result in a net reduction in the number of persons affected by pollution.

The 1973 estimate is taken from Table 17-1; the 1983 projection is explained in Table 17-2.

Table 17-2. Estimated Number of Persons Affected by Pollution, 1973 and 1983, Assuming Base Trends
(millions)

Primary Sources	Number Affected in 1973	Number Affected in 1983		
		Individual Elements	Cumulative Adjusted for Overlap within Environment	Cumulative Adjusted for Overlap, All Environments
Air				
Internal combustion powered transportation	75	55^1	55	
Stationary fuel combustion sources	20	20^2	65	
Industrial processes	20	15^3	70	70
Water				
Municipal sewage systems	25	25^4	25	
Industrial wastes	50	40^5	45	
Steam-electric power plants	5	5^2	47	90
Solid				
Agriculture	10	10^6	10	
Metropolitan solid wastes	25	25^6	35	
Soil pollution	5	5^6	37	100
Noise	80	80^7	80	106
Total (millions)	130	—	—	106
(percent of population)	62%			46%

[1] We are projecting a significant reduction in the number of people affected by vehicle emissions: 27 percent. This is an area which has already attracted widespread attention. Fairly strict control standards have been proposed and some progress has already been made. However, the validity and usefulness of these standards have been questioned. Strict standards for the internal combustion engine may also be diverting research from exploring the possibilities of new types of engines which may, in the long run, have a much greater effect on pollution reduction. This, combined with the predicted increase in the number of vehicles, may make our projection somewhat optimistic. Fuel shortages encourage both relaxation of emission standards and reduced use of fuel and development of fuel-saving technology; thus, their net effect on pollution is uncertain.

[2] Due to the anticipated increase in demand for electric power, no reduction is projected in the number of people affected by pollution from stationary fuel sources and power plants.

[3] Expect a 25 percent reduction based on serious efforts aimed at major sources.

[4] Municipal sewage is a big problem which keeps increasing as more of the population live in urban areas, and investments to cope with it beyond the point of continuing present levels are not part of the trend.

[5] A 20 percent reduction is projected although this problem is closely tied to that of municipal sewage systems.

[6] It is assumed that a concentrated effort is needed to reduce the number of persons affected by solid waste pollution.

[7] There does not yet seem to be a large enough consensus about noise pollution to include in the base trends a reduction in the number of people affected.

DISCRETIONARY ACTIVITIES TO REDUCE POLLUTION

These activities concentrate on the problems that appear to be the most immediate and are oriented toward specific sources of pollution. They include both direct pollution-control measures and indirectly related activities. Since antipollution measures appear to involve a sharp up-turn in the marginal cost at some level of reduction, the capacity output of the activities has been defined at what we have judged to be levels of abatement which appear plausible for a 10-year period and attainable at a "reasonable" cost.

Pollution control

The pollution control activity consists of subactivity elements corresponding to the principal sources of pollution: vehicle emissions and industrial emissions (air pollution); sewage systems, industrial contaminants and land runoff (water pollution); solid waste; and noise. The estimated effects and costs for these subactivities are as follows:

Activity	Percent of Population Affected by Pollution	Total 10-Year Cost (billions of 1973 dollars)
Pollution control total	−29%*	$171
Air:		
Vehicle emissions	−17	56
Industrial emissions	− 7	30
Water:		
Municipal sewage	− 4	30
Industrial and energy plants	−13	15
Solid:		
Solid waste disposal	− 7	30
Noise:		
Noise	− 4	10

*Total has been adjusted for overlaps. See Table 17-3.

Vehicle emissions (air)

Assuming that, by 1983, pollution effects from motor vehicles will be reduced by roughly 30 percent as a result of base trends[3] and that the subactivity

---

3   The Council on Environmental Quality, in its Third Annual Report, estimated that vehicle pollutants can be reduced to governmental standards by 1975 at an average cost of $350 per vehicle (p. 289).

defined here would reduce the remaining effects by 70 percent,[4] we estimate that:

● the number of people affected by pollution would be reduced by 40 million (roughly 70 percent of the 55 million affected). In 1971, there were 92.2 million automobiles and light duty trucks and 6.1 million heavy duty gasoline trucks in the United States. This number is expected to increase by approximately 3 percent annually, to a total of 140 million vehicles in use by 1983.[5]

The components of the activity include:

● enforced reduction in exhaust emissions at an average cost of $350 per vehicle by 1976-77. Operating and maintenance costs could average $65 per vehicle per year.[6] The 10-year cost of the activity is estimated at $46.5 billion;

● a research and development effort, at an estimated cost of $5 billion;

● an organization and enforcement infrastructure, at an estimated cost of $5 billion.

The total 10-year cost is therefore calculated at $56 billion, 25 percent of which is assumed to come from public funds and the remaining 75 percent to be borne in the form of higher costs to families and businesses.

Emissions (air) by industrial and energy plants

Emissions from both energy plants sources and industrial processes are included here.

The Environmental Protection Agency in 1971 estimated reductions in emissions from stationary fuel sources achievable in 298 metropolitan areas by 1976, assuming the implementation of the Clean Air Act.[7] Allowing for slippages, delays in implementation and the usual underestimation of costs, we have assumed one-third of these projected reductions to be in the base trends for 1983.

The subactivity component geared toward industrial processes is based upon similar assumptions.

We estimate that:

● the number of persons affected by pollution will drop by 17 million.

The components of this activity include:

● enforced reduction of stationary fuel emissions by such means as switching to low-sulfur fuel, separating sulfur from oil and coal, and using stack gas cleaning devices at an estimated cost of $10 billion;

---

4   We have assumed a 70 percent efficiency for this subactivity.

5   More recent projections have lower rates of growth in the number of motor vehicles or in their mileage.

6   We assume that slippages and delays in the base trends could be alleviated substantially with an additional expenditure of $350 per vehicle, *Environmental Quality*, 1972, p. 289.

7   *Economics of Clean Air Act*, March 1971.

• enforced reduction of other industrial emissions, at an estimated cost of $20 billion.

Of the $30 billion total, 25 percent is expected to come from public funds, largely for research and development, planning and enforcement, and the rest from higher costs.

Municipal sewage (water)

Assuming tertiary treatment in the metropolitan area municipal sewage systems, we estimate:

• a reduction of 10 million in the number of persons affected by pollution. The activity includes:

• the installation of advanced sewage treatment systems in 6,000 municipal areas.[8]

The $30 billion total, it is assumed, would be publicly financed.

Industrial and energy plants (water)

The major concerns here are the discharge into streams, rivers and the oceans of oxygen depleting substances which destroy water life and cause putrefaction, and of various dissolved and suspended solids which include poisonous or otherwise destructive substances.

Energy plants may also affect water quality by causing "thermal pollution," i.e., permanent increases in the local water temperature leading to possibly undesirable effects on vegetation and animal life and such changes in local weather as generation of fog.

We estimate that implementation will:

• reduce the number of people affected by pollution by 31 million.

This subactivity includes improved sewage treatment systems at industrial and energy plants and revamped production processes that minimize waste discharge, at an estimated cost of $15 billion. (The cost estimate is based upon data from the Council on Environmental Quality, which foresees an expenditure of approximately $14 billion for similar activities over 10 years, divided as follows: $3.2 billion for investment; $6.4 for operating charges; $4.0 billion to control thermal pollution.[9] Twenty percent of the cost is calculated as public funds.

---

8 Committee on Pollution, National Academy of Sciences, National Research Council, *Waste Management and Control*, A Report to the Federal Council for Science and Technology (Washington, D.C.: National Academy of Sciences, 1966), p. 191.

9 Executive Office of the President, Council on Environmental Quality, *Environmental Quality*, First Annual Report of the Council on Environmental Quality (Washington, D.C.: U.S. Government Printing Office, August 1970), p. 43.

Solid waste disposal

Solid wastes are composed of residential, commercial, institutional, indus-trial, mining, and agricultural wastes. Mining wastes are generated by mineral and fossil fuel mining. Agricultural wastes include animal wastes, residues from harvesting and greenhouse wastes. Industrial wastes are composed mostly of industrial packaging materials refuse.

We estimate that this subactivity would:

• reduce the number of persons affected by pollution by 13 million.

This subactivity includes the modernization of trash collection; the use, where possible, of sanitary landfills rather than open burning; an increased utilization of recycling techniques; and a research program concentrating on the development of incinerators that minimize pollution and on electrostatic precipitators to control particulates. Also included is the development of new methods of control of nuclear power plant materials and waste disposal. The estimated 10-year cost is $30 billion, with at least 80 percent of the outlay coming from public funds.

Noise

Reducing noise pollution from traffic, airplanes, construction, and other industry is estimated to:

• reduce the number of persons affected by pollution by 10 million.

This subactivity would include the establishment and enforcement of noise standards; the avoidance of sonic booms and similar shocks; and research and development on quiet machines and building materials that disperse and abate noise. The estimated total cost is $10 billion, 50 percent of which would be from public funds.

The cumulative effects of the pollution control subactivities

The total cost of all pollution control subactivities is estimated to be $171 billion, of which 51 percent is assumed to be public and 14 percent to be required in the first period. These activities are estimated to reduce the number of people affected by pollution by 66 million, a drop of 29 percentage points in the percent of population affected, after adjusting for overlaps. The adjusted numbers and estimated costs are summarized in Table 17-3.

Basic environmental improvements

The components of the basic environmental improvements activity are broad in nature and are much more extensive than the specific pollution control activities. They aim at both the reduction of pollution and the preservation of natural balances.

A summary of the effects and costs appears below:

Table 17-3. Costs and Effects of Pollution Control Activity
Reduction in Number of People Affected, 1983
(millions)

Primary Sources	Unadjusted	Cumulative Adjusted for Overlap within Environment	Cumulative Adjusted for Overlap, All Environments	Total Cost (billions)	Percent Public
Air			48		
Internal combustion powered transportation	40[1]	40		$ 56	25%
Stationary fuel combustion sources	5[2]	42		10	25
Industrial processes	12[3]	48		20	25
Water			58		
Municipal sewage systems	10[4]	10		30	100
Industrial wastes	30[5]	25		15	20
Steam-electric power plants	1[2]	25		7	7
Solid			63	30	90
Agriculture	5[6]	5			
Metropolitan solid wastes	10[6]	12			
Soil pollution	2[6]	13			
Noise	10[3]	10	66	10	50
Total (millions)			66	$171	
(percent of population)			29%		51%

[1] Estimated reduction is fairly large since a major effort in the area should bring substantial results. Most of the beneficial effects will be in cities where large masses of people are concentrated.

[2] Less reduction in people affected was estimated for stationary fuel sources than for industrial processes since emissions from the former are tied to the rapidly increasing output of the electric power industry. Changes in technology (i.e., nuclear power plants) could further decrease the number of people affected by this type of pollution.

[3] Substantial progress can be made with existing technology and with that likely to be developed.

[4] The close relationship between the municipal waste problem and increase in populations means that the estimated reduction attainable in 1983 in people affected will be needed.

[5] A large reduction is estimated to be possible in this area because the sources are generally concentrated at easily identifiable sites.

[6] Numbers are assumed.

[7] Included under "industrial wastes."

Activity	Percent of Population Affected by Pollution	Total 10-Year Cost (billions of 1973 dollars)
Basic environmental improve-ments	−17%	$332

This activity consists of: rehabilitation of 50 bodies of water and their surrounding land areas; rehabilitation of 50 damaged land areas; development and installation of some circulating waste disposal systems; maintenance of a balance between resource supply and use; and environmental and conservation research and development.

Rehabilitation of bodies of water

Rehabilitating bodies of water is intended to encompass both the redevelopment of bodies of water and of the surrounding waterfront areas. Major bodies of water such as the upper Chesapeake Bay and Lake Erie as well as their equivalents in smaller ones could be included. Within this activity, the ecological work would be expanded to cover entire lakes and streams and their area systems. Some relatively unpolluted waters would be set aside for preservation.

We estimate the subactivity to cost on the order of $150 billion. This is based on the assumption of rehabilitating 50 bodies of water and the surrounding land areas at $3 billion each. It is anticipated that approximately 80 percent of the expenditure would be from public funds.

Rehabilitation of land

Rehabilitation of damaged land is a comprehensive subactivity including remedies for the effects of strip mining and erosion; reforestation and planting future forest growth; and eliminating junk yards.

The effects of surface mining are aggravated by storm water gouging out additional gullies and filling streams with sediment. Replacement of topsoil and revegetation are both included in the activity. The implementation and continuation of such treatments as the planting of perennial grasses and desirable shrubs, contour plowing, terracing, and brush control to stabilize the soil and increase its water-holding capacity are necessary. The building of small dams and the institution of water control measures are also included. Selective logging and increased concern for the soils involved are necessary for improved forest management. Expenditures can be made to encourage better use of private lands suitable for tree production.

For 50 land areas, we estimate the combined cost of all of these programs at $60 billion, of which 90 percent would be public. It would probably take longer than 10 years for the effects of these programs to be fully realized.

Wastes

In general, there are three alternatives to the problem of wastes: using them again; rendering them innocuous; transporting them to places where they will not pollute the environment. Recycling has not been widely applied in the United States, and the technology of salvaging the valuable elements of collected mixed refuse is undeveloped. Lowering the costs of shredding equipment would not only increase the recycling of scrap metal but would aid in automobile disposal. Treatment processes are available for rendering wastes innocuous through the use of municipal and industrial treatment systems.

Certain salts will be virtually undetected in the ocean while the land can tolerate the insoluble salts of calcium, iron and aluminum. Land is also a good disposal area for agriculture and forest wastes since organic matter is decomposed by soil bacteria. Sludge, in the proper quantities, can be used to cover strip mining areas, and waste-waters can be disposed of through irrigation of raw crops and spraying over permanent pasture and forest lands.

We estimate the cost of waste disposal systems at $40 billion, of which 90 percent would be public funds.

Protecting essential resource balances

Maintaining the people-resource balance is another comprehensive subactivity dealing with the supply of water and other natural resources, regional ecological balances, and the supply of land where people want to live.

Processes for maintaining the fresh-water supply, such as sedimentation, filtration and aeration, regulation by storage and regional interchange are included. Some expenditures for flood control and irrigation projects are covered here although these are also included in the base. Possible courses of action to reduce depletion of mineral resources include: developing new technologies with less dependence on these resources; finding substitutes; improving extracting techniques and discovering new resources; recycling minerals.

The population problem in the United States is more a matter of too many people wanting to use the same land at the same time than a question of too many people for the food supply. Thus, most of the expenditure will be for planning and development, particularly of recreation and wildlife regions accessible to large numbers of people.

We estimate a total of $60 billion for all the people-resources programs, with public expenditures amounting to 90 percent and first period outlays to 25 percent.

Environmental and conservation research and development

Research and development concerned with land, water and materials use and reuse and maintenance of resource balances is assumed to cost $22 billion, all of which would be from public funds. Of this amount, $10 billion is estimated to be for environmental concerns and $12 billion for conservation.

Costs and effects of environmental improvement activity

The total cost for the environmental improvement activity is $332 billion , of which 90 percent is publicly financed. Most of the subactivities will take a considerable length of time. However, work must be begun early in order to achieve output in later years. Thus, we allocate 25 percent of outlays to the first period.

We estimate that this activity would reduce the number of people affected by pollution by 40 million, or 17 percent of the 1983 population, based on a comparison with the pollution control activity and its effects.

Other activities affecting pollution

Four other activities discussed primarily elsewhere in this study would probably also affect pollution. Their costs and effects are summarized below:

Activity	Percent of Population Affected by Pollution	Total 10-Year Cost (billions of 1973 dollars)
Aid to depressed communities	−2%	$171
Construction and maintenance of housing	−2	108
Design and testing of new environments	−9	202
Innovations in cars, roads and other transportation system components	−4	155

Aid to depressed communities, housing construction and environmental design activities all include upgrading of neighborhoods, which is assumed to affect pollution. (See Chapters 10 and 16 for more detailed descriptions.) Although many of the effects of the activities will take longer than 10 years to be fully realized, a fairly significant impact on pollution is expected. The innovations in cars, roads and other transportation system components are expected to affect primarily noise pollution and vehicle emissions (see Chapter 20).

INTERACTIONS AMONG ACTIVITIES

The activities discussed above have large overlapping effects. The same population is apt to be affected by some (or even all) of the activities. The offsets among activities are given in Table 17-4. Two important offsets occur among the pollution control activity (20) and the basic environmental improvements activity (21); and pollution control (20), transportation innovations (19) and the design of new neighborhoods (18). The combined effect of all activities is an estimated reduction in the percent of population affected by pollution amounting to 37 percentage points. The cost of all these activities is $1.1 trillion.[10]

Table 17-4. Effects of Activities on Pollution and Their Costs

Activity*	Cost 1974-83 (billions of 1973 dollars)	Percent of Population Affected by Pollution
Base 1973	—	62%
Base 1983	—	46
16. Aid to depressed communities	$ 171	- 2%
17. Construction and maintenance of housing	108	- 2
18. Design and testing of new neighborhood, city, regional environments	202	- 9
19. Innovations in cars, roads and other transportation system components	155	- 4
20. Pollution-control measures	171	-29
21. Basic environmental improvements	332	-17
Combined Effects		
20,21. Pollution control; Basic environmental improvements	503	-35
18,19. Design and testing of new neighborhoods; Innovations in transportation	357	-10
18,19,20. Design and testing of new neighborhoods; Innovations in transportation; Pollution control	528	-31
19,20. Innovations in transportation; Pollution control	326	-30
17,18,20. Construction of houses; Design and testing of new neighborhoods; Pollution control	481	-31
17,18,20,21. Construction of houses; Design and testing of new neighborhoods; Pollution control; Basic environmental improvements	813	-36
Total, all activities	**$1,139**	**-37%**

* The numbers preceding the activities refer to their order in the matrix, Table 2-4.

10   Since the present chapter was written, there have been several revisions of the cost estimates made by the Council on Environmental Quality and others. Many of these changes reflect general inflation and shifts in relative prices, as well as changes in the period covered by these estimates in addition to the substantive revisions. For the current set of estimates, see Executive Office of the President, Council on Environmental Quality, *The Fifth Annual Report of the Council on Environmental Quality* (Washington, D.C.: U.S. Government Printing Office, December 1974), pp. 173–179 and 219–225.

18

Outdoor recreation

OBJECTIVE

> *Active outdoor recreation.*

The present analysis is concerned with active outdoor recreation. Unlike indoor activities, it is the form of recreation not determined by individual choices alone but requires considerable public inputs. It is included as a goal here because recreation in all forms is manifestly a major objective of families and individuals, and a clearly articulated object of governmental activities at the local, state and national levels. Separate data on expenditures for outdoor recreation is not available. In 1972, expenditures for all recreational activities amounted to $50.6 billion (see Chapter 3), or roughly 6.7 percent of the total spending for all the goal categories considered in this study. Undoubtedly, a substantial proportion of this outlay was for outdoor recreation.

INDICATOR

> *Percent of those 12 years old and older participating regularly (120 or more episodes per year) in active outdoor recreational activities.*

"Regular" recreation should include more than occasional episodes of activities or those undertaken while on vacation. There is no scientifically derived consensus based on criteria for judging adequacy of outdoor recreation. A judgmental yardstick is offered here as a start for further discussion and analysis. The practical results probably are not too sensitive with respect to where exactly the criterion point is placed. Regular recreation is here defined as participation in any of the selected physical activities—swimming, boating, walking for pleasure, nature walks, playing outdoor games or sports, fishing, bicycling, camping, hiking, horseback riding[1]—120 times a year, or about every third day. Once

---

1 These are defined in U.S. Department of the Interior, Bureau of Outdoor Recreation, *Selected Outdoor Recreation Statistics* (Washington, D.C.: U.S. Government Printing Office, March 1971), p. 39.

every third day was chosen as a reasonable criterion on the basis of being a moderate figure between once a week, which is too infrequent, and a physical fitness standard which would require at least 250 episodes of vigorous exertion per year. Active outdoor recreation every third day does reflect participation of significant regularity and with some element of health promoting content.

Recreational activity and its intensity vary considerably among individuals as do both the physical and the economic access to different recreational facilities. The opportunity for recreation rather than participation in recreation is a more desirable point of measurement since it would explicitly allow for individual choice. For the time being, however, it is not practical to develop such an indicator. Even statistics on participation are undeveloped, and statistics on opportunities are almost nonexistent. Concern for freedom of individual choice is embodied here in the design of discretionary activities, which are limited to provision of facilities and information.

BASE TRENDS

Indicator	1973	1983 Projection	Projected Change
Percent of persons 12 and older participating regularly in active outdoor recreational activities	21%	54%	+33

The 1973 base and the 1983 projection were based on data collected by the Bureau of Outdoor Recreation.[2] Table 18-1 presents a summary of data for the number of recreational episodes in the active forms of summer recreation in 1960, 1965 and 1970.

To determine the base trends of the indicator, we have estimated the percent of the population participating in 120 or more recreational "episodes" a year. Those estimates were derived from the total number of recreation episodes, the average number per person 12 years of age and over, and a frequency distribution of participation which was put together from other but related data.

To project the number of recreational episodes, using the number of actual episodes for 1960 and 1970, we first excluded certain passive activities given in

---

2   Ibid.

Table 18-1. Active Outdoor Recreation Activities:
Number of Occasions of Participation for Persons 12 Years and Older
(Summer of 1960,1965 and 1970)

	Episodes (millions)		
	1960[1]	1965[1]	1970[2]
Swimming	672	970	1,423
Walking for pleasure	566	1,030	1,760
Playing outdoor games or sports	474	929	1,929
Fishing	260	322	515
Boating	159	220	388
Nature walks	98	117	337
Bicycling	228	467	1,035
Camping	60	97	355
Hiking	34	50	51
Horseback riding	55	77	177
Total episodes for the above activities	2,606	4,279	7,970
Total episodes adjusted for winter and year-round activities	2,953	4,848	9,030
U.S. population, 12 and over[3]	132.8	141.2	158.4
Adjusted episodes per person, 12 and over	22.2	34.3	57.0

[1] U.S. Department of Interior, Bureau of Outdoor Recreation, *Selected Outdoor Recreation Statistics* (Washington, D.C.: U.S. Government Printing Office, March 1971), p. 41

[2] U.S. Department of Interior, Bureau of Outdoor Recreation, *The 1970 Survey of Outdoor Recreation Activities* (Washington, D.C.: U.S. Government Printing Office, February 1972), p. 9.

[3] For 1960, U.S. Department of Commerce, Bureau of the Census, "United States Summary, Detailed Characteristics," *1960 Census of Population,* PC(1)-1D (Washington, D.C.: U.S. Government Printing Office, 1960), p. 1-358, Table 157; for 1965, U.S. Department of the Interior, Bureau of Outdoor Recreation, *The 1965 Survey of Outdoor Recreation Activities* (Washington, D.C.: U.S. Government Printing Office, 1965), p. 3; for 1970, U.S. Department of Commerce, Bureau of the Census, "Projections of the Population of the United States by Age and Sex: 1970 to 2020," *Current Population Reports,* Series P-25, No. 470 (Washington, D.C.: U.S. Government Printing Office, November 1971), p. 40, Table 2.

the surveys, confining ourselves to the active forms of outdoor recreation listed in Table 18-1 which, as shown there, totaled 2.6 billion episodes in 1960 and 8.0 billion in 1970. We then increased the number of recreational episodes in the table, which is based on summer activities, by 10 percent to include year-round activities, such as gardening, and then by 3 percent for winter sports. Divided by population 12 and over, these estimates give an average of 22 episodes per person in 1960 and 57 episodes in 1970, showing an annual growth rate of 10 percent in episodes per capita. An adjustment for shift in the age structure of the population from 1960 to 1970 between the age brackets with differing numbers of average annual recreational episodes would reduce this growth only to 9.6 percent, which is still a very high rate.[3] Such high growth rates cannot be sustained for long periods. Consequently, anticipating further demographic shifts and a reduced but still high growth in the number of recreational episodes per person, a growth rate of 7.4 percent is used to calculate the average number of episodes per person 12 and over per year for the dates after 1970. That number is thus estimated to grow to 71 in 1973 and 145 in 1983.

In order to calculate the proportion of the population with sufficiently regular recreational experiences, it is necessary to estimate the dispersion around these averages. Because no direct distribution of recreational episodes data was available, a frequency distribution (see Chart 18-1) was derived by combining the results of a survey study of intensity of engaging in outdoor recreational activity prepared in 1962 for a public commission[4] with the present estimates of the episodes per person.

Chart 18-1 was derived by extrapolating the present estimates of mean frequency of 71 and 145 episodes per person in 1973 and 1983, respectively, in accordance with the frequency distribution of point scores (which had a mean of 6.1 on its scale) in 1960, found in the Outdoor Recreation Resources Review Commission study. Because the two distributions of episodes are projected from the distribution of the score points, all three curves in Chart 18-1 are parallel.

Using the index of distribution of recreational experience shown in Chart 18-1 suggests that about 21 percent of the population 12 years and older had "regular" recreation in 1973. By 1983, that proportion is expected to expand to 54 percent. This dramatic increase for the decade is in line with observed rapid growth trends in outdoor recreation already discussed.

The volume of recreational activities depends on the number of persons having access to and the proportion actually using recreational facilities. Access, in turn, depends on institutional, financial and geographic considerations. Institutional association is a key to participation in recreation. For instance, high school and college students have access to facilities which are much more difficult for their parents to find.[5] Membership in recreational clubs, such as

---

3 High rates of growth, though not quite as high as the apparent growth rate in the outdoor recreation episodes per capita, can be noted also for some of the related series for the same period, 1960–70. Thus, the personal consumption expenditure for all recreation, including outdoor, grew during these years at 5.3 percent a year, while the number of visits to the federally owned recreation areas grew at 7.6 percent annually.

4 Prospective Demand for Outdoor Recreation (ORRRC Study Report 26), Report to the Outdoor Recreation Resources Review Commission by the Survey Research Center, The University of Michigan (Washington, D.C.: U.S. Government Printing Office, 1962).

5 In 1965, persons in the 12–17 age bracket averaged 87 recreational episodes per year, and those in the 18–24 bracket 36; the 25–44 and 45–64 groups averaged 25 and 17 episodes, respectively. Ibid., p. 19.

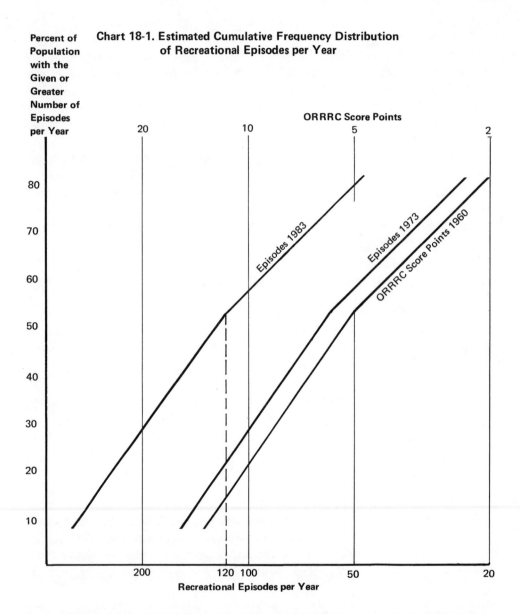

Percent of Population with the Given or Greater Number of Episodes per Year

Chart 18-1. Estimated Cumulative Frequency Distribution of Recreational Episodes per Year

ORRRC Score Points

Source: *Participation in Outdoor Recreation: Factors Affecting Demand among American Adults,* ORRRC Study Report 20, Report to the Outdoor Recreation Resources Review Commission by the Survey Research Center, The University of Michigan (Washington, D.C.: U.S. Government Printing Office, 1962), p. 11.

country, golf and swimming, depends to a great extent on income. For many forms of recreation, geography may be the main determinant of access. Some areas are rich in some or many recreational facilities while others are poor. For example, New York City has many miles of beaches and a fairly good access to winter sport sites while many cities have few natural advantages for outdoor recreation.

Access is also dependent on the quantity and quality of public inputs into recreation, whether direct (such as public facilities) or indirect (such as the recreational impact of zoning laws). The quality and effective capacity of facilities depends in turn on the balance among structures, staffing and "software." And, in any case, the use of existing facilities depends on the distance from them.[6]

ACTIVITIES TO PROMOTE ACTIVE OUTDOOR RECREATION

Seven activities discussed below affect the extent of participation in outdoor recreation.

Basic environmental improvements

Improving polluted bodies of water and their surrounding land areas, such as Lake Erie, Chesapeake Bay, Hudson River, Long Island Sound, and San Francisco Bay, would provide extensive new recreational opportunities and presumably increase the number of persons and number of groups taking part in recreational activities regularly. The effect and cost of this activity are summarized below:

Activity	Percent of Persons Regularly Participating in Recreation	Total 10-Year Cost (billions of 1973 dollars)
Basic environmental improvements	+4%	$332

We estimate that cleaning up 50 major bodies of water and rehabilitating 50 major land areas (which are assumed to be located in densely populated regions, the reason for their pollution in the first place) would:

---

6 Ruth P. Mack and Sumner Myers, "Outdoor Recreation," *Measuring Benefits of Governmental Investments*, ed. Robert Dorfman (Washington, D.C.: The Brookings Institution, 1965).

● open up regular recreational opportunities within reach of an estimated additional 15 percent of the population 12 years and older (30 million people). By assuming an effective marginal rate of recreational participation of 27 percent, which is one-half the average rate of 54 percent, the percent of population participating regularly is calculated to increase by 4 percent.

The cost of cleaning up 50 bodies of water is estimated to approach $150 billion and of restoring 50 land use areas $60 billion of the $332 billion total cost for the entire activity. A more detailed discussion of this activity appears in Chapter 17.

Recreational facilities in neighborhoods and localities

This activity includes extending and upgrading present recreational facilities plus developing natural environmental features, such as beaches or ski slopes, for a given locality.

The effect and cost are estimated to be:

Activity	Percent of Persons Regularly Participating in Recreation	Total 10-Year Cost (billions of 1973 dollars)
Local recreational facilities	+12%	$127

Through expanding and developing local recreational facilities, which is assumed to make recreational opportunities virtually universally available, we estimate that:

● of the 46 percent of the population projected not to have regular recreational experience in 1983, we again assume 27 percent will make regular use of the opportunities made available by the activity, thus increasing the percent of population participating in active outdoor recreation by 12 percent.

This activity is estimated to cost $127 billion, with 60 percent from public funds. Eighty percent of the expenditure would be made at the end of the development period.

Changes in health-related habits

This activity describes a scenario of a large-scale adoption by the public of fitness habits as part of normal personal hygiene and the provision by the public sector of the necessary infrastructure required to support such habits. This infrastructure includes building and maintaining health-oriented recreational facilities and providing educational and informational services. The effect and cost are summarized below:

Activity	Percent of Persons Regularly Participating in Recreation	Total 10-Year Cost (billions of 1973 dollars)
Changes in health-related habits	+25%	$64

We estimate that such a train of events embodying an intense public interest in physical fitness and an appropriate response to this interest from the governmental institutions would:

• increase the proportion of the population over 12 years of age regularly participating in outdoor recreational activities by 25 percent.

The cost of the physical fitness component of the activity is estimated to be $24 billion of the $64 billion for the full activity. A more detailed description of the activity appears in Chapter 5.

We recognize that this activity overlaps and in a large measure is an alternative to or a variant of the development of local recreational opportunities described earlier, but it embodies a rather plausible set of distinct developments, orientation and combination of inputs and is, therefore, treated separately.

Development of major parks and facilities

This activity is designed for output in two categories: recreation and conservation. The effects and costs are summarized below:

Activity	Percent of Persons Regularly Participating in Recreation	Total 10-Year Cost (billions of 1973 dollars)
Development of major parks and facilities	+5%	$80

Adding 50 major park areas is estimated to:

• increase participation in regular recreation by 5 percent of the population aged 12 and over. (The figure is low due to the distance many such facilities would be from population centers.)

The cost of the activity is calculated with reference to recent cost experiences of the National Park Service. Table 18-2 illustrates the costs for maintaining

**Table 18-2. National Park Service Budget for
Three National Parks, Fiscal Year 1972**
(dollar amounts in thousands)

National Parks	Acres (thousands)	Management Protection and Maintenance Cost	Construction Cost	Total Cost
Grand Canyon	673	$1,860	$ 921	$2,781
Yellowstone	2,213	4,714	3,838	8,552
Cape Cod	10	899	228	1,127

Source: National Park Service, unpublished data, 1971.

three major national parks in fiscal year 1972. The large operating cost differentials reflect variation in the intensity of use and in size.

A relatively new park in the Northern Cascades also suggests possibilities and costs of future developments. A full 80 percent of this 670,000 acre site was federally owned land before being designated a national park. In 1971, the project cost $1.4 million, 52 percent of which was operating costs.

The activity suggested here consists of:

● developing 50 major park areas, located primarily near densely populated areas. An average of 22,000 acres per park area and a total annual cost of $2,700 an acre are assumed (based on 1973 prices), including land acquisition, maintenance, operation, and improvement costs. The total yearly cost, $3.0 billion, is assumed to be 80 percent financed by public funds, allowing the remaining $0.5 billion for private development. Under such circumstances, there probably would also occur a major expansion in the private hotel and resort industry in those areas, which is implicitly treated as part of the base activities and not a discretionary activity;

● maintaining an infrastructure to support the major parks and to construct and maintain lesser public parks and facilities at an estimated annual cost of $1 billion.

The total cost for the decade is thus estimated at $80 billion, 80 percent of which would be publicly financed. Twenty percent of the cost would fall in the first subperiod, primarily for preparatory work and land acquisition.

Aid to depressed communities

This activity includes construction, development and servicing of recreational facilities in economically depressed communities, where there is generally a lack of developed opportunities for recreation. The effect and cost are summarized below:

Activity	Percent of Persons Regularly Participating in Recreation	Total 10-Year Cost (billions of 1973 dollars)
Aid to depressed communities	+5%	$171

Construction and maintenance of recreational facilities in depressed areas are estimated to:

• increase participation in regular recreation of one-third of the population of depressed and adjacent areas, thus increasing national participation by 5 percent.

The total cost of this activity is estimated at $171 billion. A more detailed description of the activity appears in Chapter 10.

Design and testing of new environments

The development of new types of living environments and the redevelopment of existing environments would necessarily include the development of recreational opportunities, be it simple bicycle paths or more intensely developed facilities such as gyms or swimming pools. The effect and cost of the activity are summarized below:

Activity	Percent of Persons Regularly Participating in Recreation	Total 10-Year Cost (billions of 1973 dollars)
New environments	+3%	$202

We estimate that the activity as designed would provide sufficiently attractive opportunities for regular recreation for about 25 percent of the population of whom 46 percent do not participate regularly in recreation. The activity thus would:

• with a 27 percent marginal utilization rate, add an additional 3 percent to the total population assumed to have regular recreation.

The cost of the full activity is estimated to be $202 billion. A more detailed description of the activity appears in Chapter 16.

Introduction of time-saving innovations

We judge that a considerable proportion of additions to discretionary time would be used for recreational purposes. The effect and cost of this activity are estimated to be:

Activity	Percent of Persons Regularly Participating in Recreation	Total 10-Year Cost (billions of 1973 dollars)
Time-saving innovations	+4%	$91

Adding an average of 70 minutes a day or 319 hours a year to the discretionary time of every man, woman and child over six years of age through time-saving innovations would, we assume:

● increase the percent of the population (12 and over) participating regularly in recreation by 4 percent.

The components of this activity include:

● innovations in home design and consumer goods resulting in reduced cleaning time, easier repair and maintenance, better food preparation and storage, and easier outdoor maintenance;

● development of large-scale service industries for repair, maintenance, shopping, and delivery;

● expanded R&D for development of time-saving devices.

The total cost of this activity is $91 billion with only 20 percent coming from public sector expenditures. This activity and its cost are described in greater detail in Chapter 20.

INTERACTIONS AMONG ACTIVITIES

A summary of the effects, costs and interactions among activities appears in Table 18-3.

All activities taken together, with allowance for overlaps, are estimated to increase recreational participation above that expected by a continuation of trends by 28 percent, giving a maximum total potential of 72 percent of population regularly participating in outdoor recreation.

Table 18-3. Effects of Activities on Percent of Persons
Regularly Taking Part in Outdoor Recreation

Activity*	Total Cost 1974-83 (billions 1973 dollars)	Percent of Persons 12 Yrs. and Older Regularly Taking Part in Recreation
Base 1973	—	21%
Base 1983	—	54
1. Change in health-related habits and patterns	$ 64	25%
16. Aid to depressed communities	171	5
18. Design and testing of new neighborhood, city and regional environments	202	3
21. Basic environmental improvements	332	4
22. Recreation facilities in neighborhoods	127	12
23. Major parks and facilities	80	5
28. Time-saving innovations	91	4
Combined Effects		
1,22. Health-related habits; Recreational facilities	191	26
21,22. Environmental improvements; Recreational facilities	459	13
16,18,21,22,23. Aid to depressed communities; Design and testing; Basic environmental improvements; Recreational facilities; Major parks	912	17
1,16,18,21,22,23. Aid to depressed communities; Design and testing; Basic environmental improvements; Recreational facilities; Major parks; Health-related habits	976	28
1,28. Health-related habits; Time-saving innovations	155	26
Total, all activities	**$1,067**	**28%**

*The numbers preceding the activities refer to their order in the matrix, Table 2-4.

19

Preservation

OBJECTIVE

> *To preserve significant natural and cultural objects and forms.*

INDICATORS

> *An index of the number of the various specific life, natural and man-made forms or objects maintained and preserved.*

There is no direct way to measure the achievement of preservation objectives. We have selected a hypothetical composite yardstick reflecting the number of diverse animal and plant species; of natural wonders, such as the Grand Canyon; of large natural preserves, such as the Adirondacks; and of significant man-made forms and structures, such as Mount Rushmore or Williamsburg, that are publicly or privately protected and maintained. We recognize that the measurement is inadequate but this formulation is provided as a beginning.

BASE TRENDS

Indicator	1973	1983 Projection	Projected Change
Index of preservation, 1973 = 100	100	110	+10

There is currently no national inventory of preservation of areas and structures. For the analysis, we have arbitrarily assumed a base of 1973 = 100 to reflect the scope of both public and private efforts.

We also assume that the level of preservation efforts will increase by 1983, and we project an increase of 10 percent. The actual content of this increase may include a number of smaller endeavors as well as major, widely recognizable projects.

DISCRETIONARY ACTIVITIES

Discretionary activities discussed below may have the capacity of raising the 1983 level of the preservation index by 60 points.

Expanding the number of major parks and facilities

This activity is expected to have its main impact on increased recreational opportunities. Its effect on preservation and costs is presented below:

Activity	Index of Preservation	Total 10-Year Cost (billions of 1973 dollars)
Major parks and facilities	+10	$80

We assume that an addition in the form of 50 major parks or an equivalent number of smaller facilities at a cost of $80 billion over the decade would effectively extend the scale of preservation efforts by 10 percent. A more detailed description of this activity appears in Chapter 18.

Preservation of wilderness, scenery and significant man-made structures

This activity would be devoted to preservation and enhancement of threatened species, natural landscapes and environments, and man-made objects of cultural or historic significance. The maximum extent to which the projected preservation efforts could actually be expanded over the next 10 years cannot be determined objectively at this time since even the present scope of preservation has not been measured or even well-defined. It is assumed here that, if preservation became a high priority objective, an intensive activity utilizing the existing and prospective knowledge and competence would raise the scope of preservation efforts by 50 percent. A summary of the effects and cost of such an activity is given below:

Activity	Index of Preservation	Total 10-Year Cost (billions 1973 dollars)
Wilderness, scenery and important structures	+50	$26

We assume that the activity would encompass the preservation of living species, of natural and man-made large-scale areas and of structures, with emphasis on beauty, historical, cultural, or scientific importance and environmental soundness.

This activity would include:

• areas to be set aside specifically for preserving endangered species. The cost could be judged from past experience. Thus, according to unpublished data from the U.S. Bureau of Sport Fisheries and Wildlife, federal expenditure to preserve the whooping crane was $103,000 in 1971; activities relating to the buffalo cost $270,000, and those relating to the bald eagle cost $142,000 plus $1.5 million for land acquisition;

• the restoration and preservation of historic and architectural landmarks. Cost estimates vary widely according to the type and size of the object and the volume of visitors. In 1971, for example, operating costs of the National Park Service for Mt. Rushmore National Monument amounted to $0.5 million, while the private program for the preservation of Williamsburg cost $28 million.

Acquisition of land in densely populated areas and its subsequent restoration would be expensive. Maintenance costs, while significant, would occur only after the initial work is completed. As an initial estimate, it is submitted that the acquisition costs (land and buildings) would amount to $12 billion over the 10-year period, other initial costs including restoration, construction and other preparations $8 billion, and operating costs $6 billion.

The activity is thus estimated to cost a total of $26 billion, with 75 percent of the expenditure in the last six years. Although some private conservationist efforts are included, primarily for historic and architectural landmarks similar to existing private projects, such as the one at Mount Vernon, the activity is assumed to require over 90 percent financing with public funds.

A SUMMARY OF EFFECTS

Both of these activities are treated as independent efforts with no overlapping effects. The output is thus additive. The combined effect of both activities, as shown in Table 19-1, is therefore estimated to be an additional 60 percentage points of the index reflecting the scope of objects of preservation to be maintained by 1983 at a 10-year total cost of $106 billion.

Table 19-1. Effects of Activities on Preservation of Life and Natural Forms

Activity*	Total Cost 1974-83 (billions 1973 dollars)	Index of Preservation of Life and Natural Forms
Base 1973	—	100
Base 1983	—	110
23. Major parks and facilities	$ 80	10
24. Preservation of wilderness, scenery and significant man-made structures	26	50
Combined Effects		
Total, both activities (output additive)	**$106**	**60**

*The numbers preceding the activities refer to their order in the matrix, Table 2-4.

20

Discretionary time

OBJECTIVE

>*Expanding the amount of discretionary time available to individuals.*

INDICATOR

>*Hours of discretionary time per person per year, for persons aged six years and over.*

Discretionary time is defined here as time free beyond that necessary for the maintenance of life and social functioning and available for discretionary use by individuals. It is measured by an indicator reflecting the amount of time spent by the population 6 years old and older on specific activities other than activities such as sleeping, eating, personal care, paid work, school, basic household chores and transportation which are considered not discretionary.[1] The estimates were made by modifying some of the allocations made in the existing time budget studies in estimating leisure time. Discretionary time is, thus, statistically a variant of the leisure time estimates. As a rule, entire categories are allocated to either discretionary or nondiscretionary activities. No attempt has been made to distinguish between discretionary and necessary components of these activities.

BASE TRENDS

Indicator	1973	1983 Projection	Projected Change
Discretionary time (hours per person per year)	2,111	2,199	+88

1 Time use of the preschool population under six years is not included since the concept of discretionary time used here is not applicable for such children. (School-age children are included.)

Historically, leisure time has been expanding. According to a recent analysis, 19th-century agricultural man lived an average of 35 years, four of which were leisure. The average American at the turn of the century lived 60 years and had an expectancy of 10 years of leisure. At present, with a life expectancy of 71 years, the leisure time expectancy over a lifetime is estimated at 25 years.[2]

The amount of leisure time available to an individual per year depends on employment status, number of young children in the family, age and educational participation. Estimates of leisure time are sensitive to definition. Much of what is considered work by many people may be considered leisure by others, and much of what is considered leisure in some calculations (for example, being involuntarily retired from work) could well be considered a chore in others. Nevertheless, the more refined definitions are not practical at present because basic analyses and even statistical observations on which they would have to rest do not exist.[3]

Estimates of time spent in leisure and nonleisure activities for 1965-66, are shown in Table 20-1. These estimates made by John R. Robinson were used to determine the base trends for 1973 and 1983. Three adjustments were made to bring the calculations in line with the concept of discretionary time employed here, one for time of illness and impairing disability, another for time spent in eating which we considered a nondiscretionary activity, and the third for time spent in school.

The 1973 and 1983 estimates were projected from the numbers in Table 20-1 on the basis of assumptions of trends in working time,[4] of productivity changes in household work,[5] and of changes in the composition of the population.[6] The resulting estimates are 2,111 hours of leisure per person in 1973 and 2,199 hours in 1983. The 1973 and 1983 figures were calculated as follows:

---

2   Geoffrey Moore and Janice Neipert Hedges, "Trends in Labor and Leisure," *Monthly Labor Review*, February 1971, p. 6.

3   Discussion of the different existing data as well as an analysis of observed changes may be found in John R. Robinson and Philip Converse, "Sixty-six Basic Tables of Time Budget Data for the United States" (Ann Arbor: Institute for Social Research, 1966), and in Angus Campbell and Philip Converse, eds., *The Human Meaning of Social Change* (New York: Russell Sage Foundation, 1971).

4   Working time for employed individuals has decreased little since 1950 and less since 1960. See Moore and Hedges, "Trends in Labor and Leisure," and Campbell and Converse, *Human Meaning of Social Change*, Table 4, p. 45.

5   A partial indicator of increases in productivity of home operations is the increase in labor force participation of women from 20 percent in 1900 to 43 percent in 1970. Increased participation also correlates with reduced family size and improved health.

6   With the decrease in retirement age, increase in life expectancy and improvement of health conditions, availability of leisure increased especially for older people.

Table 20-1. Amount of Time Devoted to Leisure and Nonleisure Activities by Type of Activity and Type of Individual, 1965-66
(hours per year)

Time Use	Employed Men[1]	Employed Women[2]	Housewives	Average for the Three Groups
Total Nonleisure	5,875	6,169	6,147	5,989
Sleep	2,774	2,738	2,738	2,738
Work for pay	1,440	782	22	720
Care of self	537	564	478	524
Transportation	734	564	368	567
Household and children	243	1,260	2,283	1,222
Shopping	147	261	258	218
Total Leisure	2,885	2,591	2,613	2,771
Eating	618	406	485	517
Visiting	488	746	847	691
Reading	301	188	245	255
Entertainment	98	108	62	87
Sports	74	14	12	73
Radio	48	43	12	36
Motoring	16	14	18	14
Clubs	48	43	74	59
Television	853	580	460	647
Miscellaneous	341	449	398	392
Population in the group as percent of U.S. population 6 years and older	27%	15%	20%	62%

[1] Arithmetic average of three groups: executives and professionals; white collar; labor.

[2] Arithmetic average of two groups: white collar and labor.

Sources: John R. Robinson, "Social Change as Measured by Time Budgets," paper presented at American Sociological Association meetings, San Francisco, 1967, cited in Philip H. Ennis, "The Definition and Measurement of Leisure," in Eleanor B. Sheldon and Wilbert E. Moore, *Indicators of Social Change* (New York: Russell Sage Foundation, 1968), p. 555; U.S. Department of Commerce, Bureau of the Census, *Current Population Reports,* P-25, No. 359 (Washington, D.C.: U.S. Government Printing Office, February 20, 1967); U.S. Department of Labor, Bureau of Labor Statistics.

Note: Assumes employed men work, on average, 40 full-time weeks per year at 7.2 hours per work day; employed women, 40 weeks at 4.6 hours a day for 4.25 days per week; and housewives, 40 weeks at 0.2 hours per day and 2.75 days per week. These assumptions are based on estimates from Bureau of Labor Statistics data. Totals for all categories were then forced to add to a grand total of 8,760 hours (24 hours per day x 365 days).

Adjustments	1966	1973	1983
Total leisure time of employed men, employed women, and housewives (from Table 20-1)	2,771		
Minus:			
Eating time (considered a nondiscretionary activity)	−517		
Illness	−113		
School	−212		
Plus:			
20 percent more leisure for the 38 percent of persons who are neither employed workers nor housewives	147		
Total discretionary, 1966 estimate	2,076		
Plus:			
Gains from estimated decrease of one hour per work week for total population, per decade	—	+35	+50
After 1973, gains from reduced child care time due to care services and birth rate decline (5% of the time requirement in Table 20-1 for household and child care adjusted for proportion of population engaged in child care)	—	0	+38
Total discretionary	2,076	2,111	2,199

DISCRETIONARY ACTIVITIES TO INCREASE FREE TIME

The activities described below represent ways to diminish nondiscretionary uses of time. Several of the activities discussed were not designed exclusively or even primarily to expand leisure time, yet they have that effect. Also, the opportunities for increasing the availability of discretionary time through reductions in working time usually would reduce incomes. Reductions in income are treated as costs analogous to expenditures for other activities. By this treatment, the difficulties of calculation involved in dealing with activities having positive and negative effects simultaneously are thus avoided.

Some of the problems of limited leisure opportunities arise from the distribution—or perhaps maldistribution—of leisure, in the sense that some persons have a great deal while others have very little. (Or that the same person may have a very uneven amount of discretionary time at different times during his life.) This situation is not treated as a distinct concern but, rather, is taken into consideration in the design of the activities.

Improvements and innovations in transportation

Time savings through improved transportation systems, primarily through the avoidance of wasted time, increases in speed and improvements of connections, appear to be a major way in which to expand discretionary time. Four distinct subactivities for reducing transportation time requirements have been identified. Their effects and costs are summarized below:

Subactivity	Discretionary Time (hours per person per year)	Total 10-Year Cost (billions of 1973 dollars)
Improved design, operation and repair of automobiles	+ 9	$ 26
Street and highway innovations	+31	45
Efficient rapid transit in major cities	+19	64
Taxi fleets	+12	20
Total	+71	$155

Improvement in design, operation and repair of automobiles

There are three principal ways in which a time savings can be effected through improvements in the automobile system: (1) avoidance of breakdowns and the resulting loss of time by passengers; (2) fewer indirect time losses for other cars, e.g., cars behind those which break down; and (3) diminished frequency and duration of repair work.

We estimate time losses in 1983 of:

● 2.5 hours per person per year due to breakdowns requiring service calls. The number of service calls in 1966 was 69 million.[7] Assuming that the direct loss was four hours per case, and that the average passenger load (population six years and older) was 1.5, there was a six-hour loss per case, or a total of 414 million hours during the year. With a 1966 population, six and over, of 170 million, that loss amounts to 2.5 hours per person per year. It is assumed that the same ratio will apply to 1983;

---

7   *1968/Automobile Facts/Figures*, Automobile Manufacturers' Association, 1968, p. 67.

● 7.5 hours per person per year for breakdowns and collisions that do not involve service calls, which are assumed to be three times more frequent than breakdowns with calls;

● 8.8 hours per person per year for time loss of persons involved indirectly in breakdowns (cars behind the broken down car, etc.), assuming a time loss of five hours per year for cases involving service calls and 3.8 hours per year for those not involving service calls;

● 4.8 hours per person per year for repair and maintenance not involving breakdowns. Repair and maintenance time not involving breakdowns is assumed to be 10 hours per vehicle, which, for the 100 million vehicles expected for 1983, yields 1 billion hours. With a population of 207 million (six and older), 4.8 hours of time are lost per person.

We postulate that 40 percent of these time losses are avoidable, thus reducing time loss from automobile breakdown and repair in 1983 by 9 hours per person per year (40 percent of 23.6).

The components of this activity include:

● research and development to improve the design of vehicles and of maintenance and repair plants, at an estimated cost of $5 billion;

● upgrading the maintenance industry through improved training of personnel, introduction of new equipment, and establishment of a necessary regulatory infrastructure, at an estimated cost of $11 billion;

● changes in the design of automobiles for better performance and the introduction of standardization of parts and components, estimated to cost $10 billion.

The total cost of this activity, an estimated $26 billion, would be mainly privately financed—and may be more than offset by reduced total transportation costs. Public outlays amounting to only about $2 billion of the total would be required for the regulatory activities and part of the R&D. All but $2 billion of total expenditures would be concentrated in the second subperiod.

Improvements and innovations in road and highway systems

This activity aims at reducing travel time requirements through improvements in transportation system design, traffic flow management and efficiency of vehicle use. The major innovative developments to be considered here consist of measures to increase the efficiency of commuter traffic (which could include computerized information systems to extend the possible range of mutually beneficial transactions in car-pooling and ride-sharing and the introduction of less synchronized hours of work to improve traffic flows), measures directed toward cars and drivers (such as the introduction of "packaged traffic control systems" to trace traffic flows and guide traffic patterns accordingly), and measures to reduce time required for long-distance travel (which might include automated highways over certain heavily traveled sections of the highway system).

Introducing innovations along these lines by 1983 is estimated to:
- cut 9 hours per person per year on work trips (18 hours per member of the labor force, which is one-half the population over six);[8]
- cut 9 hours per person per year from long-distance automobile trips for weekends, vacations, and other purposes (52 trips at 10 minutes each);
- cut 13 hours per person per year in nonwork local trips.

The estimated total cost of the reduction in time required for long-distance road transportation is on the order of $23 billion. Automating 1,000 miles of highway system, for example, assuming the necessary technological developments not yet in existence would be made,[9] at a cost of $10 million per mile, would amount to a total cost of $10 billion. Guidance devices installed in 70 million automobiles, trucks and buses, at an average cost of $100 per vehicle would require a total outlay of $17 billion. And supporting R&D is estimated to cost $6 billion.

The activity would also include capital and operating innovations permitting time and resource economies through modal integration and connections in long-distance travel.

The cost of reducing time requirements for commuting, making intermodal connections and other mainly local transportation is estimated to be on the order of $22 billion, which, for example, might cover installing and operating 100 traffic information and guidance systems at $200 million each, plus $2 billion for technical development.

Thus, the total cost for the activity is calculated at $45 billion. Public outlays for R&D and part of the construction and operating expenses (for example, for pilot projects and operating deficits) are estimated at $15 billion. Three billion of the total cost would be needed in the first four years for R&D, pilot projects and start-up costs.

Rapid transit systems in large metropolitan areas
Constructing rapid transit systems combining subways with bus lines operating on exclusive right-of-way roads in large metropolitan areas, and improving existing lines is estimated to:
- save an average of 15 minutes per trip for 16 million passengers in 1983, or a total of four billion hours per year. For the total population of 207 million aged six and over in that year, the saving will thus amount to 19 hours per person per year.

---

8   The effects of staggered work hours, which we assume could cover 70 percent of all work trips by 1983, are included here.

9   Leonard A. Lecht, *Goals, Priorities, and Dollars: The Next Decade* (New York: The Free Press, 1966), p. 179.

The estimate is calculated from a trend projection of 12 billion passengers in 1983 and an additional 4 billion passengers due to the activity. This reversal of the downward trend in mass transit riders[10] is projected to result from the combination of such factors as higher gasoline prices and the availability of highway funds for urban transit.

The total cost for this subactivity is calculated at $64 billion. This amount includes $7 billion in public outlays, primarily to cover operating deficits. An outlay of $3 billion would be needed in the first four years for planning and start-up costs.

Taxi and limousine systems

We postulate that the introduction by 1983 of a secondary network of scheduled and by-call limousine and taxi services,[11] especially in high density areas and at peak times, supplementing existing systems, would:

● give a time saving of 12 hours per person per year, assuming regular use of the system by 10 percent of the population six years and older (with regular use defined as 10 trips per week for 50 weeks of the year), a 1983 population (aged six and over) of 207 million, and an average savings of 15 minutes a trip for the 10 billion trips a year.

The cost of this subactivity is derived from load factor, operating hours and unit cost assumptions. Assuming a load factor of five, comparable to the existing factor for limousine services, and 10 billion trips a year gives 2 billion vehicle trips. Assuming the average duration of a vehicle trip to be 20 minutes, the number of vehicle hours is 670 million. We assume, further, direct labor costs of $11 an hour, direct operating and vehicle costs of $2 an hour, and overhead (including start and idle time and communications costs) of another $2 an hour. The resulting cost estimate is $10 billion a year at capacity level. Such a system requires a comparatively short phasing-in period once the decision, planning and conceptual phases have been completed. Assuming one-third of capacity operation in the first year (1981 in this case), two-thirds in the second, and full capacity in the third year, the total cost for the 1983 output, equivalent to two years of full capacity operation, is $20 billion.

Of the total, the public sector cost is estimated at $4 billion, consisting of roughly one-third operating and capital cost subsidies, one-third public maintenance of the communications and regulatory infrastructure, and one-third R&D

---

10   The number of passengers was 17.2 billion in 1950 and 7.3 billion in 1970; see U.S. Department of Commerce, Bureau of the Census, *Statistical Abstract of the United States: 1972*, 93d edition (Washington, D.C.: U.S. Government Printing Office, 1972), p. 554.

11   Some of the technical aspects of such a system are described in Sumner Myers, "Technology and Urban Transit," *Looking Ahead* (Washington, D.C.: National Planning Association, November 1966), and "Poor People–Poor Transportation," *Looking Ahead* (Washington, D.C.: National Planning Association, September 1968).

for communications systems and development of a low-cost vehicle for this purpose. Since the lead time is only two years, no outlays are entailed in the first 4 years of the 10-year period.

Summing up for all subactivities, of the $155 billion total cost, 18 percent is calculated as public funds and 5 percent is estimated as needed in the first subperiod.

Reduction in working time

This activity represents an increase in discretionary time through increases in vacation time or other reductions in work time (e.g., a shorter work-week or work-day) of a magnitude equivalent to three weeks a year. The effect and cost of the activity are summarized below:

Activity	Discretionary Time (hours per person per year)	Total 10-Year Cost (billions of 1973 dollars)
Reduction in working time	+60	$107

Reducing work time is estimated to:
● increase discretionary time by 120 hours for each member of the labor force, or by 60 hours per person six years and older.

The cost of this activity is calculated as a reduction of GNP, given an assumption for the elasticity of product with respect to the reduced man-hours. In these calculations, the reduction in working time is chargeable, conceptually, to the discretionary funds allocated to social costs. A reduction of working time by three weeks amounts to 6 percent. A straight 6 percent reduction of the 1983 GNP of $2,033 billion would amount to a GNP decrease of $122 billion in 1983, and correspondingly smaller amounts for earlier years of operation of the activity. We assume that, because of the resulting more effective use of capital and a corresponding increase in the productivity of time worked, and because the discretionary time increment probably would be financed in part by cutting less productive work, the actual displacement of GNP would be only 40 percent of the proportionate amount, or $48.8 billion for 1983.[12] The 10-year period cost

---

12   Edward F. Denison (assisted by Jean-Pierre Poullier), *Why Growth Rates Differ, Postwar Experience in Nine Western Countries* (Washington, D.C.: The Brookings Institution, 1967), pp. 59–64, contains an extensive discussion of productivity offsets to reductions in work time per year, citing a wide range of cases and studies. The present assumption is consistent with this range.

is simply assumed to be $107 billion on the basis of a 4-year build-up to introduce three weeks vacation in 4 equal percentage increments. The government share of the cost would be 20 percent, corresponding to its share in employment. All of the cost would fall in the second subperiod.

Time-saving innovations

This activity is intended to reduce time spent on "consumer production" in general and household chores in particular. Its effect and cost are given below:

Activity	Discretionary Time (hours per person per year)	Total 10-Year Cost (billions of 1973 dollars)
Time-saving innovations	+319	$91

In addition to saving time, many of these innovations would probably also save money, thus contributing to the economic welfare of the consumers. But only time savings are included in the analysis at present.

Increased mechanization of home activities and improvements in the service industries, including shopping and delivery services, inventory control services, and maintenance and repair services are, by our best judgments, estimated to:

• have the potential for a time gain of 70 minutes a day for adults or 319 hours a year for every man, woman and child over six years of age. Table 20-2 shows the distribution of reduced time requirements for specified major elements of household work on which the estimated time savings are based, i.e., food preparation, cleaning, shopping, building and appliance maintenance, and outdoor maintenance and repairs.

The meaning of the time gains needs to be clarified. For a large number of persons, such activities as home maintenance, especially outdoor maintenance and repair, and shopping are a form of recreation. If one interprets the categories of work as having chore and recreational, or even creative, elements, the time gains then represent opportunities to change work from a chore into something desirable or to use the free time in another fashion.

The components of this activity include:

• the introduction of innovations in home operations, such as appliances and materials designed to reduce cleaning time and to permit easier home repair and maintenance, more effective food preparation and storage, and easier maintenance of the outdoors by home owners. We assume an average expenditure of $650 per household unit during the period for such innovations, or a total

Table 20-2. Present and Reduced Time Requirements for Specified Household Chores

Household Chore	Time Required, as Shown in the 1954 and 1965-66 Studies (hours per person per year)	Possible Savings, 1983	
		Min. per Day Adults (18 & Over)	Hrs. per Yr. Pop. 6 & Over [1]
Total household chores	1,185	70	319
Food preparation	237[2,3]	10	45
Cleaning	529[2]	30	137
Shopping	91[2]	5	23
Maintenance and repair[4]			
(excluding automobiles)	328[2]	25	114
Indoor belongings	n.a.	5	23
Building	n.a.	15	68
Outdoor	n.a.	5	23

[1] Figures in preceding column were multiplied by .75 to conform to the definitions and the population base used here and then converted to hours per year.

[2] Spring 1954. Source: Sebastian de Grazia, *Of Time, Work, and Leisure* (New York: Twentieth Century Fund, 1962), p. 422.

[3] Eating time of 438 hours (1965-66) has been subtracted from eating and food preparation time. Source: Eleanor B. Sheldon and Wilbert E. Moore, *Indicators of Social Change* (New York: Russell Sage Foundation, 1968), p. 555.

[4] Time savings from improved automobiles and maintenance were discussed under "Transportation improvements."

cost of $58 billion for the decade. This figure includes only the net increment beyond the normal expenditure trend for household cost;

• developing large-scale servicing systems (based on expanded markets for such services) for repair, maintenance, shopping, and delivery, at an estimated cost of $26 billion;

• R&D efforts for the development of time-saving devices, services and systems, at an estimated cost of $7 billion.

The total cost is therefore calculated at $91 billion. The bulk of the activity is assumed to originate and be funded within the private sector, only 20 percent of the total cost coming from public expenditure, and that largely for supportive research and certain subsidy elements to make services generally available. Only 8 percent of the cost is incurred in the first subperiod.

Changes in health-related habits

This activity is aimed at improving health through changes in behavior. The effect and cost are given below:

Activity	Discretionary Time (hours per person per year)	Total 10-Year Cost (billions of 1973 dollars)
Changing health-related habits	+57	$64

Decreasing the number of disabled by 7.7 million (by substantially reducing smoking, alcoholism, accidents, and drug abuse and improving nutrition and fitness) is estimated to:

• add 57 hours per person (over six years old) per year of discretionary time, assuming that each person who does not become chronically disabled gains an average of 1,550 hours of discretionary time.[13]

The estimated cost of this activity is $64 billion. A more detailed discussion of the effects and components of the activity appears in Chapter 5.

Health services related to specific conditions

This activity consists of expanded efforts at diagnosis, treatment and prevention of three major conditions—arthritis, mental illness and cancer. The effect and cost of the activity are summarized below:

Activity	Discretionary Time (hours per person per year)	Total 10-Year Cost (billions of 1973 dollars)
Health services related to specific conditions	+53	$66

Reducing the number of disabled by 7.1 million (mostly by reducing disabilities primarily from arthritis and mental illness) is estimated to:

• add 53 hours per person (over six years old) per year to discretionary time, assuming, as above, that each person who does not become chronically disabled gains an average of 1,550 hours of discretionary time.

This activity is estimated to cost $66 billion. Its component parts are described in detail in Chapter 5.

---

13   We estimate the reduction in the number of disabled under six to be negligible.

General day care for children

The estimated effect and cost of introducing general day care for all children of day care age is summarized below:

Activity	Discretionary Time (hours per person per year)	Total 10-Year Cost (billions of 1973 dollars)
Day care	+117	$126

Providing general day care is estimated to:

● free 117 hours per person per year for discretionary use. This estimate is based on time spent in child care and household chores shown in Table 20-1. Of the 1,222 hours shown for household work and child care together, it is assumed that just over half or 55 percent (672 hours) is spent for child care and the remainder in household work. Of the 672 hours, 30 percent is subtracted to account for time spent with older children, leaving 470 hours per year in time spent with children of day-care age. We assume that 60 percent of these children would be in day-care centers as a result of full operation of the activity. It is further assumed that two-thirds of the time spent with children would be saved by the children's participation in outside day-care activities. The 40 percent not attending day-care centers would thus require 188 hours of care, and the 60 percent attending would require 93 hours of care, leaving a gain in discretionary time of employed men and women and housewives of 189 hours. Since these groups represent 62 percent of all persons six years or older, we estimate the effect of the activity on the latter population to be 117 hours per person per year.

The cost of this activity is expected to be $126 billion during the decade. A more detailed description of the day-care activity is given in Chapter 15.

COMBINED EFFECTS

There are no significant interactions among activities and the output is additive (see Table 20-3). Implementation of all activities affecting free time is thus estimated to raise the number of hours of discretionary time per person per year by 677 hours, to a total of 2,876 hours in 1983.

Examined on a cost per hour basis, the transportation activity is the most expensive ($10.55 per hour in 1973 prices). The time-saving innovations activity is the least expensive (about $1.40 per hour) and accounts for 47 percent of the total time gained. The cost per hour of all six activities is $4.35.

Table 20-3. Effects of Activities on Discretionary Time

Activity*	Total Cost 1974-83 (billions 1973 dollars)	Hours per Person per Year
Base 1973	—	2,111
Base 1983	—	2,199
1. Change in health-related habits and patterns	$ 64	57
2. Health services related to specific conditions	66	53
8. General day care for children	126	117
19. Innovations in cars, roads and other transportation system components	155	71
27. Reduction in working time	107	60
28. Time-saving innovations	91	319
Combined Effects		
Total, all activities (output additive)	**$609**	**677**

*The numbers preceding the activities refer to their order in the matrix, Table 2-4.

21

Science

OBJECTIVE

Discovery and diffusion of scientific knowledge.

INDICATOR

Number of scientists and engineers engaged in basic research.

The indicator represents the level of basic scientific effort. It is thus a measure of input; no direct measure of the output of science is feasible, at least at this time, especially at the level of basic science. Additional indicators which would measure the diffusion of scientific knowledge or the public understanding of science have not been developed in the context of the present study, which is limited to an indicator of the real level of scientific effort.[1] Basic research is viewed as representing efforts directed to the production of scientific knowledge as distinguished from its communication and diffusion, mainly through teaching, which constitutes the other principal activity of scientists, and also as distinguished from the production of technological knowledge through applied research and development activities directed toward specific fields of application.[2]

Professional manpower in basic research, it was decided, is preferable to a measurement of expenditure for science (which would introduce relative income trends and relative use of other inputs into the measure) or the number of scientific publications issued (which would be less complete and less stable in content and also would not permit as clear a distinction between basic and applied research as the manpower data).

---

1 Such indicators, however, are the subject of an ongoing NPA study by the author, "Indicators of the State of Science and Research," which is expected to be completed in 1975.

2 Applied research and development are treated in the present study as elements of the various discretionary activities oriented to various specific objectives.

BASE TRENDS

Indicator	1973	1983 Projection	Projected Change
Number of scientists in basic research (thousands)	81	139	+58

The number of scientists engaged in basic scientific work has been recorded for a number of years by the National Science Foundation. Data on the number of scientists in 1966, its extrapolation to 1973 and projection to 1983 are given in

Table 21-1. Basic Data and Projections Regarding the Number of Scientists in the United States, 1966,1973 and 1983
(thousands)

Scientists	1966	1973	1983
All fields	417	569	1,053
All fields, Ph.D.s	154	254	427
All in basic research	67	81	139
Ph.D.s in basic research	38	53	87
Percent of all scientists in basic research	16%	14%	13%
Science degrees awarded during the year:			
Doctorate	9	15	20
Masters	30	39	50
Science degrees as percent of all degrees:			
Doctorate	49%	43%	39%
Masters	21%	15%	15%

Sources: All fields, 1966: National Science Foundation, *Employment of Scientists and Engineers in the United States, 1950-66,* NSF 68-30 (Washington, D.C.: National Science Foundation, 1968); 1973 extrapolated on the basis of the 1966-70 growth rate, using unpublished 1970 data from the National Science Foundation; all fields, projected to 1983 by extending projected 1966 to 1975 trend, using 1975 projection from U.S. Department of Labor, Bureau of Labor Statistics, "Occupational Employment Patterns for 1960 and 1975," *Bureau of Labor Statistics Bulletin,* No. 1599 (Washington, D.C.: U.S. Government Printing Office, December 1968), p. 182.

Breakdown (for all data except that on degree awards) is based on proportions and projection of proportions from the National Science Foundation register of scientific and technical personnel.

Data on higher degrees awarded in science are from the Office of Education, National Center for Educational Statistics.

Table 21-1. While the definitions of categories in the table are subject to interpretation, the present formulation shows there were 67,000 scientists engaged in basic research in 1966, and we estimate 81,000 for 1973.

The 1973 estimate is based on the 1966-70 growth rate of research scientists, as shown in NSF data. The 1983 projection is based on the 1966-75 trend in research scientists, using NSF data and Bureau of Labor Statistics projections.[3]

Presumably, if scientific research were to be pursued intensively as a social objective, a much larger number of scientists could be engaged in basic work, since only 14 percent of all scientists have been working in basic research while science degrees have constituted 43 percent of all doctorates and 15 percent of all masters degrees granted (see Table 21-1). The potential supply of qualified and interested talent is presumably quite large and growing. With sufficiently strong incentives, the number of research scientists projected for 1983 could theoretically be tripled—or even more than tripled.

In view of this supply potential, the maximum feasible increment in the number of active basic scientists is more likely to be governed by the capacity rate of science to absorb new scientists by providing them opportunities for real and productive scientific pursuits than by the supply of potential scientists. There exists no basis for estimating such a capacity directly, but use has been made in the past of a concept of "capacity rate of growth" in research and scientific endeavors. A "magic number" of 15 percent per annum has been often used by advocates of scientific programs as the capacity of such programs to absorb financial resources productively. This may correspond to a 10 to 12 percent rate of growth of real resources. The projected rate of growth in the number of basic scientists in the base trend is 5.5 percent per year. (This rate was 5.7 percent for the period 1953-70.)[4] It is assumed that under conditions of an intense interest in science, the capacity growth of basic research could be 12 percent a year for the period 1974-83, giving a maximum feasible number of scientists in basic work in 1983 of 252,000, apparently still well within the limits of the potential supply.

---

3   See Table 21-1 notes for source information. Subsequent to the completion of the present study, more detailed research was undertaken, mentioned in note #1, with the objective of developing a wider range of indicators of scientific and technological activities than can be derived from the existing input data. As part of that research, a more detailed analysis was done of the number of scientists and engineers engaged in basic research. The estimate for 1973 was 78,000, very close to the 81,000 used here. However, the number of scientists and engineers engaged in basic research apparently has been declining since 1970, which may raise some doubt about the presently used projection of 139,000 in 1983. The 1983 projection is not being revised at this time, however, because, first, it does not affect the estimate of the activity outputs and, second, it may still be realistic in view of increased demand for basic research in the energy field and indications of a revival of interest in science and research in the most recent months.

4   National Science Foundation, unpublished data, 1971.

ACTIVITIES TO INCREASE THE NUMBER OF SCIENTISTS

Increases in the number of basic research scientists are judged to be possible through four activities, one of which is directed exclusively toward the expansion of science while the other three are oriented to higher education.

Expansion of pure science:
Institutions, education and communication

This activity describes a scenario of intensive efforts to promote the growth of science. It implies a growth rate in the number of scientists of 8.9 percent, higher than the projected base trend growth of 5.5 percent but below the theoretical maximum of 12 percent, which in view of the recent slowdown of momentum probably could not be attained over the 10-year period. The activity consists essentially of institutional expansion, improved communications and diffusion of knowledge and increased entries into the science professions. The effects and costs are summarized below:

Activity	Number of Active Research Scientists (thousands)	Total 10-Year Cost (billions of 1973 dollars)
Expansion of pure science	+51	$36

The expansion of scientific institutions and modes of scientific communication and the offering of scholarships are estimated to:
- increase the number of active research scientists in 1983 by 51,000.

The activity would include:
- scholarships for the study of science, at an estimated cost of $10,000 per student for four years, or a total cost of $2 billion;
- capital investment, research and development expenditures, and expansion and innovation in the communication of scientific findings, at an estimated cost of $26 billion; a total for the period of a half-million dollars per active basic scientist is assumed;
- operating cost, including assistants, supplies and services, at $75,000 per scientist a year for an average of two full years, amounting to $8 billion.

The cost for the activity would thus total $36 billion, with 15 percent needed in the first subperiod. About 80 percent is calculated as publicly financed, with 20 percent largely for financing by nonprofit institutions, including a small amount of business outlays in the communication elements of the activity.

Other activities

Three other activities directed toward expanding educational opportunities are assumed to affect the number of active research scientists, at the rates suggested by past relationships between academic attainment as a whole and entries into science careers. The effects and costs of these activities are summarized below:

Activity	Number of Active Research Scientists (thousands)	Total 10-Year Cost (billions of 1973 dollars)
Universal access to higher education	+20	$273
Structural improvements in higher education	+20	70
Improvement of skills	+10	342

Making higher education financially accessible to all is estimated by 1983 to:
• add 20,000 basic research scientists with masters degrees. Given the additional graduation of conventional college-age students and of older persons as a result of this activity for the years 1980 and 1981 (see Table 8-3 in Chapter 8) and assuming, on the basis of historical experience, that about 11 out of 100 bachelors degrees will lead to masters degrees in science two years later,[5] the number of graduates in sciences in 1983 would be 115,500. Of that number, 13 percent, or 15,000 conventional college-age students, are assumed to go into basic research on the basis of projected statistical ratios. From among older graduates who would resume interrupted careers, 5,000 are estimated to become scientists.

The total cost of this activity is calculated at $273 billion, nearly all of which is incurred during the last subperiod. The output of scientists engaged in basic research would thus occur in the latter years of the subperiod. A more detailed description of this activity appears in Chapter 8.

Structural improvements in higher education include more efficient techniques of communication, thus reducing the time requirements for advanced learning. They are assumed to increase the number of college graduates almost immediately, as compared with the built-in time lag for expanding access to higher education. The stock of college graduates resulting from this activity is

---

5   Office of Education, National Center for Education Statistics, unpublished data, 1973.

therefore estimated to be proportionately larger than that resulting from the fellowship program. Additionally, it is assumed that a greater percentage of those affected by this activity would continue their educational training toward a masters or doctorate degree. Therefore, although in 1983 this activity produces only one-third as many college graduates as the higher education access program, we estimate it will:

- increase the number of scientists by approximately the same number as would the higher education access activity, 20,000.

The cost of this entire activity is calculated to be $70 billion. The activity is described in more detail in Chapter 8.

Regarding the third educational activity, we assume that the increase in the number of scientists actively engaged in basic research as a result of the maintenance and improvement of skills activity would be:

- one-half of the increase due to each of the other two activities in higher education, or 10,000 scientists.

The full activity is estimated to cost $342 billion, and is discussed in Chapter 9.

INTERACTIONS AMONG ACTIVITIES

The interactions among the activities are shown in Table 21-2. The three activities oriented primarily toward higher education, combined, are estimated to add 35,000 scientists to the base projection (139,000) in 1983. This result assumes an overlap among the activities that would reduce the sum of their effects by 30 percent.

The educational and skills activities aim at a general upgrading of educational and professional attainment with their marginal effects on science following the rates from past experience. On the other hand, the activity of promoting basic science aims at shifting persons from other fields in which they are being trained into scientific fields and of researchers into basic scientific research from applied and developmental work. Since the potential supply of scientists is large and the two activity classes concern different populations, they have been treated largely as independent in their effects with an assumed reduction of the sum of their outputs by only 10 percent. Therefore, the combined effect of all four activities is estimated to increase the number of basic scientists in 1983 by 81,000.

Table 21-2. Effects of Activities on Number of Scientists Active in Basic Science

Activity*	Total Cost 1974-83 (billions 1973 dollars)	Number of Scientists Active in Basic Science (thousands)
Base 1973	—	81
Base 1983	—	139
9. Universal access to higher education	$273	20
10. Structural improvements in higher education	70	20
11. Maintenance, updating and improvement of job skills	342	10
25. Pure science—institutions, education, communication	36	51
Combined Effects		
9,25. Higher education; Pure science	309	64
10,25. Structural improvements; Pure science	106	64
11,25. Job skills; Pure science	378	55
9,11. Higher education; Job skills	615	25
9,10. Higher education; Structural improvements	343	30
9,10,11. Higher education; Structural improvements; Job skills	685	35
Total, all activities	**$721**	81

*The numbers preceding the activities refer to their order in the matrix, Table 2-4.

22

The arts

OBJECTIVE

    Creation and diffusion of artistic values.

INDICATOR

    Number of persons active in the arts.

Concern with the arts has been limited in this analysis to the "fine arts," which include the performing arts, writing, film, music, painting, and sculpture, and also a provision for the development of new forms.

    Measuring the quantity of artistic output directly in terms of artistic creation is not feasible. Therefore, at the level of broad public concern, artistic activity, like science, is measured here in terms of level of effort; i.e., the number of persons active in the arts (the number of active artists). The analogy between science and art is very strong and their treatment in this study is quite similar. However, unlike science where the inputs are covered by reasonably solid statistics, the data regarding inputs in the arts are virtually nonexistent.[1]

BASE TRENDS

Indicator	1973	1983 Projection	Projected Change
Number of persons active in the arts	265,000	323,000	+58,000

1   Indicative of the lack of statistical information on the arts is the fact that the only entries for the arts in the index of the *Statistical Abstract of the United States: 1972* are "art works, imports" and "performing arts." See U.S. Department of Commerce, Bureau of the Census, *Statistical Abstract*, 93d edition (Washington, D.C.: U.S. Government Printing Office, 1972).

Table 22-1. Number of Artists by Field*

Field	1960	1970
Actors	11,656	15,083
Painters and sculptors	83,904	105,036
Dancers	4,535	7,020
Musicians	76,999	96,315
Authors	28,691	26,388
Total	205,785	249,842

Source: U.S. Department of Commerce, Bureau of the Census, *1970 Census of Population*, "United States Summary, Detailed Characteristics," Table 221.

* Experienced civilian labor force 14 years of age and over.

Even determining the number of persons active in the arts is not simple. Numbers obtained from membership and directory listings of leading artistic institutions and groups are too restrictive since they primarily cover only the more eminent professionals.[2] On the other hand, participation in amateur artistic activities is very widespread with hard-to-define limits which might conceivably be stretched to include everybody. We therefore compromised with an estimate based on the number of actors, painters and sculptors, dancers, musicians, and authors in the experienced civilian labor force. According to the U.S. Census of Population, these numbered 206,000 in 1960 and 250,000 in 1970 (see Table 22-1), an annual average increase of 2.0 percent. At this rate of increase, we estimate that in 1973 there were 265,000 persons active in the arts.

The 1983 trend projection assumes a continuation of the 2.0 percent annual rate of growth exhibited by the Census group total. On this basis, we project 323,000 persons will be active in the arts by 1983. The increasing support of the arts by the federal government as well as the continued interest by the public suggest that the number of active artists may continue to grow faster than the labor force.

ACTIVITIES TO INCREASE THE NUMBER OF ARTISTS

A combination of activities is estimated to have the capacity to increase the

---

2   Following such narrow definitions, we estimate from the information obtained in the Rockefeller Brothers Funds, Inc., *The Performing Arts: Problems and Prospects, Rockefeller Panel Report* (New York: McGraw-Hill, 1965) and from data provided by a local professional theater and symphony orchestra the following number of artists in the different fields: 1,650 actors and 5,400 musicians. The number of artists is about 5,000 based on *Who's Who in American Art,* ed. Dorothy B. Gilbert (New York and London: R.R. Bowker and Co., 1970).

number of active artists by as much as 315,000 above that projected by a continuation of base trends. Aside from comparatively smaller "fallout" effects from general expansion in higher education, such increases would have to come from special efforts to promote the arts.

Special efforts to promote the arts

Both supporting individual artists and developing means of communication and institutional arrangements for bringing the public and the artists together are a part of this activity. The effect and cost of the activity are summarized below:

Activity	Number of Active Artists (thousands)	Total 10-Year Cost (billions of 1973 dollars)
Promotion of the arts	+300	$28

We estimate the following results under such conditions of maximum encouragement of the arts:

• an expansion in the number of active artists of 300,000. This number represents a judgment about the size of the latent pool of competent artists who could enter active careers in the arts under conditions of maximum encouragement of the arts. The number was derived by assuming that, under the base trend conditions, only one-third of the talented enter active careers in the arts. One-half of those with artistic talent but not engaged in the arts are assumed to enter careers in the arts as a result of this activity. With a 1983 projection of 323,000 active artists, we have thus calculated the latent pool roughly at 300,000.

The components of this activity include:

• institutional development and support, at an estimated cost of $9 billion. This activity would provide 250 new art centers at an average initial cost of $25 million, plus a total operating outlay of $3 billion;

• educational, training and support subsidies for the 300,000 new artists, at an average cost of $55,000 for the period, or a total cost of $16 billion;

• the development and promotion of new art forms, at a cost, arbitrarily assumed, of $1 billion;

• the establishment of effective two-way communication between artists and the public, at an assumed cost of $2 billion.

The total cost of the activity is thus estimated at $28 billion, with 15 percent needed in the first subperiod. Nearly 70 percent of the cost is assumed to be public, with the private share including direct purchase of art objects and outlays of nonprofit organizations.

These estimates are extremely speculative not only with respect to the potential capacity for increasing the number of artists but also regarding the cost and its composition between public and private sources. The activity structure reflects the assumption that the maximum potential expansion in the number of artists would require that a large number of art students complete art schools at a comparatively high average cost and largely with public financing. There may, however, exist possibilities for increasing artistic activity through institutional improvement which would develop the incentives and the market system for the arts and increase private initiatives by such means as providing the artists with access to debt and equity financing, audience sponsorship ventures and large-scale use of prizes and direct purchases. Such approaches may reduce total cost and especially public cost far below the level involved in the indirect stimulation through the educational system, but they have not been included so far.

Other activities

Three other activities are assumed to add to the number of active artists. They are universal access to higher education, structural improvements in higher education and the improvement of job skills. The effects and costs of these activities are summarized below:

Activity	Number of Active Artists (thousands)	Total 10-Year Cost (billions of 1973 dollars)
Universal access to higher education	+32	$273
Structural improvements in higher education	+11	70
Maintenance, updating and improvement of job skills	+16	342

Universal access to higher education is estimated to:
• increase the number of active artists by 32,000. This number was derived by applying double the ratio of artists to college graduates in 1973 (1:200) to the total projected stock of college graduations in 1983 resulting from the activity (3.2 million).

The total activity is estimated to cost $273 billion. For a more detailed description, see Chapter 8.

Technological improvements and enhancement of supporting staffs and communication techniques are assumed to increase the number of college graduates in 1983 by one-third the output for the universal access to higher education activity, thus:

- adding to the number of active artists by 11,000.

The total cost of this activity is estimated at $70 billion. A more detailed discussion appears in Chapter 8.

The improvement of skills activity is estimated to increase the number of college graduations in 1983 by one-half the output of the universal free higher education activity, thus:

- increasing the number of active artists by 16,000.

The cost of the entire activity is estimated at $342 billion. The activity is described in Chapters 9 and 10.

INTERACTIONS AMONG ACTIVITIES

The effects of the individual activities on the number of active artists are shown in Table 22-2. There are substantial overlaps among these activities, especially between universal access to higher education (9) and structural improvements (10) and structural improvements (10) and job skills (11). Effects of all three higher education activities together (9, 10, 11) on the number of artists are offset in nearly the same proportion as their effects on the number of persons completing higher education, leading to a 36 percent reduction of their combined totals. Thus, the simultaneous operation of these three activities suggests an increase of 38,000 artists.

When the education activities are combined with the activity designed especially to promote the arts, 61 percent of the effects of the education-oriented activities are subtracted, resulting in a total output for all activities of 315,000 additional artists. If universal access to higher education (9) and structural improvements (10) alone were combined with the activity to promote the arts (26), the output would be an increment of 314,000 artists; if structural improvements (10) and job skills (11) were combined with the promotion of the arts (26), the effect is estimated to be 304,000 additional artists.

Table 22-2. Effects of Activities on the Number of Active Artists

Activity*	Total Cost 1974-83 (billions 1973 dollars)	Number of Active Artists (thousands)
Base 1973	—	265
Base 1983	—	323
9. Universal access to higher education	$273	32
10. Structural improvements in higher education	70	11
11. Maintenance, updating and improvement of job skills	342	16
26. Promotion of the arts— institutions, education subsidies, new forms	28	300
Combined Effects		
9,10. Higher education; Structural improvements	343	36
10,11. Structural improvements; Job skills	412	18
9,10,26. Higher education; Structural improvements; The arts	371	314
10,11,26. Structural improvements; Job skills; The arts	440	304
9,26. Higher education; The arts	301	310
9,10,11. Higher education; Structural improvements; Job skills	685	38
Total, all activities	**$713**	**315**

*The numbers preceding the activities refer to their order in the matrix, Table 2-4.

23

Discretionary activities and economic growth

Many of the discretionary activities discussed in the preceding chapters are estimated to have a considerable effect on the level of the gross national product in 1983.

Economic growth has not been treated as a category of concern because this study does not address itself to macroeconomic goals. It may become desirable in the future either to include such macroeconomic variables as employment, growth, price level, productivity, and the balance of payments in the goals accounting framework or to develop a new framework combining the quality of life and growth accounting. Also, economic growth is a source of resources with which to undertake discretionary activities and, insofar as the choice of the discretionary activities affects the rate of economic growth, it therefore has a feedback effect on the feasibility of these activities. For these reasons, a review of the effects of the discretionary activities on economic growth is provided here following the format used for the other indicators in the study.

BASE TREND

In the trend projection of the gross national product, GNP is estimated to rise from under $1,275 billion in 1973 to $2,033 billion (in 1973 prices) in 1983. This projection, which is based on the National Economic Projection Series of the National Planning Association, corresponds to a 4.8 percent rate of growth.[1]

ACTIVITIES AND GNP

Certain standard assumptions have been made in estimating the effects of discretionary activities on GNP. In projecting manpower productivity, an in-

---

1 As explained in Chapter 3, the 4.8 percent rate of growth was derived from an earlier NPA projection. NPA's most recent 10-year projection contains an average annual growth rate of 3.9 percent. See Robert Dennis, *Clambering into the Eighties* (Washington, D.C.: National Planning Association, December 1974), p. 1.

crease in productivity has been considered equivalent to an increase in wage. Also, by assumption, the wage increases have been divided by 0.7, reflecting a 70-30 percent split of GNP between components attributable to labor and components attributable to capital income which has been historically stable. Since many activities have GNP effects resulting from an increase either in manpower productivity or in manpower input, we have estimated the effect of the activity on earnings, which is then raised to a full GNP effect in 1983. The specific activities that are estimated to affect GNP are discussed below.

Remedial education

Remedial education, described in Chapter 7, consists of extensive tutoring of students, both high school and elementary, with the objective of improving their school performance, especially in language and mathematics. The activity is estimated to raise the educational attainment of high school graduates by 16 index points in 1983 and to result in a median wage improvement for wage earners amounting to $100 in 1983. However, significant improvements would occur below the national median because many entrants into the labor force would not have earned incomes at the median earnings level by 1983. The activity effect is equivalent to an average increase of 1.9 years of schooling (e.g., 16 percent of 12 years) for the 16 million graduates affected, of whom an estimated 11.2 million would be new entrants into the labor force. By 1983, we project a year of school to be worth $1,500 in 1973 prices. These new workers would thus gain an average of $2,800, representing a total wage increase of $31 billion. When raised to allow for property income, this yields a GNP increment of $44 billion.

Improved educational technology in basic education

This activity, also described in Chapter 7, consists of thorough modernization of educational technologies and processes. Since the activity is directed toward all students, it would affect many who are not likely to enter the labor force by 1983, either because they are going to college or because they are not yet 17. The full effect of this activity would therefore occur at dates later than 1983. The 11.2 million graduates affected who are estimated to enter the labor force by 1983 would have gained an average of 2.52 years of schooling. At $1,500 per year, this represents increased earnings of $3,780 for these new workers, or a $42 billion increase in total earnings. Allowing for property income, GNP would thus rise by $60 billion.

Universal access to higher education

The effects of universal access to higher education on economic growth are calculated on the basis of assuming a rate of return to human capital in the form of earnings. It is assumed that, of the education completed in 1983, 25 percent can be counted as consumption and 75 percent as investment. Of the additional 3,150 persons graduating as a result of this activity, 24 million, or 75 percent, are assumed to become employed. Their increased earnings are estimated to amount to $8,500 by 1983, yielding a total wage increment of $20 billion. When raised to allow for property income, this amounts to a $29 billion increase in GNP. This activity is discussed in Chapter 8.

Structural improvements in higher education

This activity, described in Chapter 8, has an impact on economic growth calculated in an analogous fashion to that of the increment for the activity of universal access to higher education. The relationship of output of the number of graduates to additional GNP is assumed to be the same as for the preceding activity. The increment to GNP from this activity is estimated then at $10 billion.

Maintenance, upgrading and improvement of skills

The increase in total GNP of $34 billion from this activity is assumed to amount to 10 percent of the cost of education completed in 1983 as a result of the activity. Of the total amount, $24 billion (70 percent) would be wages and $10 billion property income. This activity is more fully described in Chapter 9.

Specialized training for those outside the mainstream of the labor force

This activity, which is explained in Chapter 10, is predicated on placing 5 million persons into the mainstream of the labor force. An average increase in earnings of those persons is estimated at $3,000 per year. That increase yields $15 billion aggregate income in wages or a $21 billion gain in GNP.

Aid to depressed communities

This activity, described in Chapters 9 and 10, contains rather massive investments in human and physical capital in low productivity areas and communities. The activity is aimed at raising total and per capita income earned and output produced in these depressed areas. Assuming a 10 percent rate of return on the outlay of $171 billion for these areas, GNP would increase by $17 billion in 1983.

General day care for children

This activity, described in Chapter 15, raises GNP through increasing the supply of labor by encouraging the entry of parents into the labor force and increasing the hours they can work as well as by improving the flexibility of time schedules with which parents can hold jobs. An estimated 5.5 million new women workers would enter the labor force, adding an average of 1,107 hours of work. The increase of 6.1 billion hours worked for an average 1983 wage of $5 per hour in 1973 dollars (lower than the median, since these are additional new workers) yields $30 billion additional labor income and $43 billion of GNP.

Time-saving innovations

The introduction of more time-saving innovations, as described in Chapter 20, is estimated to produce 319 hours of additional discretionary time in 1983 for each person six years old and older. We assume that of this amount 20 percent, or 6.7 billion hours, would be used for gainful employment and that these hours would average 60 percent of the productivity of the average hour of work in the base. The projected 1983 GNP per member of the labor force is $19,361 in 1973 dollars which at 1,550 hours per worker gives $12.50 per hour worked. At 60 percent productivity an hour worked yields $7.50. Adding 6.7 billion working hours at this rate increases the GNP by $50 billion in 1983.

COMBINED EFFECTS OF ACTIVITIES

The combined effects of these activities result in substantial offsets. In large part, the overlaps occur within the three principal groups of activities shown in Table 23-1, although substantial interference effects also occur among groups. The total offset is estimated to lead to a reduction by 29 percent from the unadjusted aggregate output of the individual effects. The result of all the activities combined would be an increase of $220 billion in the projected 1983 GNP, which would then rise from $2,033 billion to $2,253 billion.

The higher GNP implies an annual rate of economic growth of 5.9 percent over the 10-year span. This represents a very large increase of 1.1 percent a year (especially from activities not designed to stimulate economic growth) when compared with past experience, but it is not out of line with selected periods in American economic history or with international experience.[2] Intermediate

---

2 Edward F. Denison (assisted by Jean-Pierre Poullier), *Why Growth Rates Differ, Postwar Experience in Nine Western Countries* (Washington, D.C.: The Brookings Institution, 1967); and Edward F. Denison, *Accounting for United States Economic Growth, 1929–1969* (Washington, D.C.: The Brookings Institution, 1974).

Table 23-1. Effects of Activities on GNP in 1983
(in 1973 prices)

Activity*	Billions
GNP 1973	$1,275
GNP 1983, projection	$2,033
Education	**$116**[1]
6. Remedial education	44
7. Educational technology	60
9. Universal access to higher education	29
10. Structural improvements in higher education	10
Manpower	**51**[1]
11. Maintenance of skills	34
12. Specialized training	21
16. Aid to depressed communities	17
Time-saving Activities	**88**[1]
8. General day care	43
28. Time-saving innovations	50
Other Combined Effects	
9,10. Higher education; Structural improvements	34
10,11. Structural improvements; Skills maintenance	40
9,11. Higher education; Skills maintenance	48
9,10,11. Higher education; Structural improvements; Skills maintenance	53
6,7. Remedial tutoring; Educational technology	82
6,7,8. Remedial tutoring; Educational technology; Day care	125
7,8. Educational technology; Day care	103
12,16. Special training; Aid to depressed communities	34
8,12,28. Day care; Special training; Time savings	80
8,12,16,28. Day care; Special training; Aid to depressed communities; Time savings	93
Total, all activities	**$220**[2]

*The numbers preceding the activities refer to their order in the matrix, Table 2-4.

[1] Total for activity area adjusted for overlaps and offsets within that area.
[2] Adjusted for overlaps and offsets among activity areas.

levels of activities or combinations of selected activities would produce smaller increments to the 1983 GNP and would imply correspondingly lower growth rates. The correspondence between growth rates and the 1983 GNP are shown below:

1983 GNP (in billions of 1973 dollars)	Annual Rate of Growth (1974-83)
$2,033	4.8%
2,097	5.1
2,157	5.4
2,220	5.7
2,283	6.0

Index

Page numbers for tables and charts are in italics.

National planning association

NPA is an independent, private, nonprofit, nonpolitical organization that carries on research and policy formulation in the public interest. NPA was founded during the Great Depression of the 1930s when conflicts among the major economic groups—business, farmers, labor—threatened to paralyze national decision making on the critical issues confronting American society. It was dedicated, in the words of its statement of purpose, to the task "of getting (these) diverse groups to work together . . . to narrow areas of controversy and broaden areas of agreement . . . (and) to provide on specific problems concrete programs for action planned in the best traditions of a functioning democracy." From the beginning, NPA has been committed to the view that the survival of a functioning American democracy under the increasingly rigorous conditions of the 20th century could not be assured only by more effective governmental policies and programs. Equally essential, NPA believes, are the preservation of private economic initiative and activity dispersed throughout the society and the continuous development by the major private groups of a substantial consensus on how to cope with the problems confronting the nation at home and abroad.

NPA brings together influential and knowledgeable leaders from business, labor, agriculture, and the applied and academic professions to serve on policy committees. These committees analyze and agree upon recommendations for dealing with domestic and international developments affecting the well-being of the United States. The research and writing for these committees are provided by NPA's professional staff and, as required, by outside experts.

In addition, NPA's professional staff undertakes a wide variety of technical research activities designed to provide data and ideas for policy makers and planners in government and the private sector. These activities include the preparation on a regular basis of economic and demographic projections for the national economy, regions, states, and metropolitan areas; program planning and evaluation for federal, state and local agencies; research on national goals and priorities; planning studies for manpower training, vocational education, medical care, environmental protection, energy needs, and other economic and social problems confronting American society; and analyses and forecasts of changing international realities and their implications for U.S. policies. In developing its staff capabilities, NPA has increasingly emphasized two related qualifications—the interdisciplinary knowledge required to understand the complex nature of many real-life problems, and the ability to bridge the gap between the theoretical or highly technical research of the universities and other professional institutions and the practical needs of policy makers and planners in government and the private sector.

All NPA reports have been authorized for publication in accordance with procedures laid down by the Board of Trustees. Such action does not imply agreement by NPA Board or committee members with all that is contained therein unless such endorsement is specifically stated.

NPA officers and board of trustees

*Executive Committee member.

Recent NPA publications

NPA reports

#142   *Improvements in the Quality of Life: Estimates of Possibilities in the United States, 1974–1983,* by Nestor E. Terleckyj, 298 p (June 1975, $10.00)

#141   *Upgrading Low-Level Employment: A Major National Challenge,* NPA Joint Statement, 32 p (February 1975, $1.50)

#140   *Effects of R&D on the Productivity Growth of Industries: An Exploratory Study,* by Nestor E. Terleckyj, 72 p (December 1974, $4.50)

#139   *Technical Change and American Enterprise,* by J. Herbert Holloman, 52 p (October 1974, $1.50)

#138   *Proceedings of the Conference on Revenue Sharing Research,* edited by Robert W. Rafuse, Jr., 124 p (July 1974, $3.00)

#137   *A Public Service Employment Program: Effective Manpower Strategy,* NPA Joint Statement, 32 p (July 1974, $1.00)

International relations

BN-16   *Completing the GATT: Toward New International Rules to Govern Export Controls,* by C. Fred Bergsten, 72 p (October 1974, $2.00)

CAC 38   *A Balance of Payments Handbook,* by Caroline Pestieau, 134 p (October 1974, $2.00)

The Fortunes of the West: The Future of the Atlantic Nations, by Theodore Geiger, 316 p (January 1973, $10.00), published by Indiana University Press, Bloomington, Indiana and also available from NPA

Other NPA studies

Federal Health Spending, 1969–74, by L.B. Russell, B.B. Bourque, D.P. Bourque, C.S. Burke, 150 p (August 1974, $3.00)

Chartbook of Federal Health Spending, 1969–74, 70 p (August 1974, $2.50)

Evaluating Vocational Education—Policies and Plans for the 1970s, by Leonard A. Lecht, 206 p (1974, $15.00), published by Praeger Publishers, NYC, and also available from NPA

Dollars for National Goals: Looking Ahead to 1980, by Leonard A. Lecht, 214 p (1974, $17.50), available from John Wiley & Sons, NYC

A complete list of publications will be provided upon request. Quantity discounts are given.

Please address all orders and inquiries about publications to:

NATIONAL PLANNING ASSOCIATION
Publications Distribution Department
1606 New Hampshire Ave., N.W., Washington, D.C. 20009
(202) 265-7685